D1470054

Robert E. Lee

ROBERT

E. LEE

THE MAN
THE SOLDIER
THE MYTH

BRANDON MARIE MILLER

CALKINS CREEK
AN IMPRINT OF HIGHLIGHTS
Honesdale, Pennsylvania

Text copyright © 2019 by Brandon Marie Miller
All rights reserved. Copying or digitizing this book for storage, display, or
distribution in any other medium is strictly prohibited.

For information about permission to reproduce selections from this book,
please contact permissions@highlights.com.

Calkins Creek
An Imprint of Highlights
815 Church Street
Honesdale, Pennsylvania 18431
calkinscreekbooks.com
Printed in China

ISBN: 978-1-62979-910-0 (hardcover)
ISBN: 978-1-68437-625-4 (eBook)
Library of Congress Control Number: 2018962588

First edition
10 9 8 7 6 5 4 3 2 1

Design by Barbara Grzeslo
The type is set in Sabon.

For Elizabeth,
who doesn't have much history yet

CONTENTS

A PARTIAL FAMILY TREE OF
ROBERT E. LEE AND

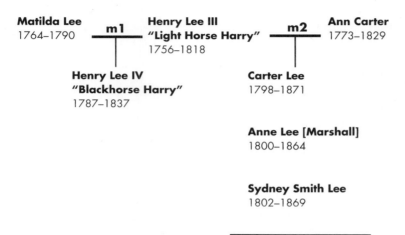

Matilda Lee
1764–1790 ——— **m1** ——— **Henry Lee III**
"Light Horse Harry"
1756–1818 ——— **m2** ——— **Ann Carter**
1773–1829

Henry Lee IV
"Blackhorse Harry"
1787–1837

Carter Lee
1798–1871

Anne Lee [Marshall]
1800–1864

Sydney Smith Lee
1802–1869

Robert Edward Lee
1807–1870

Mildred Lee [Childe]
1811–1856

MARY ANNA RANDOLPH CUSTIS

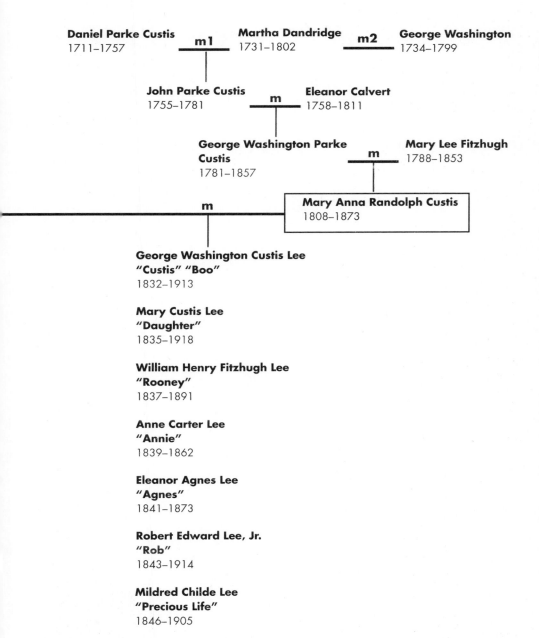

Daniel Parke Custis
1711–1757

m1

Martha Dandridge
1731–1802

m2

George Washington
1734–1799

John Parke Custis
1755–1781

m

Eleanor Calvert
1758–1811

George Washington Parke Custis
1781–1857

m

Mary Lee Fitzhugh
1788–1853

m

Mary Anna Randolph Custis
1808–1873

George Washington Custis Lee
"Custis" "Boo"
1832–1913

Mary Custis Lee
"Daughter"
1835–1918

William Henry Fitzhugh Lee
"Rooney"
1837–1891

Anne Carter Lee
"Annie"
1839–1862

Eleanor Agnes Lee
"Agnes"
1841–1873

Robert Edward Lee, Jr.
"Rob"
1843–1914

Mildred Childe Lee
"Precious Life"
1846–1905

BEFORE YOU BEGIN . . .

During the time that I was researching and writing this book, Robert E. Lee was in the news a lot. Every day I heard things, or read things, or saw things, about Lee. People freely shared statements like these:

- Lee hated slavery.
- Lee did not believe in slavery.
- Lee never owned slaves.
- Lee was an emancipator—he freed slaves.
- Lee was against secession.

But are these statements about Lee true? Or are they myths that still shape our memory of the Civil War?

What did Lee himself write? You can read his words on these pages. What did he do? What was happening in his life that affected how he thought and acted?

Robert E. Lee, like each of us, was a complex human being. Sometimes we are torn; we aren't sure what we believe. Sometimes we hold different beliefs at the same time, or our views change as we change. It may be hard to come up with the (one and only) truth. So, what comes closest to the truth about Robert E. Lee?

See what you think.

Lee never called himself Robert E. Lee. For some reason, newspapers started emphasizing his middle initial during the Civil War. To those who knew him, Lee was plain Robert Lee. He signed his letters RE Lee. His brothers sometimes called him Old Bob.

—*Brandon Marie Miller*

ACKNOWLEDGMENTS

I am grateful to the many people who have helped me with this book, but most especially to the following:

To Matt Penrod, National Park Ranger and historian at Arlington House, The Robert E. Lee Memorial.

To Kimberly Robinson, Museum Curator, Arlington House, The Robert E. Lee Memorial.

To Lucy Wilkins, Director of University Collections and the Lee Chapel & Museum, Washington and Lee University.

To Robert E. May, Professor Emeritus of History, Purdue University.

To Ruth Ann Coski, former supervisor of The White House of the Confederacy and manager of the Eleanor S. Brockenbrough Library, The Museum of the Confederacy, Richmond, Virginia.

To Tom Clemens, Civil War historian focusing on the battle of Antietam.

To my husband, family, and friends, who have listened so kindly—and then listened more—to my questions and thoughts and discoveries about REL.

Lastly, my warm thanks to Carolyn P. Yoder, senior editor at Calkins Creek, and to everyone who has worked so hard to create this book.

Thank you all so much!

A view of the Hudson River with West Point in the background, watercolor by Michael Seymore, 1846

CHAPTER ONE

ESCAPING FAMILY HISTORY

One day, Robert E. Lee would face gut-wrenching decisions about honor, and country, and sending young men into ferocious battles. One day, he'd fear charges of treason and imprisonment. One day, he'd have to start life again, sick and exhausted, in a world he didn't want or recognize.

But on a late June morning in 1825 he was just an eighteen-year-old boy who'd traveled far from his home in Virginia.

Robert caught his first glimpse of the United States Military Academy at West Point from the deck of a steamboat chugging up the Hudson River. Gentle mountains framed the water on both sides, offering glorious views. West Point loomed above as the steamboat docked at the base of a cliff. As they stepped off the boat, an old man with a hook in place of his hand greeted Robert and other young men offered an appointment to the academy.

Robert stood out among the arrivals—handsome, rosy-cheeked, with wavy dark hair and dark eyes. His family included signers of the Declaration of Independence. His father had fought in the American Revolution. Lees had served the country since before the nation's birth. But a childhood marked with scandal and uncertainty had also formed the Robert Lee who arrived at West Point.

The young men trudged uphill to the campus built on the site of an old Revolutionary War fort. The academy itself—founded in 1802—proved less impressive than the Hudson River shimmering like a ribbon below. A wide and windy forty-acre parade ground marred by stray boulders promised hours of marching and practicing maneuvers. A mess hall and two large, rather bleak dormitories, or barracks, flanked the parade ground. A two-story building held everything else—a chapel, the library, and classrooms.

Sylvanus Thayer, the superintendent of West Point, greeted each of the young men. Thayer had transformed the academy into one of the toughest places in the country to get an education. Alongside the other young men, Robert bent his head to the entrance exam—reading, writing, and simple math—meant to quickly weed out boys not up to speed.

On June 27, as a fading sun softened the mountains, Lee lined up on the parade ground with one hundred and four others. Those who'd passed the test heard their names called out in alphabetical order. "Lee!" Robert must have let go a breath of relief. He took four steps forward, as they'd been told to do. At the end, about two dozen young men remained standing behind.

The next morning Robert and the other new cadets set up summer camp. Their first duty made plain the lowly status of the "newies"— digging latrines. For two months that summer the cadets crammed into tents, broiling under the sun or drenched by pelting storms.

Each morning Robert woke to the trumpet's prod of reveille. Newies spilled from their tents for mornings of marching and drilling. Shallow trenches dug twenty-eight inches apart forced the long lines of sweating young men to take precisely measured and matched steps. Afternoon classes followed morning drills and bled into evening hours of study before lights-out at nine o'clock.

Cadets learned to stand at attention. Their new gray uniforms fitted so tightly about the chest that the young men *had* to stand straight. Shoulders thrust back. Chins leveled perpendicular to the chest. Stomachs pulled in. Arms stretched straight at their sides. No bend in the elbows. Fingers pressed against the seams of their trousers. Feet planted at an angle of forty-five degrees. Tall and ramrod straight, Robert would never lose the soldierly posture drilled into him at West Point.

Robert survived the summer camp, his first test as a soldier. On September 3, 1825, he signed papers officially giving the next five years of his life to the army in exchange for his West Point education. Along with his classmates Robert spoke his oath: "I do solemnly swear that I will bear true allegiance to the United States of America, and that I will serve them honestly and faithfully against all their enemies . . . ; and observe and obey the orders of the President of the United States . . ." Rigorous training lay ahead to mold these young men into army officers who could lead soldiers, build roads and forts, and protect America's shores and far frontiers.

In his spotless uniform young Robert Lee represented a family known for both glory and misdeeds, for service and scandal. He understood what he had to do. The long shadows of childhood stood with Cadet Lee as he began his West Point years.

WAR HERO OF A NEW NATION

Robert's father, Henry Lee III, had been a dashing young cavalry officer in the Revolutionary War. Lee's Legion served as scouts, the eyes and ears for General George Washington and, later, General Nathanael Greene. Henry's lightning-quick attacks on horseback harassed the British lines; his bold moves and coolness under fire earned him the nickname Light Horse Harry Lee. He possessed a "quickness of talent, a genius sudden," a family friend recalled. He was "dazzling and always at command."

There was recklessness in Henry Lee, too. He won a gold medal from Congress for his victory at Paulus Hook, New Jersey, but also faced a court-martial for some of his actions during the battle. Lee was acquitted on all charges. In another instance, Washington reined in Lee's plan for dealing with army deserters. Yes, Washington told Lee, executing deserters discouraged the practice, but it must be done "with caution and only when the fact is very clear." Washington rejected Lee's proposal to cut off a runaway soldier's head and display it to the troops. This "appearance of inhumanity," Washington noted, might only "excite resentment."

In 1782, the twenty-six-year-old hero returned home from war. A few weeks later he married his cousin, Matilda Lee, the wealthy heiress to her family's imposing plantation, called Stratford. Henry and Matilda had two surviving children, a daughter and a son, Henry Lee IV. But as Light Horse Harry settled down as a husband and the master of Stratford, the brash and daring side of his nature needed new outlets.

* * * * *

Henry Lee believed in the greatness of the new nation born of war. As a speaker and writer, Henry had "an eloquence which seemed to flow unbidden." Not surprisingly, he entered politics. As Americans wrestled

Robert's father, Henry Lee (1756–1818), by Charles Willson Peale, painted from life, about 1782

18

with the best way to build their new nation, Henry's neighbors elected him to Congress. Lee believed the country needed a strong national government instead of thirteen individual states each pulling its own way. He fought for ratification of the United States Constitution in 1787, and in 1791 Virginians elected Henry their governor.

Like many others, including George Washington, Henry turned to the wheeling and dealing of land speculation. Fortunes could be made purchasing thousands of wild American acres, buying cheap and selling high. At a time when Americans hungered to surge west and expand their country—eager to buy land of their own—speculators could turn huge profits.

Henry Lee was a smart man, but his horse may have had more money sense. A friend recalled that in his "unhappy rage for speculation," Henry bought huge tracts of land on credit. He borrowed from everyone—family, friends, and acquaintances—and it added up to thousands of dollars he could not pay back. George Washington, who'd loaned Henry money, eventually had to write, "The period for payment of the second Instalment of your Bond is past, and the first Instalment is only partially complied with. . . . It, Cannot be more unpleasant for you to hear, than for me to remind you of these things." Alarmed, Matilda put Stratford and her estate in a trust for her children. Henry could live at Stratford for his lifetime, but he could not sell Matilda Lee's family home. Soon after, in 1790, Matilda died.

Devastated by Matilda's death, Henry threw himself into politics. Though he was governor of Virginia he considered sailing to France to fight in the French Revolution. He continued gambling in land speculation and was gutted when certain deals he'd relied on to save his finances came to nothing.

BUILDING A NEW FAMILY

On June 18, 1793, Henry Lee settled down once more to wedded life.

He married twenty-year-old Ann Carter at the bride's home, Shirley plantation, on the banks of the James River. Ann was a dark-eyed beauty, well educated, musical and dignified, graceful on horseback. Though Stratford remained their home, the couple moved to the governor's house in Richmond and later to Philadelphia when Henry again served in Congress. When George Washington died in December 1799, it was Henry Lee who made the formal eulogy before Congress. He summed up Washington's life with the iconic words "First in war, first in peace, and first in the hearts of his countrymen."

Over the next few years, Ann and Henry added children to the Lee family, naming them after beloved relatives: a son, Charles Carter Lee; a delicate daughter named Anne; another son, Sydney Smith. Henry was often away from home, following the scent of new deals. Ann's father worried when Henry began selling lands that belonged to Ann. He amended his will in 1803 to protect Ann's inheritance "from the claim, demand, let, hindrance or molestation of her husband, General Henry Lee or his creditors."

Ann was pregnant again in early July 1806 when she and the children traveled to Shirley in a broken-down carriage only to discover her father had died. "The eyes which used to beam with so much affection on me, were veiled for ever!" she wrote Henry. Young Carter was ill and "our unfortunate little Smith" so sick that four different doctors had seen the boy but could offer no help. She begged Henry to come and fetch his family by the end of July. "Do not disappoint me," Ann pleaded.

But Henry did not come for grieving Ann until late autumn. Then, in the heart of cold January she had another son, born at Stratford on January 19, 1807, named Robert Edward after two of Ann's brothers. Ann grew frail after Robert's birth, her health uncertain. One friend thought her not long for this world. Ann, frail or not, and Henry Lee had one more child, a second daughter, whom they called Mildred.

"THAT SWINDLING HENRY LEE"

Little Robert Lee had no idea that his father's actions caused such hardships. Henry's brothers worried they'd lose their own homes because of money he had borrowed and didn't repay. One newspaper called the former hero "that swindling Henry Lee." Creditors banged on Stratford's door, demanding payment. In place of cash, they took enslaved human beings who worked in the Lees' house and fields; they carried off livestock; they carted away furniture—all as payment for Henry's debts. People filed lawsuits against Henry, and he hid from the sheriff. A depressed Ann felt cut off from friends who'd suffered losses at Henry's hands. She seldom left the house, sometimes remaining inside for months, forgetting the world and "by the World forgot," she confessed.

Fifteen months after Robert's birth, Henry surrendered to the sheriff of Westmoreland County, who locked him in jail. In April 1809 a new arrest warrant moved him to another jail, one he called "this depot of misery." During the year Henry Lee spent in jail, apart from his family, he kept himself sane writing a six-hundred-page history of the American Revolution in the Southern states. He turned over the rights to the book to one of his brothers as part of his debt repayment.

Henry owed money to at least twenty people, including the estate of George Washington. To try and pay off his huge debts, Henry handed over thousands of acres of land. He gave up his life interest in Stratford to his son, Henry Lee IV, and came up with a payment schedule for working off the rest. Henry Lee walked out of debtors' prison on March 20, 1810. Robert and the rest of the family left Stratford and moved north to Alexandria, Virginia, just a few miles from the new capital city taking shape, Washington D.C.

The town of Alexandria, where George Washington once did business, sat on the banks of the Potomac River. The hills of Maryland

21

rose in the distance. Rows of wood and brick houses, shops and offices, lined the streets that ran down to the wharves and warehouses along the riverfront. Here, tall-masted ships unloaded cargo from around the world. The town offered banks, apothecary shops, schools, taverns, and a fire company.

What made Alexandria most appealing to Robert's family was the vast network of relatives who lived nearby. Henry's brother Edmund was the mayor. Another brother, Charles, a former attorney general of the United States, lived a few blocks away. Aunts, uncles, and cousins, by blood or marriage, lent support, advice, and built-in playmates for the Lee children. They visited one another and married one another. For the rest of his life Robert Lee felt most comfortable sheltered within this close and ever-widening circle of kin.

Though Alexandria had a population of free black people, the town maintained a booming market in selling, renting, and buying the enslaved. Robert's family on both sides had owned slaves for generations. Northern states had gradually ended slavery by the early 1800s, but in the South, slavery had grown; large numbers of enslaved laborers toiled growing cash crops of tobacco and, later, cotton. As slavery spread to new states, Alexandria profited. Most days Robert could have witnessed lines of chained people driven through the streets. Carts crammed with shackled slaves parked before the pens and jails where human property waited for the auction blocks.

CHILDHOOD DAYS AND FURTHER DISGRACE

As a young child Robert saw little of his father. He grew up a bashful boy, often teased by his brothers and sisters. He loved animals of all sorts and even had a pet hummingbird and lobster as a child. Later letters show a close relationship between the siblings. Carter Lee recalled a childhood of playing marbles and hopscotch, learning to swim, hunt, fish, shoot, skate, and ride horses. Most likely Robert followed in his brother's footsteps. The boys also shadowed the Alexandria militia, loving the military pageantry. And they had their father's swords and pistols from the Revolutionary War to wonder over.

Henry's political voice remained as firm as ever. He feuded with Thomas Jefferson and James Madison. "Those insects," Jefferson called the Lee family. In July 1812, when Robert was five, Henry rode to Baltimore to support a newspaperman named Alexander Contee Hanson. Hanson's paper, the *Federal Republican*, had criticized President Madison for taking the nation into a new war against Great Britain. A mob destroyed Hanson's printing press. Lee was there, in support of freedom of the press, when Hanson started up his paper once more.

A full-scale riot erupted. The mob beat Henry with swords and clubs, sliced his cheek to the bone, and poured hot candle wax into his eyes to test whether he was dead. Henry lay on the street for hours before doctors carried him to safety. He barely survived. Weeks later he returned to Alexandria, a fifty-six-year-old man bandaged and broken in body and spirit. Disfigured by the attack, he must have seemed a frightening figure to his youngest children. To make matters worse, creditors once more hounded the family. In 1813 Henry fled the country, sailing to the West Indies. The family put on a brave face. Henry, they said, had moved for health reasons; he'd return when he felt better. But six-year-old Robert never saw his father again.

***** *

Over the years the Lees lived in several houses around Alexandria, relying on the charity of relatives. A cousin offered Ann's brood a property he owned on Oronoco Street. This large, red-brick house, complete with slave quarters, had a garden out back where the Lee children played among the snowball bushes. The house sat on the edge of town near swampy areas plagued with mosquitoes. Half the house was a separate dwelling rented out to boarders who shared the kitchen with the Lee family. Unfortunately, little had been done to keep the place up; the paint peeled and soot blackened the walls. Life seemed far from the splendor of Shirley or Stratford, places the Lees visited but no longer called home.

Ann worried about putting enough food on the table. She wrote Carter, away at school, not to ask for pocket money, as "all of my expenses must be diminished." There was little meat for a family of five, "to the great discomfort of my young Ladies & Gentlemen," Ann lamented. Robert never ate much, though, and was often sickly. To make ends meet, Ann sold what she owned—enslaved people she'd inherited and some horses.

While Ann scrimped, in Nassau Henry ordered flanks of beef, venison hams, and gallons of oysters for himself. He lived on his wits, charming people out of their money. He speculated on shipping ventures. He passed out worthless banknotes from a fake account.

Ann Lee did her best to raise her large family on her own. On top of the constant money worries she suffered from what may have been kidney or heart disease, or tuberculosis. With his older brothers gone from home and his sisters too young or fragile, responsibilities fell to Robert. He acted as his mother's nursemaid. He mixed Ann's medicines, ran errands, and carried messages for her. He did household chores and tried to cheer his mother.

Ann carefully supervised her children's moral upbringing. She warned her sons against drinking too much wine or gambling, even on a game of chess. They should never spend their time idle and useless. After getting into debt at college, Carter promised his mother, "I am determined then never to spend a cent unless I have it in my pocket." Robert learned similar lessons at Ann's side. And always, there was the poor example set by his father overshadowing all.

Even with tight finances Ann saw that each of her children had a good education, something she considered more important than any short-lived pleasure. Robert attended family plantation schools. Around

Robert's mother, Ann Hill Carter Lee, by an unknown artist

age fourteen he entered the Alexandria Academy. George Washington had provided a fund for the school to educate poor boys and girls. Here Robert buckled down to classical languages and literature, reading some of the masters of ancient Greece and Rome: Homer, Caesar, Virgil, and Tacitus. He studied algebra, the first six books of Euclidean geometry, and English grammar. He also earned distinction for his gentlemanly behavior.

Light Horse Harry Lee, once the dashing young hero, died in 1818. He'd fled creditors yet again, talking his way onto a ship that landed him in Georgia, where he spent his final weeks, racked with pain and screaming at those who tried to care for him.

Robert and Henry Lee never knew each other. But as the years passed, Robert felt some pride in Henry, or at least in the idea of his father as a hero. Years later, he had a copy made of Gilbert Stuart's painting of Henry Lee to hang in his home. In his wallet he carried an old clipping of his father's eulogy for George Washington. He visited his father's grave in Georgia at least twice. His West Point friends all had fathers who'd also served in the American Revolution. And on his West Point application, Robert changed his birthday from January 19 to his father's birthday of January 29.

SCANDAL AT STRATFORD

Robert's half brother, Henry Lee IV, owner of Stratford, was twenty years older than Robert. He'd fought in the War of 1812 and then married an heiress named Anne McCarty. When the house on Oronoco Street was sold, Henry IV invited his stepmother and her children to return to Stratford. He knew that Ann was "a well tried disciple of adversity," and told her that her happiness, and that of his half siblings, was "necessary" to his own.

Stratford Hall in Westmoreland County, Virginia, birthplace of Robert E. Lee and scene of Lee family scandals

But tragedy marked the family's days at Stratford. In 1820 Anne and Henry IV's two-year-old daughter died after tumbling down the steep stone steps in front of the mansion. The Stratford household plunged into mourning. Heartbroken, Anne McCarty Lee soothed herself with laudanum and ended up addicted to the dangerous opium mixture. She also sought comfort from her nineteen-year-old sister, Elizabeth. Henry IV served as Elizabeth McCarty's guardian, responsible for her welfare, her money, and her property.

The scandal broke in 1821 when someone discovered a baby's body in one of the outbuildings at Stratford. "Major H Lee . . . has seduced his sister in law, Miss McCarty," wrote Nelly Custis Lewis, "defrauded her of great part of her property, & they would have gone to South America together after deserting his wife, had not Miss McC's unexpected confinement [to give birth] disclosed the nefarious business. He is justly detested, & she is miserable—has returned to her poor Grandmother who must think that she has lived too long."

The news spread like a stain across Virginia society. "You have no doubt heard of H. Lee's adventure & Miss McC—s disgrace," wrote one of Robert's aunts, "therefore I can *will not* sully this paper with the relation of such black deeds. . . . I have been wretched about my poor Sister L[ee]'s boys, being confined to such a malignant spot of vice. . . . It is a most improper place for them." Robert's family, hoping he and his brother Smith might "escape pollution," removed the teenagers from Stratford. No longer able to show his face, Henry Lee IV lay low in France for a while. He sold Stratford in 1822, the last of the Lees to live in the great house.

Robert was fourteen when this scandal tainted the Lee name. For years afterward he feared the shame would blight his own future. What decent Virginia family would let him marry their daughter? How could he change his family's situation? How could he "escape the sins into which they have fallen"? "I hope the blame which is justly their due, will not be laid to me," he wrote a few years later to the girl he loved.

* * * * *

Ann tried to talk her son out of entering the army. But in April 1824 she sat down with Robert, and each of them wrote to the Secretary of War. Robert accepted the slot at West Point with which he had been "honnoured by the President," binding himself to serve in the army, and Ann, as Robert's surviving parent, gave her consent. But when it turned out that the Secretary of War had admitted too many young men, Robert had to wait a whole year to enter.

Robert spent much of that extra time buried in study with the Quaker teacher Benjamin Hallowell. And when the Marquis de Lafayette, a Revolutionary War hero, visited Alexandria on his American tour, Robert served as part of the honor guard. Thousands lined the streets to cheer for the old soldier. People tossed bouquets and waved handkerchiefs, and a tethered eagle perched on a triumphal arch flapped its wings and screeched as Lafayette passed beneath.

When the time came for Robert to leave for New York and his trip up the Hudson River, Ann broke down, unable to face his absence. A cousin remembered Mrs. Lee crying, "You know what I have lost. He is son, daughter and everything to me." But Robert was ready. Hardworking, bright, and strong in his sense of duty, he needed to prove himself in the classrooms and on the windswept parade ground of West Point.

CHAPTER TWO

CORPS OF CADETS

"I hope to see both my dear Boys at home in June. Robert will then have been absent two years. He is much pleased with his situation at West Point."

—*Ann Lee to her son Smith,*
April 10, 1829

By September 1825 Robert had survived the entrance exam and summer camp and taken his oath. But he wasn't off the hook yet. Superintendent Thayer placed new cadets on probation for their first six months at West Point. They studied mostly math and French, the language of the military arts. They drilled with their weapons, practiced maneuvers, and adapted to the superintendent's expectations for the Corps of Cadets.

Thayer demanded that cadets embrace a devotion to duty, honor, and truthfulness—in other words, behave like gentlemen. He expected them to shun vices like drinking, gambling, and cheating. And they had to master unrelenting amounts of work. In January Robert passed the first of two yearly exams that weeded out more men from his class. Lee was now a full-fledged West Point cadet.

CADET LIFE
Robert was assigned to North Barracks, a four-story building with four or five young men crammed into each of the eighteen-by-eighteen-foot

Brigadier General Sylvanus Thayer, superintendent of the United States Military Academy, turned West Point into one of the toughest educational institutes in the country. Painted by Robert Weir, academy drawing instructor, 1843.

rooms. A partial wall divided his room into sleeping quarters and a study area taken up almost entirely by a table and chairs. A fireplace provided heat and light but did little in winter to warm the room. Cadets studied wrapped in their blankets, scorched on the side facing the fire and freezing on the other. At least one water-filled bucket stood ready at all times in case the room caught fire.

Cadets could purchase a cot if they had the funds, but most slept wrapped in bedrolls on the floor. Each morning, bedding had to be folded away into a bag. Gun racks and firearm accessories stood near the door. Cadets stored their clothes in trunks. The army issued each cadet one candle, a glass, and a washbasin. Overturned crates, boxes, and the cadets' trunks served as chairs and tables.

Bootblacks shined the cadets' shoes and washerwomen did their laundry about every two weeks. Otherwise, the young men did the chores themselves—fetching water and firewood and cleaning. They took turns serving as the room orderly, who made sure the space remained spotless, weapons stacked and furniture arranged just so. The orderly banked the fire at night and placed the fire fender in front before snuffing out the candles.

As a nod to equality among cadets, no one could use money from home. Each cadet received $28 a month for food, uniforms, blankets, books, trips to the barber, and whatever else was needed. Thayer did not want the young men going into debt. If a cadet emptied his account, the superintendent denied further purchases until the next pay day.

Robert's long days, with nearly every minute scheduled, began when reveille sounded at dawn. He had twenty minutes to dress and tidy his shared room for morning inspections by the officer of the day. Then cadets drilled until breakfast at 7:00 a.m. Classes met every day but Sunday. After classes, cadets practiced company and battalion drills and then marched in the daily parade. Supper break brought some relief for the hours of study still ahead until taps played at 10:00 p.m. Any cadet with his candle burning after the bugler played would be reported. In the cold, dark days of winter, the academy suspended morning and afternoon drills.

Sundays meant formal room inspections and attendance at chapel. In the afternoon the corps lined up in front of the superintendent's house in dress uniforms: white pants and gray jackets, shoes and bullet-shaped buttons gleaming, black plumes on tall leather hats floating on the

31

breeze. Guests and official dignitaries reviewed the corps. Shouldering their polished muskets, cadets marched and wheeled in perfect lockstep and honored the crowd with artillery salutes.

The academy served notoriously bad food—mostly "well boiled" mushy vegetables and boiled or roasted meats. Saturday, Sunday, and Monday, the mess hall treated cadets to "a pudding with sauce" for dessert. Seven waiters delivered the food and cleaned up. But most cadets remained hungry and smuggled food from the mess hall into their rooms—bread toasted in the fireplace was a favorite snack.

Cadets had time for themselves at lunch and a couple of hours on Sunday afternoons. Free time meant hiking, fishing, and swimming in nearby Gees Point, where the cadets also bathed. Winter replaced swimming with ice-skating. Occasionally there were dances. Robert learned how to dance from a dancing master brought in for the Point's summer camps. Dancing well was a gentlemanly skill important in society.

Life at West Point was harsh and rigid, and the young men bonded in their shared misery. They marched, polished weapons, starved, froze, and sweltered together. They suffered through hours of tough classes and study, hours of drill and practice and maneuvers. Some buckled under the strain of hard work, constant regulations, and very little free time, and not surprisingly, many young men balked at Thayer's stern rules. When cadets did amuse themselves, it often involved rule breaking.

RULES AND PUNISHMENTS

The year Robert entered West Point, Thayer instituted a new discipline program. Any cadet breaking rules, or engaging in other poor behavior, received demerits—black marks listed under their name. Thayer hoped that this clear, daily record of student behavior would be a fair way to show why a student was expelled. Anyone earning over two hundred demerits in a year was dismissed—the "awful 200," Robert later called them.

Regulations and endless rules governed a cadet's life. Rooms were usually checked four times a day to make sure the furniture appeared in good order and the cadets diligent. Hair hanging below the upper edge of a coat collar—demerit. Spitting on the floor—demerit. Weapons not polished—demerit. Cooking in the barracks—demerit. Candlesticks placed haphazardly—demerit. Slouching—demerit. Lying in bed after reveille—demerit. Stepping out of line—demerit. Swearing—demerit. Throwing rocks on the Plain (parade ground) or at buildings—demerit. Whistling in quarters—demerit.

Gambling was strictly forbidden. "The practice of chewing, snuffing, & smoking tobacco," deemed bad for health and an expensive habit, was off limits as well. And any cadet caught with liquor in his possession, or caught smuggling it into the barracks, faced dismissal.

Many cadets risked sneaking off the post to enjoy food and drink at Benny Havens, a tavern soon memorialized in the cadet song "Benny Havens, Oh!" Here, cadets raised their tankards with their backs to one another, so if asked, they could truthfully say they had not seen their fellow cadets drinking.

One cadet a year ahead of Lee survived a court-martial for visiting Benny Havens. Jefferson Davis, future president of the Confederacy during the Civil War, ranked low on Thayer's list of promising cadets. Davis also instigated one of the most notorious incidents at West Point during Lee's years at the academy. In the early hours of Christmas Day 1826, Davis smuggled alcohol into the barracks, resulting in a late-night spree known as the Eggnog Riot. Drunken cadets, some armed with swords, muskets, and bayonets, turned violent and destroyed property.

To Thayer's horror, an investigation revealed that seventy cadets, nearly a third of the Corps's two hundred and fifty men, were involved.

The scandal threatened the academy itself. Many in Congress already resented providing funds for West Point. People feared that academy graduates would become a gang of military elite run by wealthy and influential families.

Nineteen cadets faced a court-martial, and out of those, Thayer dismissed eleven. Though invited to Davis's party, Robert had stayed in his room while revelers wreaked havoc in North Barracks. But he sat with the corps and listened as President John Quincy Adams voiced his disappointment in "Young Men from whom their Country had a right to expect better things." Jefferson Davis was not among those dismissed. He graduated just eleven demerits shy of dismissal for misconduct, his work in the classroom as dismal as his behavior.

Punishments for minor rule breaking included extra drill, called "walking the area," or extra tours of guard duty. Not only tedious, these punishments meant one more thing crammed into a cadet's overflowing schedule of classes, drill, and study. Cadets could also be confined to their rooms for punishment or confined to one of two cells in the barracks. The light prison had windows; the dark prison did not. "Unsoldierlike and disorderly conduct" often meant time spent locked in the guardhouse. The worst offenders faced a court-martial and dismissal from the academy.

CLASSES AND EXAMS

Classwork at West Point encouraged problem solving over simple memorization, the teaching method at most schools. West Point's classes in science, math, and engineering exceeded anything taught at other American universities. Until 1835, West Point was the only school that offered an engineering degree. When colleges opened their own engineering departments they hired West Point instructors and copied academy materials.

Over his four years at West Point, Robert's courses included natural and experimental philosophy (science and mechanics), mathematics (calculus, trigonometry, and descriptive geometry), engineering, military tactics, and artillery training. He also studied French, astronomy, technical drawing, surveying and mapping, chemistry, geography, mineralogy, English, grammar, history, constitutional law, and political economy. Students took notes in class, worked problems at the blackboard, and defended their answers.

In June, members of a Board of Visitors descended on West Point to witness the end-of-term exams—"a wearisome & painful season," Lee later called it. Cadets sat on benches facing two long tables. The Board of Visitors sat at one table. The Academic Board and teachers, with Thayer in the middle, filled the other. An officer sat between the tables and asked questions.

Two large blackboards loomed in front of the tables. Thayer called four cadets forward at a time, two young men standing at each of the blackboards. One cadet figured out the problem given to him, then turned and explained his answer to the Board of Visitors and the Academic Board; the other three cadets worked on their own problems and then took their turn answering. Each cadet was examined for about an hour in each subject over the course of five stomach-twisting days.

The event moved like clockwork. Cadets were either answering questions or working at the blackboards every moment, and no one left the room without Thayer's permission. As one observer noted, "Thirteen men were under the screw for four hours, on a single branch [subject]." The exams continued for two weeks.

Afterward, the Board of Visitors prepared reports for the War Department, praising much of what Thayer had achieved, and hoped to achieve, at the academy. Only about half of an entering class made it through to graduation four years later. That toughness in the classroom served as another bond among the cadets who survived.

* * * * *

35

This George Catlin painting of West Point, done around 1830, shows (from left to right) North Barracks, South Barracks, The Academy, and Mess Hall.

Robert must have had true talent in math: he performed so well on his first-year exams that Thayer named him an acting assistant professor of mathematics for his second year, which carried a welcomed bonus of $10 more in his monthly pay. But it also added more to his workload.

After the first year, Lee ranked third in his class; he soon moved up to the second spot, chasing Charles Mason of New York. Lee was promoted to staff sergeant, sergeant major, and, in his final year, Adjutant of the Corps. But Mason earned the distinction of Captain of the Corps and the glory of leading the long gray line of cadets on parade.

Still, Robert had the respect of all around him. As he walked down the lines inspecting the cadets, he rewarded good work with a smile or nod. One cadet remembered that it felt like receiving a nod "from Olympian Jove" when Lee singled him out.

At the end of four years Charles Mason stood first in the class, just ahead of Robert. Lee graduated without a single demerit against his name, though his page in the record book was marred by the overflow demerits of a dismissed cadet named Pleiades Orion Lumpkin. With great relief Lee received his diploma in June 1829. Of the one hundred and four young men entering West Point with Robert, only forty-six remained at graduation. The graduates smashed their slates on the large boulders of the parade ground and fired off guns in celebration. Robert's excellent standing earned him a commission as a second lieutenant in the prestigious Army Corps of Engineers.

West Point served as an important touchstone in Robert's life. He possessed Thayer's most sought-after qualities of a soldier within himself. Duty and dedication came naturally, and West Point strengthened these intangibles in Lee. West Point played to Lee's strengths academically, too—classwork based in math, science, and engineering that stressed how to build and solve problems. He made lifelong friends at the Point. But for all of his success there, the years at the academy were tough ones.

None of Robert's letters from West Point have survived (or at least none have been found). But an 1851 letter written to his son Custis, then a cadet at the academy, offers insight into Lee's own experience there. "I pray you may have *strength* [and] *fortitude* . . . to accomplish the course before you," Robert wrote. West Point demanded stamina, resolve, and hard work to make it through. But most of all, Lee told his son, West Point required a young man's "*courageous heart.*"

CHAPTER THREE

"WORTHY OF EACH OTHER"

"Do you ever think of me My own Sweet Mary? And how much do you want to see me? Not half as much as I want to see you."
—*Robert Lee to Mary Anna Randolph Custis,*
May 13, 1831

As his friends left West Point for a celebration trip to Niagara Falls, Robert headed home to Virginia, a newly minted army officer with $100 in his pocket. He found his mother in failing health. Robert nursed and comforted her, and when she died a few weeks later he was too shattered by grief to attend the funeral.

Another shadow reached from the past. Robert's half brother, Henry Lee IV, again made news when he was appointed by his friend President Andrew Jackson to a foreign post. Henry still hadn't paid back the money he'd stolen from his young sister-in-law, and the Senate refused to confirm his appointment. All the old scandal resurfaced.

Grieving, gloomy, and lonely, Robert set out for his first army assignment. The War of 1812 had revealed America's poor seaside defenses. The army now planned an ambitious program of fort building and repair. Robert arrived in mosquito-and-sandfly-infested Cockspur Island, Georgia, assigned to build a new fort at the mouth of the Savannah River. He begged for letters from his family. Making matters more depressing, he'd fallen in love with a distant cousin and childhood

Wildlife sketches Lee drew while stationed in Georgia

friend, Mary Anna Randolph Custis. But he couldn't even write to her without permission.

"MY SWEET COUSIN, MARY"

Unlike Robert with his rather uncertain upbringing, Mary Custis grew up the beloved only child of one of America's most famous men. Her father, George Washington Parke Custis, was the grandson of Martha Washington, raised by Martha and her second husband, the first president. As a young man Custis had built a grand house, called Arlington, on the heights above the Potomac River. The home's mighty white columns—inspired by Greek temples—stood visible from a distance, framed by lush woods. From the wide front portico the Custis family looked out over the nation's new capital across the river below.

A growing, bustling, youthful nation needed its own heroes, and Americans revered no man more than George Washington. It had fallen to G. W. Custis to keep that spirit of his illustrious grandparents and the American Revolution alive. He turned Arlington into a lived-in museum of all things Washington. Even the elderly people Custis enslaved— who'd once served the Washingtons—were sought out and interviewed.

Custis filled Arlington with Washington treasures and welcomed friends and strangers alike to view the relics. Washington's war tent hosted celebrations on the Arlington lawn and traveled on loan. The family used George and Martha's furniture, and dined with their silver and dishes, while family portraits hung on the walls. Special occasions called for the Washingtons' punch bowl with a frigate painted on the bottom, the ship's hull visible only when the punch ran low. Custis passed around fragile family letters, some a hundred years old, for guests to read aloud. Lucky friends might receive a letter bearing Washington's signature as a souvenir.

G. W. Custis wrote histories and biographies, including *Recollections of Washington*. In high demand as a public speaker, he also penned popular plays. He painted large-scale canvases, usually depicting events in the life of his step-grandfather, George Washington. He dabbled in agriculture and offered prizes for American sheep breeding.

The Custis name, wealth, and intimate association with the Washingtons granted Miss Mary Custis a lofty spot in American society. She thought nothing of sitting down to dinner with a president across the table. She was somebody special, the great-granddaughter of Martha Washington, an heiress to land, money, and enslaved human beings.

The enslaved made possible the Custis family's comfortable life at Arlington. There were rumors that Mary had a half sister, a former slave who'd been freed and granted seventeen acres of land by G. W. Custis. Neighbors talked about the "yellow" servants at Arlington, meaning those of mixed race. They commented on how some of the Arlington slaves could pass for white.

* * * * *

A well-educated, clever young woman, Mary read poetry and novels, and stayed current by reading four newspapers a day. She rode horses and took long walks. She sewed and she painted. She wrote engaging letters and inherited a passion for gardening from her mother, the generous and kind Mary Fitzhugh Custis.

But the dark-haired, brown-eyed Miss Custis also spoke her mind, sometimes with a sharpness that discouraged her beaux. Robert's younger sister Mildred advised Mary to act more like other ladies and soften her behavior. Mary's aunt, Nelly Custis Lewis, thought her niece a "sweet modest girl, so humble & gentle with all her classical attainments. She has wit & satire too, when they are required." Aunt Nelly wished her own son would wed his cousin, noting, "There are few worthy of her I think."

When Mary's favorite uncle died suddenly in 1830, she experienced a sudden and profound religious conversion. She worked to curb her temper and become a more selfless person, devoting hours to contemplating God, her feelings, her motives, her sins.

Mary Anna Randolph Custis, painted by Auguste Hervieu in 1830, during her courtship with Robert Lee

"SHE MUST WRITE TO ME"

Robert and Mary's friendship deepened on his few visits home from West Point. But courting Mary meant following certain rules. Robert pestered his brothers and sisters to support his cause with Miss Custis. In May 1830, he enlisted Carter, then visiting Arlington, to tell Mary that "if she thinks I am going to stay here, after you go away, without hearing any thing of her, . . . she is very much mistaken. So . . . she must write to me, & if she does not I'll tell her mother. Or if she will say that I may write to her, she will have to answer me through common politeness."

Things moved quickly; after all, the two already knew each other well. Six months later, Mary agreed to marry Robert. The young couple won her mother's approval. But Mary's father had "not yet made up his mind, though it is supposed [he] will not object," Robert wrote Carter. Still, he feared the worst—that Mr. Custis would not look past the Lee family scandals. And would Custis want his only child to wed a poor soldier who'd move her about the country? Mary worked on her father, and when he finally gave his consent in March 1831, Robert rejoiced: "If *you* 'felt so grateful' to your Father for his kindness, what must I feel."

Robert, down in Georgia with the army, yearned for Mary—to read to her, walk with her, ride with her. He wooed her with snippets of poetry from Byron and Shakespeare, and quoted the novels of Sir Walter Scott. But he was frustrated that Mary's mother, too, read his letters. "And now My sweet Mary I must end, you know what I would say to you if I was there, but I cannot write it."

Lee felt overburdened with work, stymied by hurricanes and rain that washed away his efforts. He described for Mary the harsh conditions as they built canals through the island, a wharf, and houses for the builders to live in, often working in water and mud. They had laid out the fort, he told her, and made a great embankment all around

43

it in case of storms. They had created machines—pumps, pile drivers, and cranes—to use in the process. They'd made surveys and drawings and dug foundations in the sandy soil. One hundred and fifty men, some enslaved, labored to build Fort Pulaski. "Now call us lazy," he challenged Mary.

On those still and beautiful nights, with the stars reflected on the water, Robert told Mary he'd entered the army because "I thought & intended always to be *one* & alone in the World for I never expected You *would* be mine." In his loneliness he confided, "The truth is, that I have been for so many years in the habit of repressing my feelings."

Mary wished Robert might turn his heart more to God, and "then I should have nothing more to wish for on earth with regard to you." Robert told her not to expect miracles, but to give him time. To Mrs. Custis he wrote a teasing note of complaint against her daughter. Each of Mary's letters carried a little sermon aimed at him, he said, and she never passed up an opportunity to comment on "the wickedness of men, that's at me."

The realities of army life meant packing on short notice and moving to a new post. In late March 1831 Lee was ordered to Hampton Roads, Virginia—and he was not unhappy to be heading home, closer to Mary and his family.

"TOO LATE TO CHANGE YOUR MIND"

Robert applied for furlough to begin June 30 and rejected Mary's talk of delaying their wedding until fall. He began making arrangements for them to live at his new post. Mary was glad to hear he'd found them two rooms, but would she be so pleased, he wondered, if "one of them is the 'size of a piece of Chalk'?"—more like a closet with a window in it. "I am sure you would like better to have a house to yourself, where your mother could stay with you," he wrote. He advised Mary she could also bring Cassy, her enslaved maid.

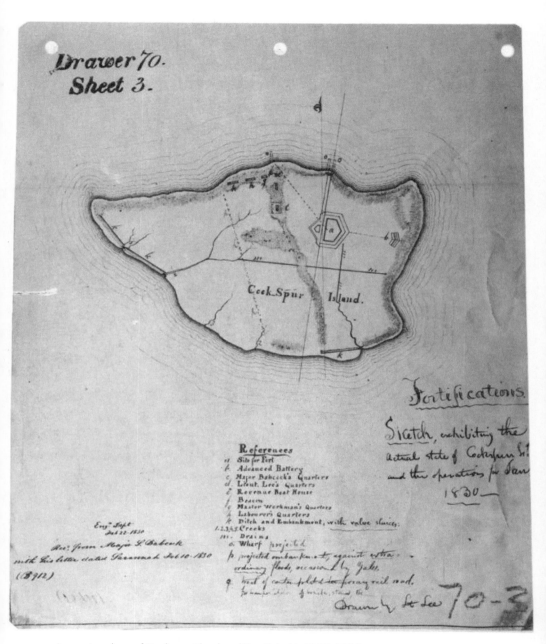

A map Lee drew of Cockspur Island and Fort Pulaski, 1829–1830

Still Mary hesitated. Marriage meant leaving Arlington and her parents. It meant losing the freedoms of young womanhood and facing the scariest part of being a wife—the dangers of childbirth. But she mustn't change her mind at this late date, Robert told her. He feared that her courage was "oozing out" at her fingertips and cautioned, "Do not let it all escape." He offered Mary a final warning about the new life that awaited her. She had been so sheltered by home and parents that "the change from Arlington to a Garrison of wicked & Blasphemous soldiers will be greater & more *shocking* to you than you are aware of."

Robert and Mary wed at Arlington on the evening of June 30, 1831. Robert reported to an absent friend that there'd been no fainting or fighting, "nor anything uncommon which could be twisted into an adventure." As rain stormed against the windows, they stood in the parlor and repeated their vows. The bride's fingers trembled in the groom's hand, who noted he felt "bold as a sheep." Friends and

George Washington Parke Custis, grandson of Martha Washington and owner of Arlington; Mary Fitzhugh Custis, a kind and humble woman who became a second mother to Robert Lee

relatives pronounced the bride never lovelier and the groom handsome, with merry eyes and high color in his cheeks. "They are worthy of each other," noted a cousin.

"THIS WILL NEVER DO"

Robert and Mary Lee spent years adjusting to their differences. Mary was not easily led, as society expected of a woman. Robert once asked a female friend at a party to tell Mary her petticoats showed beneath her dress. If *he* told her, she'd pay no attention. On another occasion, bedridden after a long illness, Mary took scissors to her matted hair in a fit of frustration. Lee told a friend, "When I left today she talked of having it shaved off and I expect on my return to find her *bald*."

Mary freely gave her husband unwanted advice, and Robert bullied and scolded his wife. Zealously punctual, Robert found Mary's tardiness annoying. Robert needed "order & methodology" and found Mary slack in housekeeping matters. Mary observed that once her orderly husband had arranged things to his liking, even in the dark he could grab any piece of paper or clothing he wanted.

Robert questioned his wife's money management. Above all, he feared and hated debt. Mary told him her accounting methods may not be "your nice mode of keeping yours," but she paid off everything she owed just the same. "Do not be uneasy about me," she reminded her husband.

One bit of household management Robert gladly pushed onto Mary was dealing with their enslaved household servants, especially the few he'd inherited from his mother. "I do not know what to do with [them]," he wrote his wife. Robert found slavery messy, the slaves irritating. It was an inefficient system forcing "unwilling hands to work." He disliked the responsibility of slavery—having to feed, clothe, house, and doctor people whom he saw as lazy and ungrateful.

He complained about the poor work done by his slaves. They gave him "useless trouble." When he thought of renting out a woman called Nancy to a fellow officer, Robert realized that he could not "*recommend her as a good cook and washer*" and would not be willing to take her himself. "In the meantime," he wrote Mary early in their marriage, "you may do with them as you please. . . . But do not trouble yourself about them, as they are not worth it."

The biggest challenge for Robert and Mary was his army career. As a young army wife, Mary missed her parents and Arlington. She felt herself a wanderer without a permanent home. She made the best of their cramped army quarters but resented the public nature of fort life. "What would I give for one stroll on the hills at Arlington," she wrote her mother from Fort Monroe in Virginia.

A watercolor of Arlington painted in 1853 by Benson Lossing

Just months after the wedding Mary returned to Arlington for a long visit, leaving an unhappy husband behind. "This will never do Molly," he wrote, using a nickname for his wife. When she returned to the post, Mary brought her mother with her. Another time when his wife returned to Arlington, Robert vented, "This is a terrible life we lead Molly, unsatisfactory, profitless & irksome."

Robert did not wish to rely on Mary's parents for anything. He loved Arlington, and he loved and admired her parents, too. They'd been an important part of Lee's life since childhood. But he wanted to have his own home with Mary. When the army transferred Lee to a desk job in Washington D.C., he looked for a house he and Mary could rent. As there was nothing suitable and affordable, Robert rented a room in a boarding house for those nights he couldn't make the trip across the river and up to Arlington, where Mary stayed with her parents.

Time and effort on both their parts soothed their differences, though separations remained hard, especially for Robert. Eventually, he encouraged Mary to visit Arlington, but she often decided to stay by his side and give her husband "some comfort at home."

CHAPTER FOUR

"THE LITTLE LEES"

"I still feel the glow of your infant cheek as I carried you in my arms. I yet feel your arms clasping my neck as I swam with you on my back, & I love to think of the many, many times I have hugged you to my heart."

—*Robert Lee to his son Fitzhugh "Rooney" Lee,*
November 1, 1856

Over the next fourteen years Mary Lee gave birth to seven children—and amazingly for the time, they all survived into adulthood. The first child, a son Mary named after her father, was born at Fort Monroe. All the other Lee children entered the world at Arlington in a tiny dressing room off of Mary and Robert's upstairs bedroom. Nicknames promptly took the place of the little Lees' formal names:

George Washington Custis Lee (born in 1832) became Boo, and
   later Custis.
Mary Custis Lee (1835) was called Mee or Daughter.
William Henry Fitzhugh Lee (1837) became Rooney, and later
   Fitzhugh.
Anne Carter Lee (1839) became Annie.
Eleanor Agnes Lee (1841) was called Wiggy, and later Agnes.
Robert Edward Lee Jr. (1843) became Rob or Robertus.
Mildred Childe Lee (1846) was called Precious Life or Milly.

Mary struggled with childbirth, a dangerous time for mother and baby. She developed a serious groin infection after the birth of Daughter in 1835. Confined to bed, even four months later she couldn't stand, let alone walk. Robert's brother Carter wrote a relative he'd received alarming news about Mary's health and dreaded the arrival of the next mail. Robert, away on assignment surveying in the Great Lakes region, knew nothing of Mary's condition.

When Mary wrote and asked him to come home, Robert responded sharply. How could she ask him to leave early "from the performance of a duty imposed on me by my profession"? She should encourage him to perform his best, not entice him to shirk his job. Mary must cheer up and carry on.

But when Robert arrived home several months later, his wife's condition and appearance shocked him. Nine months after Daughter's birth, she could barely walk. Robert wrote Carter that his wife was "much shattered" and depressed. Although she would have five more children, Mary never recovered her full strength. The infection may have contributed to the crippling arthritis that tormented her in the coming years.

From this time forward, there was no more talk of the Lees having a permanent home away from Arlington. Mary must always be safe at Arlington with her mother when the babies came. And while Mary made a point of not complaining to Robert about her health (even though she often suffered), he became more sympathetic to her needs.

"YOUR AFFECTIONATE FATHER"

In an age when most fathers practiced hands-off childrearing, Lee ached to be involved. Children found Robert Lee a magnet—even in his darkest days, he always took time to talk to a child. With his own children he romped and played. When away he longed to hug and press them with kisses.

A handsome Robert Lee in his dress uniform as a First Lieutenant of Engineers. Painted by William West in 1838.

Rob recalled how he and Mildred enjoyed crawling into bed with their father, snuggling close as he talked "in his bright, entertaining way." Lee fretted about their teething and sat up nights with his sick children. He joined his older sons and their friends trying to high-jump on the lawn at Arlington. He taught his children to swim and ride; in winter he took them sledding and skating. His sons tagged along to see the engineering projects he was working on. He brought home a pony and stray dogs and cats, and teased the girls about their pet chickens.

With the family all at Arlington, Lee awoke early and snipped roses to set at the breakfast plates of his wife and daughters. Little Mildred got a rosebud. When Lee sat down to tell his children a story, he liked to have his hands and feet tickled, sliding off his slippers and putting his feet in someone's lap. "No tickling, no story," he'd say when the tickler's fingers lagged at an exciting spot in the tale.

A daguerreotype of Robert Lee with his son William Henry Fitzhugh Lee, nicknamed Rooney

He wanted to raise and shape his children, to help them in their lives. But army duty often stood in the way. "You do not know how much I have missed you and the children, my dear Mary," he wrote. At another time he wrote her, "Oh, what pleasure I lose in being separated from my children! Nothing can compensate me for that." He dreamed of Daughter and Boo nearly every night. He described one vivid dream to his wife: "Our last romp together was a race up the hill, in which the little woman flew like a gazelle, and far outran the *Boo*. . . . How is the little darling and her bright eyes." No persnickety detail was too small for his worry or comment. He told Mary she must make the girls wear their sunbonnets, for "Annie is getting horribly freckled and I can't allow it."

When Lee returned home from the Mexican War after an absence of two years, young Rob waited to greet his father. Scrubbed, dressed, his hair curled in fashionable ringlets, Rob gathered with the household in Arlington's large entry hall. After a moment Lee pushed through the crowd, asking, "Where is my little boy?" He then picked up and kissed another child, not knowing his own son, to poor Rob's humiliation.

"THEY *CAN* IF THEY *TRY*"

Robert shared a glimpse of the family whirlwind at Arlington with a friend. "I have been made a horse, dog, ladder, & target for cannon by the little Lees since I have been writing," he noted as he hurriedly finished his letter, "so I wish you well over it." He had more patience than Mary with their brood. The demands of motherhood often irritated her. Along with the difficult pregnancies, she faced an endless round of nursing babies, teaching the older children to read and write, instructing them in religion, and figuring out how to dress them all. The constant frenzy of young voices jangled her nerves, and she could "scarcely get a moment to think or read." In frustration, she sometimes called them brats.

Robert had a solution for all this. To succeed, he believed, his children needed to learn obedience, practice self-denial, and give every situation their best. Throughout his life, people greatly admired Lee himself for these qualities. But he didn't make it easy for those around him. His letters to his children mixed longing and loving words with a barrage of dos and don'ts.

A daguerreotype of Mary Lee, probably with her youngest son, Rob. Boys wore dresses and long curls until about the age of five.

When Custis entered West Point in 1850, Robert escorted him to the academy and helped him settle in—no traveling alone and arriving as a stranger, as Robert had done. Lee wrote his mother-in-law, "It seemed to be a great comfort to him to have me along, & lightened considerably the pain of leaving home." Two years later he pressured Custis to claim the number one spot in his class, the honor that had eluded Lee despite his exemplary work. "You must be No. 1," Robert preached. "It is a fine number. Easily found & remembered. Simple and unique. Jump to it fellow."

In much of his haranguing, Lee the father sounded like Lee the soldier. He preached duty all day long. He saw his second son, Rooney, as thoughtless and impulsive. At age eight, the boy had accidentally sliced off the ends of two fingertips with a hay cutter, and years later Lee still worried that Rooney had not learned self-control and the principles of duty. Until Rooney did, Robert told Mary, he could "never feel assured of his conduct."

He urged Mary to make sure eleven-year-old Rob learned "obedience, regularity & precision in the discharge of his duties." The boy needed to know that work was a necessity and he had to apply his abilities. "If he is *made* to know them now, *habit* will make them easy."

The girls, too, enjoyed their share of fatherly expectations. Foremost, they must be *"regular, orderly & energetic* in the performance of all their duties." When Annie and Agnes said they didn't want singing lessons, pleading that they had no talent, Robert exploded. *Can't* was not a word he wanted to hear. "They *can* if they *try* & I say in addition they *must,*" he wrote his wife. In 1853 he offered Annie his mixture of love and nagging: "I hope you will always appear to me as you are now painted on my heart, and that you will endeavour to improve and so conduct yourself as to make you happy and me joyful all our lives. Diligent and earnest attention to *all* your duties can only accomplish this."

He also expected his children to excel at school. Custis *did* graduate number one in his class at West Point. Rooney, never a great student, went to Harvard before leaving to join the army. Rob later recalled his father patiently helping him with schoolwork and remembered how hard he had tried to please him.

Lee sent Agnes and Annie to a boarding school that went beyond the typical education for young ladies. Along with the usual music, drawing, and French, the Lee girls studied algebra, chemistry, botany, theology, political economy, geography, philosophy, logic, and Latin. A misspelling in a letter from Mildred prompted her father to tease, "I noticed that you spelt Saturday with two ts (satturday). One is considered enough in the Army, but perhaps the fashion is to have two."

So often far from home, Lee knew he was "most vulnerable" when it came to his children's welfare. Perhaps he tried so hard because his own father had tried so little. But however much Robert pushed, prodded, and counseled, his children mostly responded with affection over irritation. Even the most independent of his children, bossy and adventurous daughter Mary, felt pride in her father. In the coming crisis of Civil War that defined their young adult years, and for the rest of their lives, the Lee children stood by Robert's side.

CHAPTER FIVE

"HERE WORKING FOR MY COUNTRY"

PART I

"The object is . . . to get a channel through the Rapids for S[team] Boats during the stages of low water and will consist in blasting the rock under water and rem[oving] it from the channel."

—*Robert Lee to John Mackay,*
a West Point friend and fellow soldier,
writing from St. Louis, June 27, 1838

Robert Lee arrived in St. Louis, Missouri, in late summer of 1837. Mary and the children remained at Arlington, so Robert faced the sweltering heat and humidity, the droning mosquitoes, the choking dust, and the danger of cholera alone. He'd been sent to clear and tame the mighty Mississippi River, one of the nation's most important waterways. Over time the river's current had deposited a growing island of mud, silt, and sand—nearly two hundred acres covered in cottonwood trees—that blocked the harbor of St. Louis. The island threatened steamboats and trade. Congress allocated funds for the project and, for the first time, the army put Lee in charge.

This project was one of many taken on by the Army Corps of Engineers. When Robert graduated from West Point, he became one of only twenty-six engineers working in the field. Their efforts pushed America's frontier westward. This elite group surveyed new territories, dug canals, and laid roads and railroad tracks stretching into America's interior. They strengthened defenses, constructed lighthouses, and built bridges and forts. Along the way, they developed new ways to keep records and oversee large projects. One prominent general said the army had traded swords, guns, and cannon for shovels, picks, and saws.

*****

At St. Louis, Robert faced a daunting task—earlier efforts to control the Mississippi had failed. And he was supposed to figure out what to do with a boulder-strewn section of rapids two hundred miles upstream, where the waters were impossible to navigate when the river ran low. Lee and another army engineer, Montgomery Meigs, surveyed the situation at St. Louis and then traveled north to inspect the Des Moines rapids from a dugout canoe. Lee recorded information about the depths and currents, made surveys, and developed plans, while Meigs drew the final maps.

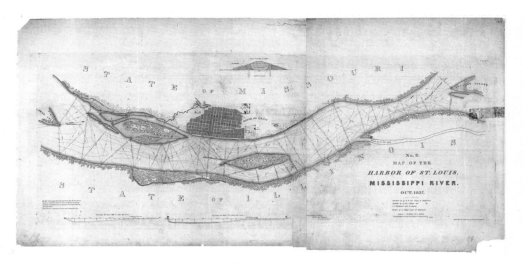

Robert Lee and Montgomery Meigs created this map of the harbor at St. Louis in 1837.

Lee's plans proposed blasting away the rock that caused the rapids and keeping the natural course of the river. For St. Louis he proposed building a pier to "give direction to the current." He suggested driving deep pilings into the water for the pier, surrounding the pilings with stone, and filling them with brush to let the river wash through without too much pressure on the structures. The brush would also act as a filter and catch silt and branches carried by the river. Lee also proposed building a wing dam that extended partway into the river. At 1,300 feet long, the wing dam was meant to direct the river current, force away the island, and make a new shipping lane.

In late 1837 Lee returned east to present his plans to Congress and seek funding. Despite the "crowding, squeezing and scrambling" on the train and steamboat, Mary and sons Custis and Rooney made the long trip back to Missouri with Lee, leaving Daughter behind at Arlington with her grandparents. Lee admitted it was "a rough country" to bring them to, but having family soothed life for Robert "most marvelously." Mary and the boys stayed with Robert for a year before he took them home to Arlington—Mary was eight months pregnant—to await the birth of their fourth child.

* * * * *

Congress did give money for the project, but not as much as Lee had hoped for. St. Louis added funds, too. But buying a steamboat, store boats, and a machine to drive in the pilings ate a huge chunk of the money right away. Robert needed a pile engine thirty to thirty-five feet tall, worked by a horse, with a ram of 1,600 to 2,000 pounds. He hired eighty men and fitted up keelboats to house them. He dealt with heat, troublesome mules, and grumpy workers, and with water levels either too high or too low.

Lee joined his workforce every morning at sunrise and supervised the day's efforts. At night he drew new plans and figured estimates. He wrote orders for everything from rice to rope. Lobbying Congress and the War Department for continued funding became an unpleasant part of his job. Improvements to the river "will be repaid an hundred fold," he reminded the purse-holders in Washington.

While in Missouri, Lee did more than make accurate soundings and studies of the Mississippi. He noted the beautiful prairie that lured

Americans west. Prairie hens and partridges roamed so thick on the ground, Lee marveled, that he could hardly keep from stumbling over them. He dug down three feet into the black prairie soil, so much richer than Virginia's clay, that "you could cultivate it with your feet." Lee measured black walnut trees and sugar maples. He hunted turkey and fished. He also observed "plenty of Indians" and made note of their blankets, buffalo robes, and painted faces.

With his Virginia upper class snobbery showing, Robert told family he found the rough Missourians "somewhat amusing." They were "a swaggering, noisy set," he said, "careless of getting work." Those of the "higher order" were not much better, "engrossed" only in business and piling up money. Even the children seemed dirty and "uninteresting."

Lee's efforts began paying off. The Mississippi ran deeper and broader along the St. Louis waterfront, and the massive island had begun shifting downriver. Lee's men had blasted and cleared tons of rock at the Des Moines rapids, widening the shipping channel. But in spring 1839, as a financial depression gripped the nation, Congress cut funding for the project.

Lee returned to Washington, frustrated at not completing his assignment. But he was thrilled to escape the West, see his new baby, Annie, and be back in Virginia. "I felt so elated when I again found myself within the Confines of the Ancient Dominion [Virginia], that I nodded to all the old trees as I passed," he wrote a cousin, "chatted with the drivers and stable boys, Shook hands with the land lords, and in the fullness of my heart—don't tell Cousin Mary—wanted to kiss all the pretty girls I met."

ARMY FRUSTRATIONS

Though a soldier to the core, many things about army life discouraged Lee. He thought about quitting nearly every year. Why should he spend so much of his life lonely and away from his family? And for what—low pay and snail-paced promotions? The army did not promote on merit. Congress set the number of officers the army could have at each rank. The only way to move up was if someone above you got promoted, retired, or died, opening a slot. The slots were usually filled by the most senior officers moving up, leaving younger men to fret that they'd never get ahead.

Lee followed news of the yearly army bills as they moved through Congress; he hoped for pay raises or more chances for promotion. "The manner in which the Army is considered and treated by the Country and those whose business it is to nourish and take care of it, is enough to disgust every one with the Service," Lee wrote his friend John Mackay. Such treatment, Lee felt, would drive good soldiers from the army and embitter those who stayed. "Oh we have been horribly shamefully treated," Lee wrote passionately in June 1836 when it seemed no promotions were coming. "In fact I am in *dis-g-u-s-t*." Later that year the army did promote Lee from second lieutenant to first lieutenant. Two years later, while he was in St. Louis, Robert advanced to the rank of captain.

The only way to get more pay was to get promoted. Lee always felt a money pinch, and if Congress voted to cut army salaries everything looked even bleaker. One year the army cut his pay by $500, and then lopped off another $300 the following year. He needed to get ahead in his career, even if it called for sacrifices, so he and Mary could "give our dear children such an education and standing in life as we could wish," he explained to Mrs. Custis. To his brother Carter he complained, "I never felt poorer in my life & for the first time in my life I have not been able to pay my debts." Having Arlington as a refuge for his family did make things easier for Lee.

He was good at his job, careful and meticulous. Other army engineers left the service for better paying jobs in business and industry.

"I shall make a strong effort to leave it [the army]," Lee announced in 1848. Family encouraged him to resign; he could manage Arlington or another Custis plantation. But Lee never made the decision, never took action. "I am waiting, looking and hoping, for some good opportunity to bid an affectionate farewell to my dear Uncle Sam," he wrote a friend. But waiting and hoping was all he ever did. No new job dropped into his lap "like a ripe pear."

Robert valued the friendships he made in the army. This, he told Mary, was what kept him in the service so long and now made him afraid to leave it: "I do not know where I should meet with so much friendship out of it." Most people commented on Lee's great dignity, but he also had a common touch. He joked with fellow officers and shamelessly flirted with the ladies.

*****

From 1841 to 1846 Lee worked at Fort Hamilton on the western end of Long Island overlooking New York harbor. The lengthy stay allowed the family time together in New York mixed with trips back home to Arlington. Mary shopped in the city and daringly took the children sea bathing. Her modest bathing costume included stockings, a corset, and a long skirt.

If Mary and the children were away, Lee kept company with Spec, a black-and-tan terrier. Robert wrote the family that Spec "has become so jealous now that he will hardly let me look at the cats." But the sameness of the work plagued him. Martha Williams, nicknamed Markie, was one of Mary's cousins and a close friend of Robert's. To Markie he confided, "My thoughts are engrossed . . . in the construction of cranes, Diving bells, Steam Pile drivers &c [etc.]. . . . If it was not for my heart, Markie, I might as well be a pile or stone myself, laid quietly at the bottom of the river."

In August 1846 Robert Lee received orders that energized his

Lee worked at Fort Hamilton on Long Island, New York, shown on the far right, from 1841 to 1846.

Martha Custis Williams, nicknamed Markie, was one of Mary's cousins and a close friend to Robert Lee. Markie's father, who painted this picture, was killed in the Mexican War.

military career. Three months earlier the United States had declared war on Mexico. All around him soldiers readied for battle: they sharpened swords and bayonets and prepared equipment for the field. Mustaches even seemed to bristle in a warlike fashion, Lee noted. But as weeks passed and others headed for Mexico without him, Lee feared he'd be left behind filing reports at Fort Hamilton.

Now his orders had come. After years in the army Robert would get his first taste of action and a new chance to prove himself as a soldier.

CHAPTER SIX

WAR WITH MEXICO

"I wish to assure you of my safety, about wh[ich] you might be doubtful if no letter arrived. The battle [took place] this mor[ning] shortly after Sunrise."

—*Robert to Mary,*
from the hacienda of Mexican general
Antonio López de Santa Anna,
April 18, 1847

Before he left for Mexico, Robert drew up his will, providing for Mary and the children in case he never returned home. He made special provision for his second daughter, "gentle Annie," who'd injured an eye in a scissor accident at Fort Hamilton and might be "more in want of aid than the rest." Then, saying farewell to the family at Arlington, Robert began his long journey west, first to New Orleans, then Texas, which had entered the Union as a slave state in 1845. There he met up with General John Wool's troops, and finally, in October 1846, Lee crossed the Rio Grande into Mexico.

For years, newspapers in Mexico had warned that the United States' unrestrained growth signaled trouble. They perceived Americans as greedy and ambitious, with a "fanatical intolerance" for nonwhite peoples. Americans did believe it their destiny to control the entire continent clear to the Pacific shores. Not many cared that Spaniards, Mexicans, and Native Americans already lived in those western lands.

President James Polk had acquired the vast Oregon Territory in the Northwest from Great Britain in 1846. American settlers swarmed by the thousands over plains and mountains to reach Oregon. Now Polk and Congress turned their attention to American expansion in the Southwest. A boundary dispute with Mexico over Texas became the catalyst for war.

Some Americans saw the war as a land grab and an excuse to spread Southern slavery westward. President Polk, a slave owner, said slavery would never flourish in the deserts and mountains of the West. But some Northerners warned that cotton grew just fine along the rivers of Texas and New Mexico, and slaves had been forced to work in California's mines. If the United States won territories from Mexico, most of that land lay south of the 1820 Missouri Compromise line that banned slavery north of latitude 36°30′ and marked the boundary dividing free and slave states. The Massachusetts legislature saw in Polk's plans the threat "of extending slavery, of strengthening the slave power, and of obtaining control of the free states."

Even with these questions, most Americans favored the war—the United States stood to gain even more vast territories if victorious. Lee wished himself "better satisfied as to the justice of our cause." But the war offered him a chance for "distinction & honour," and he wasn't going to regret the opportunity.

GENERAL SCOTT'S PLAN

Lee's first weeks involved the dull work of road building and cutting into riverbanks, but things picked up in January 1847 when he joined the command of General Winfield Scott. Larger than life in size and personality, "Old Fuss and Feathers" Scott had written the book on army procedures and regulations. Along with men like Thayer at West Point, Scott helped create the country's professional army. Scott, who knew Lee from the various assignments he'd had in Washington D.C., immediately put Lee on his staff.

Scott planned to capture the Mexican port of Vera Cruz—now

known as Veracruz—and from there march overland to the capital of Mexico City, 250 miles away. It was a bold plan. Mexico had the larger army and the advantage of fighting on home soil, and Scott's forces would have to march across rugged and mountainous country, maneuvering cannon and supply wagons as they moved.

MAJOR GENERAL WINFIELD SCOTT.
GENERAL IN CHIEF, UNITED STATES ARMY.

General Winfield Scott relied on army engineers, like Lee, during the Mexican War. Lee came to admire Scott a great deal.

Scott believed in outthinking his enemy and dealing with a crisis calmly—using his head before sending a single soldier into battle. Reconnaissance and reliable information were his best tools, and he meant to use the Army Corps of Engineers in a new way. Engineers became Scott's eyes and ears; he sent them on reconnaissance missions to size up the situation. What was the best way to use the terrain? Was it possible to change the landscape to get his army through? Scott didn't want to attack Mexican strongholds straight on. Was there a way to maneuver his forces for side and rear attacks? The more he knew, the more easily Scott could hit the enemy at their weakest point.

Captain Lee excelled at this headwork. His strengths meshed perfectly with the general's strategy. One impressed junior officer wrote his wife about a staff meeting. Calmly speaking in "well-weighed words," Lee suggested various methods they might try and offered "his own services and exertions" to carry out Scott's vision for the campaign. Lee served as Scott's chief scout, and the general trusted Robert's abilities like no other. Lee was, Scott would write, "the very best soldier I ever saw in the field."

VERA CRUZ

Scott prepared to attack Vera Cruz and the fortress protecting the town, San Juan de Ulúa. The army crowded aboard U.S. Navy ships and waited at sea for several weeks. Lee shared space with his old West Point (and miserably seasick) friend Joseph E. Johnston. A chilled rain fell on the night of March 9 as the Americans loaded onto specially designed landing craft and moved toward shore—troops, cannon, horses, and supplies. They brought three of the largest naval cannon from the ships to pound the fortress and city walls, dragging the monster guns and cannonballs across the sand. Lee chose the spots and began building earthworks to protect the gun batteries.

After waiting several weeks aboard a U.S. Navy ship, Lee landed on the beach at Vera Cruz in March 1847.

The guns opened a constant barrage of fire during the night of March 24. The lit cannon fuses blazed in the darkness. Shells whistled and burst overhead like fireworks, "so beautiful in their flight and so destructive in their fall," wrote Robert. His brother Smith, a naval officer, manned one of the guns. Lee worked to keep the earthworks repaired and sometimes fired the guns himself. He kept near Smith whenever possible, spying his brother's white teeth through the smoke and fire. Later Robert confided in Mary, "I . . . am at a loss what I should have done had he been cut down before me."

After three days of battering, the shattered city of Vera Cruz surrendered on March 29, 1847. It had been Robert's first experience under fire. Though glad of the victory, "my heart bled for the inhabitants," he wrote home. "The soldiers I did not care so much for, but it was terrible to think of the women and children." The United

States now had a base from which to continue Scott's march to Mexico City. In dispatches to Washington, Scott praised the work of his tireless army engineers.

CERRO GORDO

Scott's army pressed forward. The Mexican forces under General Santa Anna had dug in at Cerro Gordo, a narrow and easily defended mountain pass protected by fortifications, cliffs, and a river. Robert took on the dangerous scouting mission to find a way to flank Santa Anna's stronghold. At one point Lee and his guide lay hidden beneath a fallen tree, surrounded by Mexican soldiers, until darkness covered their escape.

Robert discovered a small path through the wasteland on the Mexican left that could be widened to get American troops and wagons through. The Americans cleared the road under cover of darkness and moved up the artillery in pieces. Scott ordered a three-pronged attack on Cerro Gordo on April 18. As a shower of bullets rained down, Lee guided troops along the trail he'd discovered. The Mexicans suffered heavy losses; the Americans captured several thousand soldiers, guns, wagons, and horses. Santa Anna retreated in a rush, leaving his wooden leg behind. "It was a beautiful operation . . .," Robert wrote Mary. "All of our Eng$_{rs}$ are safe & have done good work." But he'd also had his first close-up look at the aftermath of a battle, the mangled bodies and anguished wounded.

Robert earned praise from all sides for his work, for his coolness under fire and nerve-jarring conditions. Lee could take in a situation and instinctively get an impression that would have taken others time and study to figure out. He had nearly superhuman endurance, untouched by fatigue that felled other men. General Scott made special mention of Robert's valuable contribution to the victory, as he had done at Vera Cruz. War had cast the gentlemanly army engineer in a new light.

71

ON TO MEXICO CITY

After a lull to wait for reinforcements, the American army pushed on in August toward Mexico City. Several Mexican strongholds lay ahead. One of the biggest obstacles was an impassable bed of old lava, a broken plain of razor-sharp rock called the Pedregal. Lee needed to find a way through so Scott could once more flank Santa Anna's army.

Robert found a trace of a path he thought could be turned into a road. He led an advance party to begin the work, often under fire from the Mexicans. When rumors flew that Santa Anna was massing a large army to block Scott's attempt to get around the Mexican forces, Lee volunteered to report back.

In a pouring storm, with only flashes of lightning to mark his way, Robert made the hazardous journey alone across the Pedregal. Hours later, he delivered his message to Scott. There was little time to lose.

Lee was slightly wounded during the storming of Chapultepec, the fortress protecting Mexico City.

The general sent Lee back again across the jagged fields with orders for General David Twiggs to lead an assault. Scott called Robert's crossing of the Pedregal "the greatest feat of physical and mental courage" he'd seen. On August 18, using the route Lee found, Twiggs's troops attacked from the rear. American forces routed the Mexican army in less than twenty minutes at the Battle of Contreras.

At Chapultepec a few weeks later the Americans attacked the mighty stone fortress protecting Mexico City. American troops used ladders to storm the walls. Lee was slightly wounded in the battle. Having not slept for days, he passed out in the saddle and fell from his horse. On September 14, Mexico City surrendered. Lee rode with General Scott and his staff—in full dress uniform—into the Mexican capital.

Lee joined Scott's Grand Entry into Mexico City, September 14, 1847.

With the Treaty of Guadalupe Hidalgo, signed in February 1848, the United States gained clear ownership of California and the New Mexico Territory (the future states of New Mexico, Arizona, Utah, Nevada, and parts of Colorado) in return for payment of fifteen million dollars, plus five million more to settle war claims.

LESSONS

Lee spent the winter drawing maps for the War Department. He'd received three promotions for valor, making him a brevet (or honorary) colonel. Robert was proud of how the West Point men had shown themselves. He took pride in how all branches of the service, even the volunteer soldiers, worked together for a common cause.

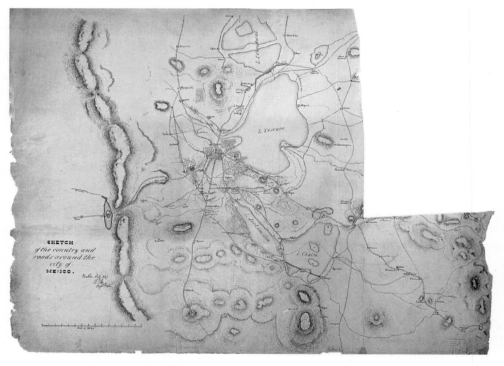

Lee's sketch of the "Country and Roads Around the City of Mexico," signed and dated "July 1847, RELee Capt Engrs."

Lee admired Winfield Scott, both the man and his strategies. He'd seen how Scott's confidence in his troops gave the men pride. He'd seen Scott win with a smaller force. He'd seen victories earned by first battering the enemies' stronghold with artillery. He watched how Scott turned the enemies' flank and hit Mexican forces at their weakest

74

points instead of making frontal charges. Lee's efforts as a scout and his careful use of the terrain had been central to Scott's plan to strike at the political heart of Mexico.

But Lee had not led men or commanded troops in this war. He had tasted neither retreat nor defeat in Mexico. And he was not alone—other officers gaining their first impressions of war under Scott were Ulysses S. Grant, George B. McClellan, George Gordon Meade, James Longstreet, and Thomas Jonathan Jackson. On battlefields in the distant future, these men would put their deadly knowledge to use against one another.

FAR FROM HOME

What Lee had most desired during his months in Mexico were letters from home. Envelopes addressed in a familiar hand had become "tantalizing" treats. Often, Robert had to wait to find a time when he could sit quietly, absorb every word, and lose himself in his family. And he found joy in writing to his family and friends, too.

Mary needed those letters. Her worries for Robert had deepened as the months dragged on and as family members and friends lost loved ones in Mexico. Robert wrote about battles and army life—the food, the fleas, the heat. He compared, summed up, and noted his own strengths in wartime. He entertained his children with tales of birds and animals, sent sketches home, and even bought a white pony (named Santa Anna) to have shipped back to the States for the little Lees. Christmases apart were lonely, and Robert wished that "good Santa Claus will fill my Rob's stocking tonight & that Mildreds, Agnes, & Annas may break down with the good things."

Lee found Mexico breathtaking. His pen couldn't do justice to the lush flowers and trees. From a ship anchored "Off Lobos" he wrote Mary's father, "The surf is constantly breaking over the [coral] reef & the Isd [island] is enclosed by a white wall of foam." He described in detail the foods in the Mexican markets, even noting, "The fish were beautiful to behold." He appreciated the dark chocolate and how the señoritas' skirts showed their bare ankles.

But he found little to admire in the Mexican people or their way of life. He described Mexicans as idle, weak, worthless, and vicious. "It is a beautiful country," he wrote, "& in the hands of proper people would be a magnificent one." He advised opening Mexican ports to European immigrants, breaking down the power of the Catholic Church, and allowing "free opinions of government & religion."

Robert left Mexico in early June and arrived home before the end of the month. On June 30, 1848, his wedding anniversary, he wrote his brother from Arlington:

> Here I am once again, my dear Smith, perfectly surrounded by Mary and her precious children, who seem to devote themselves to staring at the furrows in my face and the white hairs in my head. . . . I find them, too, much grown, and all well, and I have much cause for thankfulness, and gratitude to that good God who has once more united us.

CHAPTER SEVEN

"HERE WORKING FOR MY COUNTRY"

PART II

"I can advise no young man to enter the Army. The same application, The same self-denial, the same endurance, in any other profession, will advance him faster & farther."

—*Robert Lee to Markie Williams,*
September 16, 1853

L ee emerged from the Mexican War with a golden reputation. He'd earned the admiration and trust of many in the military, including General Winfield Scott, now the nation's highest-ranking soldier. A fellow officer called Lee a man without fear, a brave knight beyond reproach. Yet for all this, in his twenty-six years of military service Lee had risen only to the rank of captain. The brevet colonel rank won in Mexico was honorary.

After the war, it was business as usual. Lee pushed papers in Washington and traveled to Florida and Alabama to pick sites for future defenses. By the autumn of 1848 he had received orders to supervise the building of a new fort in Baltimore's harbor. Lee needed to construct a man-made island of several acres to hold the fort—a planned stronghold of brick with forty-foot-high walls holding three hundred cannon.

Though Maryland was a slave-owning state, Baltimore had a thriving population of free black people, twenty-five thousand strong. The city's bustling trade and busy harbor provided perfect hiding spots and escape routes for runaway slaves. Lee worried about the influence of both free blacks and Northern white abolitionists on his enslaved servants. He settled in, focused on his job, kept a close eye on his slaves, and sought a house in Baltimore's sky-high-priced market.

A year passed before Lee found and renovated a long, narrow, three-story home large enough for his family. Mary and all the children but Custis, at school in Virginia, joined him. Robert's older sister, Anne Marshall, lived in Baltimore with her family, and she introduced the Lees around. Robert and Mary had time to socialize. Decades later their son Rob remembered the glittering gold epaulets on Lee's dress uniforms as his parents set out for an evening.

The children's education was important to both Robert and Mary. Custis finished school in Virginia and then entered West Point in 1850. Rooney and Daughter went to school in Baltimore, while Agnes and Annie returned to Arlington to study with their grandmother and then a governess. That left only Rob and Mildred at home, but the house remained crowded with visiting hordes of family and friends.

Lee was making slow but steady progress building Fort Carroll when fresh orders arrived in May 1852: he'd been appointed superintendent of the United States Military Academy at West Point. Lee did not want the job. "I learn with much regret the determination of the Secretary of War to assign me to that duty," he wrote. Couldn't they appoint someone else? But Lee had his orders. Once more the family returned to Arlington and prepared for the move to New York. In September 1852 Robert went on ahead to take up his new duties.

BACK AT THE POINT

West Point had changed in the years since Lee's graduation, although the academy still trained two hundred and fifty cadets. New buildings had replaced old. More books on more subjects filled the library shelves. New equipment, like telescopes, offered better scientific study. The Plain

Robert Lee, sporting a new mustache, photographed around 1851

lay mostly cleared of boulders, and trees planted in Lee's cadet days now shaded the campus.

The biggest change had come in America's attitude toward West Point. The earlier criticism and suspicions about the academy had vanished. West Point officers distinguished themselves during the war with Mexico; the difference their superior training made shone clearly. And it wasn't just what West Pointers were doing on the battlefield. Former students like Robert built the country's infrastructure as engineers. Men of the Long Gray Line served in government and as American diplomats. They worked as teachers, lawyers, judges, doctors, and clergymen.

While most of the old curriculum remained, updates had been added at every level. The Mexican War and the army's presence in the vast western territories showed the need for training with horse-drawn artillery and more instruction in horsemanship. Cadets now practiced maneuvering the big guns into position. Lee began building a new riding hall and stables, since the upper floors of the old riding hall were supported by iron pillars that, despite padding, injured cadets and horses. Cadets learned to ride and move as cavalry units, mastering how to fight on horseback. J. E. B. Stuart and Philip Sheridan, future standout cavalry generals, trained during Lee's time as superintendent at West Point.

The army needed Spanish-speaking officers in the Southwest, so Spanish classes were added. Cadets spent more time in hands-on designing and building. Army officers had immense lands to survey, map, and explore, so West Point devoted more coursework to mapmaking and drawing skills. All of this meant an even larger study load piled on the overworked cadets.

FAMILY LIFE AT WEST POINT

The Lee family lived in the superintendent's quarters, built during Thayer's years at West Point: a roomy house with a garden, stable, pasture, and greenhouse where Mary propagated plant cuttings from Arlington. They brought their own furniture—red velvet sofas and chairs bought in Baltimore, and items like the Custis silver and china.

The Lee children came and went, depending upon their schooling. Robert and Mary sent Rooney, who'd grown so tall and broad that Agnes called him "perfectly enormous," to school in New York City. Eighteen-year-old Mary attended a female academy where she adopted the fancier name "Marielle." Rob and Mildred went to the school for officers' children on the post. Agnes—homesick for "my precious Arlington"—and Annie studied French and music with academy instructors.

Lee went out of his way not to favor the family members attending West Point, including his son Custis and his nephew Fitz Lee. Robert warned that Fitz would rack up "200 demerits the first year and that would be an end to all his military resources." The misbehaving Fitz nearly lived up to his uncle's prediction. He narrowly escaped being kicked out and finally graduated fifth from the bottom of his class.

"We always have a no. [number] of cadets at our house," Agnes wrote in her journal. Their presence intimidated Agnes and made her uncomfortable at first. At receptions and parties she and Annie set tables, helped entertain, and longed for the moment they could steal away, sit on the stairs, and enjoy a good cry over their lives.

As a twelve-year-old, Agnes chafed at her parents' fussing: "I must sit up & talk & walk as a young lady and be constantly greeted with ladies do this & that—& think so—all as if I was twenty." Annie, too, faced criticism. Lee teased his daughter that she must mind her posture. "I do not know what the Cadets will say if the Supt's *children* do not practice what he demands of them. They will naturally say he had better attend to his own before he corrects other people's children, and as he permits his to stoop it is hard he will not allow them."

Agnes and Annie soon lost their fear of the cadets. "We know almost all of Custis' class," Agnes noted. And they gossiped over the young men in their cousin Fitz's class, labeling one cadet "the greatest lady's man" and another "a perfect bore."

Robert and Mary entertained faculty and their wives and opened their home to officers and cadets. Lee also hosted West Point's first-ever alumni reunion. They held parties for the girls and their friends. On New Year's Day they filled the house with guests, who dined on a long parade of sweets. Mary also presided over an elaborate Valentine's Day party. Agnes noted that Rob and Mildred received and sent at least a dozen homemade valentines. Their sister Mary "had a good many too. Annie & I considered ourselves much neglected I only had one."

But all this entertaining and fuss tired Lee. It usually came after a long day spent at his desk. Mary wrote Rooney once that when the rest of the family attended a concert, they left Superintendent Lee behind "stretched out full length on the sofa."

DEALING WITH CADETS

Lee understood the tremendous pressure cadets lived under. He complimented cadets who did well. He sat down and advised those struggling with classwork or mounting demerits. But he was a tough taskmaster, even if he did feel sympathy for the cadets. Why couldn't the young men just do what was right, he wondered, and save them all trouble? Under Superintendent Lee, cadets earned demerits for the tiniest infractions.

Lee trimmed the number of demerits needed for dismissal from two hundred for the year to one hundred in six months. He hoped the change would force cadets to face their bad behavior sooner and improve. If anything, cadets rebelled more. The demerit system under Lee was "carried to such an extent" that it was impossible to avoid the black marks, one cadet complained.

Robert penned stacks of letters to parents. He wrote about sick cadets. He expressed concern for cadets in trouble. He refused leave requests for frivolous matters like attending a wedding, for "what is granted to one must be given to all." Cadets needed every minute of their attention focused to "master their Course at the Academy." When Lee did grant consent for a cadet to leave, it was only after talking to the young man's professors. Then Lee wrote out a detailed timetable for the young man's departure and return, including train schedules.

The hardest part of his job was sending home cadets who failed their exams—"I hope not many," he wrote Markie as exams loomed one June. He told Rooney, "I fear we shall lose some of our friends," when two cadets performed badly. "Two nice lads too," Lee wrote, "but they preferred their own ease & pleasure to their clear & imperative duty." Agnes and Annie watched some of the end-of-year exams. Agnes attended one on international law. Everyone told her she wouldn't understand a word of it—"but to my great satisfaction I did . . . & liked it very much."

"IN THE HANDS OF A KIND GOD"

A sad event rocked the family in April 1853 when Mary's mother, Mary Fitzhugh Custis, died suddenly at Arlington. It proved to be a turning point for Robert. Now he'd lost a second mother, a woman he greatly admired, who had offered him a home and sympathetic ear since his boyhood.

She'd been in her rose garden one day, gone the next. "The blow was so sudden & crushing," Robert wrote Markie, "that I yet shudder at the shock & feel as if I had been arrested [halted] in the course of life, & had no power to resume my onward march." He wept uncontrollably at her grave and reminded his children that the best way to honor their grandmother was to live as she had lived—with humility and kindness.

A few months later Robert made the religious commitment he'd avoided his whole life. Along with his daughters Mary and Annie, he knelt before the altar rail at Christ Church in Alexandria and took his first communion as a member of the church. "We are all in the hands of a kind God," he wrote Mary, "who will do for us what is best, & more than we deserve, & we have only to endeavour to . . . do our duty to him and ourselves."

Religion meant a new duty he must fulfill—a duty toward God. Robert's outlook on life turned more rigid over the next few years as he struggled with his own sins. He sometimes felt that God was punishing him, that he must always try harder. He hoped for the best, but the end result lay in the hands of God, not his own.

The peace and beauty he found in nature had always uplifted Robert, and it was here that he saw most clearly the hand of God. Lee felt pleasure in the sweet yellow blooms of Arlington's hillsides in spring. He noted the stately trees, the shape of clouds, the majesty of mountains. "I enjoyed the Mountains as I rode along," he wrote from western Virginia in 1861. "The views were magnificent. The valleys so beautiful, The Scenery so peaceful. What a glorious world Almighty God has given us. How thankless & ungrateful we are, & how we labour to mar His gifts." If much of his religious life seemed dark and somber, this brought him joy.

"HE IS NOW IN TEXAS"

In March 1855, Secretary of War Jefferson Davis, who'd known Robert since their West Point days, offered a tempting promotion. Lee could become a lieutenant colonel in one of two new cavalry regiments being formed for the western frontier. It was a major expansion for the army, and Davis selected his officers based on merit rather than the old order of taking the next man in line for promotion. For Lee, the promotion meant leaving behind the Army Corps of Engineers. But Davis offered a jump in rank two grades higher, and a larger salary. Robert accepted.

The Corps of Cadets serenaded the family before they left West Point, singing "Home Sweet Home" and "Carry Me Back to Old Virginny." The family departed in a driving rain, a fitting end to a job Lee had not wanted and was not sorry to leave.

The summer passed quickly back at Arlington. Robert designed and ordered a grave monument for Mrs. Custis that included a carved wreath of her favorite flowers. He drew plans for a new furnace system and a remodel of the south wing of the house. The main room, home to dust and cobwebs, had never been finished in all these years—the walls not plastered, the woodwork not painted. Here the Lee children had played among unframed paintings and old furniture. Now everything was mended, plastered, painted, and stained. The Lees had red velvet draperies installed to match the furniture bought in Baltimore. Marble mantels, family portraits, and a crystal chandelier made an elegant room. When Robert left, Agnes noted, "He is now in Texas O so far away he seems. I love him so much."

* * * * *

Lee's tasks in Texas included training recruits, purchasing horses and equipment, gathering provisions, and handling ill, homesick, and discouraged young men. Most importantly, his 2nd Cavalry Regiment was meant to protect the flood of American citizens arriving in Texas.

The white settlers displaced and attacked Native nations like the Comanche. They killed and scattered the buffalo and other game the Indians relied on for survival. The Comanche lashed back with raids on white settlements, killing, burning, stealing horses, and taking captives. While these marauding bands of Comanche roamed free, the army had rounded up about fifteen hundred Indians onto two reservations. One of the tasks for Lee's cavalry was to keep them there.

Lee considered the Comanche an inferior people and hoped the United States government could "humanize" them. He thought their painted faces made them "more hideous than nature made them, & the whole race is extremely uninteresting." He told Mary the Comanche gave "a world of trouble to man & horse," then, using one of his favorite dismissive phrases, added, "they are not worth it."

In the spring of 1856 Robert led troops to chase down Comanche raiders after a bloody attack, intending to impress the Comanche with a show of U.S. Cavalry might. It turned into a 1,100-mile trip of frustration. The 2nd Cavalry's only claim to victory was against a small band of Comanche not even involved in the raiding. The expedition dissolved

85

Comanche Feats of Horsemanship, painted by George Catlin in 1834–1835. Catlin traveled extensively among Native nations, sketching and painting portraits and scenes of everyday life.

into a miserable search for grass and water in a land parched by drought and wind. Soldiers battled fleas, mosquitoes, and rattlesnakes. A sudden storm from the north swept in freezing temperatures. Lee termed these useless maneuvers "wandering over the plains," a land seeming vast as an ocean where bands of Comanche could easily escape. He had too few troops to make any real difference in stemming raids by the Comanche or Mexican bandits.

Robert's time in Texas was frequently broken by another job he disliked—serving on numerous court-martials around the country. In early 1857, one of the times Lee was absent, he learned his young lieutenants had intercepted a Comanche raiding party and "chastised them severely." His men killed a dozen Comanche, wounded more, and captured horses and all the Indians' belongings. "It is a distressing state of things," he wrote Mary, "that requires . . . such treatments, but it is the only corrective they [the Comanche] understand, & the only way in which they can be taught to keep within their own limits." When Lee heard that a group of civilians had killed ten Comanche and recovered stolen horses, he was "glad of it, & only wish it had been accomplished by the Cavalry."

Missing his home and family made the job even worse. The barren world of Texas, with plants that stung and water so filthy even the army mules refused to drink it, made the distance from his beautiful Virginia even starker for Lee. He spent one Fourth of July, a holiday lavishly celebrated at Arlington, sheltering under his blanket spread over four stakes he'd stuck in the ground. "The Sun was fiery hot, the atmosphere like the blast from a hot air furnace, the water salt," he wrote. Even his candles melted in the Texas heat. Depressed at the separation from his family, Lee wrote Annie, "I know it is useless to indulge these feelings, yet they arise unbidden & will not stay repressed. They steal on me in the business hours of the day & the waking hours of night, & seem to hover around me waking or sleeping."

He tried to convince Mary and his daughters to visit. Mary begged off. Her arthritis had grown so bad she needed crutches and a wheelchair, and she often slept on a daybed downstairs at Arlington. "I almost dread him seeing my crippled state," she told a friend.

When another Christmas rolled around Lee made the best of things, remembering "dearest Mary the many happy Xmas' we have had together, & the pleasure I have enjoyed with you, your dear parents & the children around me." Robert often rode out by himself to see the birds and snakes. He wrote a cousin that a man might show his joy, "but he should conceal & smother his grief as much as possible." Lee's fellow soldiers saw none of this sadness. To them Robert presented a quiet front: dignified, capable, striking in appearance, impressive.

Adding to Lee's depression was the death of his younger sister,

87

Mildred. It deeply preyed on his mind, especially the fact that he had not seen Mildred for so long and now never would. He fortified himself with comforting thoughts that his mother-in-law, Mary Fitzhugh Custis, would welcome Mildred into heaven. "God knows how I cherish her memory," he wrote Mildred's son. Lee confided how much he missed his wife and children and added, "I do not know how long I can stand it." Again Lee wondered why he stayed in the army.

* * * * *

The remoteness of Texas cut Robert off from news of the nation as well as news of his family and Virginia home. Eastern newspapers, including Lee's local paper, the *Alexandria Gazette*, had to travel across the country and arrived in Texas on steamships out of New Orleans. After Lee received a bundle of newspapers in late December 1856 he penned Mary, "We are now assured, that the Govt: is in operation, & the Union in existence, not that we had any fears to the contrary, but it is satisfactory always to have facts to go on."

Lee believed that a soldier should stand above partisan politics. The military had no business trying to influence civilian voters. He seldom wrote about politics, and when he did, it was only to family and close friends. But like the rest of the nation, he followed the debates shaping the United States in the 1850s as slavery drove a deepening wedge between North and South.

Events in Kansas had especially gripped the nation for two years. The Kansas-Nebraska Act of 1854 did away with the old Missouri Compromise of 1820. Both the Kansas and Nebraska territories would be open to slavery, and at some point, under the doctrine called popular sovereignty, people would vote on whether to keep slavery or do away with it. Nebraska, which was mostly settled by free-soil pioneers, remained peaceful. But in Kansas the situation exploded.

Proslavery Missourians stormed voting places in Kansas. The town of Lawrence was destroyed by white Southerners bent on avenging the shooting of a proslavery sheriff. In early 1856 a fiery Northern abolitionist named John Brown and his sons retaliated by murdering five slaveholding Southerners at Pottawatomie Creek. In the local war that followed, fifty-six more people were killed while the shocked nation watched events unfold in what became known as "Bleeding Kansas."

Violence had even erupted in the U.S. Senate. Preston Brooks, a congressman from South Carolina, claimed that the admission of Kansas as a slave state was now a point of honor for the South. Senator Charles Sumner, a Northerner, delivered a two-day speech titled "The Crime Against Kansas." The speech incited Brooks to beat Sumner with his gold-headed cane until the man fell bleeding and unconscious to the floor of the Senate chamber.

Each side infuriated the other. "Are we to be chastised as they chastise their slaves?" asked a Northern newspaper. Must the North bow down and please "our Southern masters"? Meanwhile, the *Richmond Enquirer*, a Southern paper, claimed, "The vulgar Abolitionists in the Senate are getting above themselves." How dare they speak rudely about Southern gentlemen? "They must be lashed into submission."

In December 1856 the outgoing president, Franklin Pierce, criticized Northern abolitionists who pressured the South over slavery. Lee wrote Mary from Texas that he was "much pleased with the Presidents message." As a Southerner, Lee resented Northern abolitionists who meant to "interfere with & change the domestic institutions of the South"—code words for slavery. Lee labeled abolitionist actions "evil," "unlawful," and "irresponsible." Abolitionists could recklessly incite what white Southerners feared most—a murderous uprising of enslaved black people. Lee believed abolitionists had no business meddling with a Southerner's right to own slaves. They had no business trying to block Southerners from moving slaves into any territory to the west.

Lee's time in Texas came to an abrupt halt in October 1857 with the death of his father-in-law, George Washington Parke Custis. Custis had named Robert an executor of his will. Lee received a two-month leave of absence from his military command and returned to Arlington to settle the estate. "He has left me an unpleasant legacy," Robert wrote his son Custis. Complications would extend Lee's two-month leave into two difficult, miserable years.

CHAPTER EIGHT

TROUBLE WITH "THE PEOPLE"

"Slavery as an institution, is a moral & political evil in any
country. . . . I think it however a greater evil to the white than to
the black race."

—Robert to Mary,
December 27, 1856

O ne thousand people attended the funeral of George Washington
Custis. Robert arrived at Arlington a few weeks later and found
his family "sad, suffering & sick." He recalled his father-in-law's great
"kindness & affection" toward him, and it struck Robert forcefully that
now Custis's chair sat vacant.

In his will, G. W. Custis left his daughter Mary the Washington
family treasures. Arlington would remain her home as long as she lived;
then the house would pass to her eldest son, Custis. The second Lee
son, Rooney, inherited White House plantation, built on land where
George Washington courted and married the widow Martha Custis. G.
W. Custis left his third grandson, Rob, his Romancoke plantation. The
estate would pay each of the four granddaughters a $10,000 legacy. The
will specified that land should be sold to pay the legacies and pay off
Custis's debts.

George Washington Custis included another condition in his will.
Encouraged by the wishes of his deceased wife and the example set by
George Washington, Custis freed his slaves, to be carried out within five

years of his death. Custis owned about two hundred enslaved people, more than $100,000 worth of valuable "Negro property." Around sixty-three of them worked and lived at Arlington. The rest labored at White House or Romancoke or were hired out to other people.

Charles Syphax with his grandson William. Syphax oversaw the dining room at Arlington and was considered the unofficial leader of Arlington's enslaved community. G. W. Custis inherited Charles Syphax from his grandmother Martha Washington in 1802. Syphax married Maria Carter, an enslaved woman, and the couple had ten children. According to Syphax family tradition, G. W. Custis was the father of Maria Carter Syphax. This seems likely as Custis freed Maria and her children in 1826 and gave her seventeen acres of land at Arlington. Charles Syphax remained enslaved.

As he grew older, G. W. Custis had neglected the management of his enslaved laborers. Markie Williams, who stayed with her great uncle at Arlington, recorded his claims that his slaves had little to do but eat, drink, and sleep. The enslaved had, he said, "comfortable homes, their families around them and nothing to do but to consult their own pleasure." Markie noted his words: "And truly in many instance[s] the master is the only slave."

Custis's comments revealed how many white Southerners viewed the condition of enslaved lives. And yet the Custis slaves, especially those at Arlington, did have a better life than many enslaved people. For the most part, Custis kept slave families together. He recognized marriage among the enslaved, though it was not legal under Virginia law. Selina Norris and Thornton Gray, two of Arlington's enslaved, married in the same parlor where Robert wed Mary. The Grays raised their eight children in the one room allotted them in Arlington's slave quarters.

Selina Norris Gray, shown with two of her daughters, around 1861–1865. Selina married Thornton Gray, an enslaved man, in the parlor at Arlington. The couple had eight children. Selina served as Mary Lee's personal maid and later as housekeeper at Arlington. When Mary Lee fled Arlington in April 1861 she entrusted the house keys to Selina Gray.

At Arlington, slaves had not only first names but also last names, something rare among the enslaved. Mary Lee, her mother, and the Lee daughters taught slave children to read. Again, this was against Virginia law. Slaves at Arlington raised their own chickens and tended their own gardens—a benefit for Custis as well, since he could then provide less, and spend less, on his slaves.

None of this made up for a life trapped in perpetual servitude passed from parent to child. And outside the slave quarters at Arlington stood that cruel symbol of slavery—a whipping post. Like other enslaved people, the Custis slaves fought back in small ways with everyday resistance. They worked slowly. They pretended not to understand. They broke things. They built roaring blazes in Arlington's fireplaces on blistering hot days to annoy the Custis and Lee families. Slaves stole items—Lee even had a new pair of trousers disappear. They ran away. They pushed the limits of being rude and ignoring orders. For a man like Robert Lee, this disobedience was inexcusable.

A master's death usually left enslaved people even more vulnerable, and wondering what would happen to them. But the Custis slaves knew they had been freed. It didn't matter that the will stated they might remain enslaved for up to five years; they considered themselves free people from the moment G. W. Custis died. The power to decide when the slaves gained their legal freedom, however, rested in Robert's hands as executor of his father-in-law's will. And he held a different view.

＊＊＊＊＊

Lee had immediately taken stock of what needed doing and doubted he could complete the work in five years. Arlington leaked and needed repairs. Outbuildings, slave dwellings, and the mill were falling apart. Neglected farmlands at White House and Romancoke yielded scant crops. Debts poured in from all sides, amounting to nearly $10,000. For some properties that Custis listed as "I may own," Lee unearthed no legal deeds.

On top of putting the Custis homes and farms to rights, Robert had to pay out the legacies listed in the will, adding to the estate's burdens. He himself had little to offer his seven children—no permanent family home, no wealth in land or slaves, no heirlooms. It weighed on Lee that the Custis inheritance must be made whole and profitable for his sons' and daughters' futures.

Robert thought the will itself posed problems. There seemed to be contradictions—he was told to do things but given no way to pay for them. According to Virginia law, freed slaves had to leave the state. But what of those who could not leave, the young, old, or sick? The will made no provisions for how Robert should care for them. And when Lee did free the slaves, sending them out of Virginia would be wildly expensive—how should he pay for that? Mary had a solution. When that moment came, let those "kind friends" of the slaves—the abolitionists—purchase them, free them immediately, and take them away.

Robert submitted questions for a court ruling. He would free the Custis slaves, but not right away; he wanted at least the full five years. The slaves were his property. He needed them working hard, and he needed the money he could make hiring them out. He asked the court to postpone emancipation until he'd fixed the Custis properties and earned enough money to pay the legacies and the estate's debts. The court ruled against Robert, saying he needed to sell land to pay off the debt and pay the legacies. Robert balked at the ruling—he needed the land. Lee took his claims to the Supreme Court of Appeals of Virginia.

"REBELLED AGAINST MY AUTHORITY"

Meanwhile, using some of his own money, Lee began work to restore Arlington and make the estates profitable. Unlike most men of Virginia's upper class, Lee had never managed a large enslaved workforce. At his military posts he usually had only two slaves, a woman who cooked and washed clothes, and a valet who looked after Lee's other needs. Now,

Lee was out of his element, feeling harassed with "cares and trouble."

The enslaved people of Arlington refused to cooperate with Lee's tidy world ordered by duty, discipline, and obedience. They ran away. Lee advertised for the return of runaway slaves, usually offering a $10 reward, plus payment for transporting the runaways to jail in Alexandria. The slaves' "ingratitude & bad conduct" wounded Mary's feelings. At every turn, Robert rid himself of troublemakers. He sent slaves to Richmond to be "disposed of . . . to the best advantage." He hired out others. His letters show that he knew these people: their names, their ages, their jobs, their children, their larger family ties. But he never understood how badly they desired freedom.

Mary Lee painted this watercolor sketch of Lawrence Parks, an enslaved man at Arlington. He served as one of the pallbearers who carried Mary Fitzhugh Custis's coffin to the gravesite.

Robert did not recognize humanity or intelligence in the slaves at Arlington or elsewhere. He called the black children of Arlington "all the little Ebony bipeds on the hill." He wanted to be "considerate & kind to the Negroes," but they needed a firm overseer who would "make them do their duty." He brushed aside the cruel punishments of slavery. "The painful discipline they are undergoing, [is] necessary for their instruction as a race," Robert wrote Mary, "& I hope will prepare & lead them to better things."

White Southerners had once called slavery a necessary evil. But by the 1850s they talked of slavery as beneficial to both slave and master. Lee agreed—slavery offered a needed step for African Americans as part of God's plan to improve black people. Were they not better off here, in a condition of slavery, than in Africa? Lee asked. As a race, they were morally unfit for freedom. They were untrustworthy and thieving. They were idle. They were not as capable of learning, Lee believed, as white people.

How long enslaved blacks must endure bondage was up to God. Lee believed emancipation *would* come one day, but only when God saw fit, perhaps centuries in the future, for, to the Almighty, "two thousand years are but as a single day." This removed any decision from Lee's hands and the hands of other Southern slave owners.

In a letter to Rooney in May 1858, Robert wrote that he'd had "trouble with some of the people." Three men, "Reuben, Parks & Edward, . . . rebelled against my authority." They refused to obey Lee's orders and told him they were as free as he was. Lee captured them, tied them up, and sent them to jail. "They resisted till overpowered," he told Rooney, "& called upon the other people to rescue them." The men remained jailed for two months before Lee hired them out through a slave trader. He also sent three women to be hired out—he suspected them of stealing some jewelry. Lee washed his hands of any slave who gave him trouble.

Inside view of the slave pens and jail at Alexandria, Virginia

"TAMPERING WITH THE SERVANTS"

If the decision to end slavery lay with God, it wasn't up to Northern abolitionists to interfere. Lee and other slave owners blamed abolitionists for stirring unrest and inciting disloyalty in the slave quarters. Mary wrote a friend that abolitionists poked around Arlington, "tampering with the servants & telling them they had a right to their freedom *immediately* and that if they would unite & *demand* it they would obtain it."

For Lee, abolitionists meddled irresponsibly and illegally with Southern slavery. The abolitionists knew this. "If he means well to the slave," Lee wrote, the abolitionist "must not create angry feelings in the master." Lee claimed abolitionist actions forced white Southerners to use harsher treatments to keep their property in line.

In late spring of 1859, three Arlington slaves—Wesley Norris, his sister Mary, and a cousin, George Parks—fled Arlington. They hoped to reach free soil in Pennsylvania, but were seized in Maryland, thrown in jail, and then returned to Arlington for punishment.

The runaways told Lee they considered themselves free. Lee said he would teach them a lesson. Lee ordered the overseer to whip the two men fifty lashes and Mary Norris twenty. The overseer stripped the three slaves to the waist, but he refused to do the whipping. Lee sent for the county constable, who carried out the punishment. "Not satisfied with lacerating our naked flesh," Wesley Norris later said, "Gen. Lee then ordered the overseer to thoroughly wash our back with brine, which was done." Lee then sent the slaves to a Richmond slave trader to hire out.

The incident became fodder for abolitionist newspapers, which added lurid details not in Norris's account. In the papers, Lee himself whipped the female slave, Mary Norris, thirty-nine times. Such an action seems out of character for the hands-off Lee, who avoided dealing with slavery as much as he could and preferred hiring someone to do the job.

"The *N.Y. Tribune* has attacked me for my treatment of your grandfather's slaves," Robert told Custis, "but I shall not reply." Mary angrily denounced "the most villainous attacks upon my husband." Years later Lee claimed there had been "not a word of truth in it." No one he'd ever employed, said Lee, could charge him with "bad treatment." But Lee probably did not consider having a runaway slave whipped bad treatment—whipping was the lawful punishment for a slave who had disobeyed or run away.

* * * * *

On October 17, 1859, Lieutenant J. E. B. Stuart galloped up to Arlington with a message for Lee: the Secretary of War in Washington requested Robert report to him immediately. Without even changing out of his civilian clothes, Lee hurried to the War Department. President James Buchanan and the Cabinet had received a panicked report from a conductor on the Baltimore & Ohio Railroad—armed abolitionists had blocked and shot at his train in Harpers Ferry, Virginia. These raiders had possession of the only bridge into town and had grabbed control of the armory of the United States. By ten o'clock that night Lee and Stuart had boarded a special train chugging toward Harpers Ferry. Lee had command of ninety marines to deal with the situation.

He may have already known that the abolitionist John Brown was at the center of things at Harpers Ferry. Since 1856, when Brown and his followers murdered proslavery men in Kansas, his name had spiked fear across the South.

CHAPTER NINE

"I SHALL MOURN FOR MY COUNTRY"

"I only see that a fearful calamity is upon us, & fear that the country will have to pass through for its sins a fiery ordeal."

—Robert Lee to Markie Williams,
January 22, 1861

The little town of Harpers Ferry lay in western Virginia on a wedge of land where the Potomac and Shenandoah Rivers met. Sheer cliffs of gray stone rose beyond the town. John Brown had scouted the area in the summer of 1859. Then, using an alias, he'd rented a farm about five miles away on the Maryland side of the Potomac River. He'd focused on Harpers Ferry for one reason—the town was home to the United States Armory and Arsenal.

Brown had spent the last few years raising money, gathering weapons—including pikes to arm slaves unfamiliar with guns—and recruiting followers. Unlike the abolitionists who supported peaceful means to end slavery, Brown believed violence alone could destroy the evil of human bondage. He hoped to seize the armory's weapons and build an army to free Virginia's slaves.

On the night of October 16, 1859, Brown's band of twenty-one raiders—both white men and black men—set out for Harpers Ferry. He'd planned to rally larger numbers to his cause, but decided to go ahead with the followers he had. They crossed a wooden bridge into town in the dark early hours of October 17. Quickly they cut telegraph wires, captured the armory from the lone night watchman, and proceeded to the Harpers Ferry train station, where they killed a station worker and blocked the B&O train pulling in. Brown eventually let the train go, and at the next stop the conductor telegraphed for help.

Abolitionist John Brown led a raid on the U.S. Armory and Arsenal at Harpers Ferry, Virginia.

At daylight on October 17, alarmed local citizens formed a militia company that fired on Brown's men, killing several. The militia seized back the bridge, blocking Brown's escape. Brown had taken thirteen hostages and now retreated to the armory's fire engine house, a small building with half-moon windows high up in the thick brick walls.

"A FANATIC OR A MADMAN"

Robert Lee arrived in Harpers Ferry around midnight, the start of a new day, October 18. He immediately took charge, sending the local militia home. He conferred with the young marine lieutenant, Israel Green, and decided not to act until daylight.

Lee wrote a letter telling Brown and his followers that if they peacefully surrendered "they shall be kept in safety." Escape was impossible, Lee warned, for marines now surrounded the armory. Lee couldn't answer for the raiders' safety if he had to seize the engine house by force. He doubted that Brown would accept his terms, however, and Lee planned swift action to protect the hostages if Brown failed to surrender.

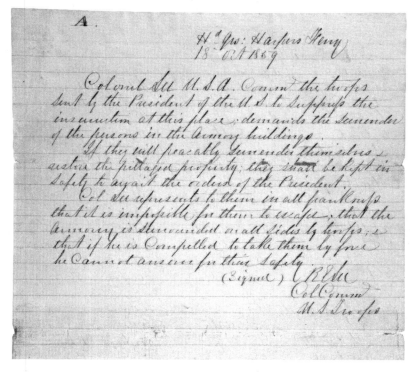

The letter Lee wrote demanding Brown's surrender, October 18, 1859

Tactfully, Lee offered the local militia captain the chance to lead any assault on the engine house. The man declined. Lee then asked Lieutenant Green to handle the attack if Brown failed to surrender.

Operations began at seven that morning. J. E. B. Stuart approached the wooden doors of the engine house under a white flag. The door opened a crack, a gun pointed at Stuart's face, and Stuart handed over Lee's letter. As Lee had expected, Brown refused to surrender. Instead, he tried to negotiate his own terms, demanding safe passage out of Harpers Ferry.

But Lee was not there to negotiate. At his command twelve marines charged the engine house door with a heavy ladder, battering against it until the boards splintered. Lieutenant Green shoved inside. Lee had ordered the use of bayonet and sword only, to keep stray bullets from injuring the hostages. Green slashed Brown with his sword, gashing Brown's head and knocking him out. The skirmish ended quickly with the death of several men, including one marine, and injury to others. The hostages all survived unharmed.

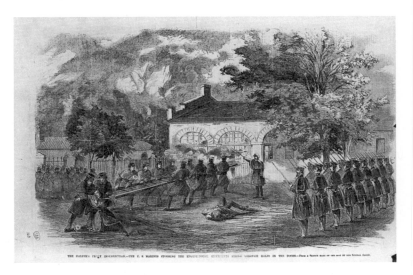

On Lee's command, marines storm the engine house where John Brown has holed up with his hostages. Depicted in *Frank Leslie's Illustrated Newspaper*, October 29, 1859.

Lee ordered medical attention for the wounded. He had Brown carried to an office in the armory where marines propped up the abolitionist on the floor. The governor of Virginia and two congressmen soon arrived and questioned the infamous prisoner. Even with his face, hands, and clothes covered in blood, Brown talked willingly of his cause. A reporter described the abolitionist's wiry body, restless gray eyes, and tangled hair. Lee listened as Brown proclaimed himself an instrument of God meant to destroy slavery. They could easily dispose of him, Brown said, but the crisis would not end with his death. The South, he warned, would answer soon for their sin of slavery.

Abolitionists disgusted Lee, and an extremist like John Brown earned even more of Lee's contempt. Lee placed little importance on the events at Harpers Ferry. Having done his duty, he dismissed the raid as "the attempt of a fanatic or a madman that could only end in failure" and left for Arlington the next day. Robert's success and the way he handled operations at Harpers Ferry, however, won him praise. President James Buchanan even invited him to dinner.

Unlike Lee, many in the South feared that John Brown's raid was only the first attempt by Northerners to arm Southern slaves and incite rebellion and murder. And it infuriated white Southerners that some in the North expressed sympathy for Brown and his rampage. With anger, dread, and rumors swirling, the state of Virginia quickly charged Brown with murder and conspiring with slaves to rebel. His trial ended with a sentence of death.

In late November Lee returned to the area to make sure John Brown's December 2 execution moved forward without trouble. As Brown left his cell for the last time he handed a note to one of his jailers. Brown was certain, he wrote, that "the crimes of this guilty land will never be purged away but with Blood." Lee dismissed Brown's hanging in a letter—"'Poor fly he done buzz'"—little suspecting that John Brown's death marked the beginning of a year that would shake the nation.

Lee spent Christmas with his family at Arlington and then visited his son Rooney and his new wife, Charlotte, at White House plantation. Lee had known Charlotte since her childhood; "she was as dear to me as my son," he would later write. Charlotte charmed Lee with her devout character, "affectionate nature," and "attractive manners."

But Lee's time with family had run out. He had spent over two years trying to resolve his father-in-law's affairs. He worked hard to build up Arlington again, as well as White House and Romancoke, but confided to Rooney, "I succeed badly." Lee's case in the Virginia Supreme Court concerning the Custis will remained unsettled when he returned to active military duty—back to Texas—in early 1860.

* * * * *

The temperatures spiked to 110 degrees as Lee hunkered down to business as acting head of the U.S. Army's Department of Texas. He trained new troops, replaced worn-out cavalry horses, fixed forts, and handled cases of discipline and desertion. Lee even tested the use of camels as supply-carrying animals in the arid Texas heat—a failure. His thoughts, as always, drifted homeward, and as spring approached, he wrote his daughter Annie that she must eat plenty of strawberries and raspberries with chilled cream for him.

The staggering division between North and South over slavery stood foremost on the minds of the military men in Texas, as in the nation as a whole. Lee had seen far more of the country than most Americans dreamed of. His military service had taken him north, south, east, and west, from lonesome outposts to bustling cities. He had a sense of the entire nation, and he believed in the Union. But he also believed in the South and loved his Virginia home above all. As a conservative man, Lee wanted things to remain as they had always been. He both resented and mourned the fact that the world seemed crazy and ready to fall apart. As the nation struggled, so did Robert Lee.

"I FEEL THE AGGRESSION"

Lee had grumbled for years about a deepening Northern hostility toward the South over slavery. "I believe that the South justly complains of the aggression of the North," he told Markie Williams. He made the same point in a letter to Rooney—"The South . . . has been aggrieved by the acts of the North"—and added, "I feel the aggression." He resented the North's attempts to block the spread of slavery into the west. Lee believed this threatened "the equal rights of our [Southern] citizens." All Americans should have access to the west. If Congress blocked slave owners from the territories, it would eventually mean more free states than slave states in the Union. The North, along with gaining congressmen and senators, would gain political and law-making power to threaten slavery in the South.

As protection, Southern leaders demanded a federal slave code promising that no one, even Congress, could restrict a slave owner's constitutional right to move his property wherever he wished, meaning that all future states would be slave states. Others schemed to buy Cuba, or take it by force, along with Nicaragua or Mexico, as places to expand a Southern empire of slavery and boost Southern political power. Lee had been approached to lead one of these expeditions, which he flatly turned down.

All eyes watched that summer of 1860 as the political parties gathered to name their candidates for November's presidential election. The Democrats met in Charleston, South Carolina. William Lowndes Yancey, a famed orator from Alabama, harangued Northern Democrats as he argued for the slaveholding rights of the South: "Ours are the institutions which are at stake; ours is the property that is to be destroyed; ours is the honor at stake." In the end, many Southern delegates walked out of the convention, angering the Northern Democrats.

The Democrats attempted a second convention in Baltimore six weeks later. Here they nominated Stephen A. Douglas, a Northerner, for president. Douglas supported the idea of popular sovereignty, letting people in a territory or state vote to keep slavery or do away with it. The men who'd bolted from the Charleston convention nominated their own presidential candidate—John C. Breckinridge of Kentucky—on a platform that endorsed a national slave code. Another candidate muddied the situation further when the Constitutional Union Party nominated a Southern slaveholder, John Bell, for president.

In Chicago, the Republican Party nominated Abraham Lincoln on a platform against the spread of slavery. Lincoln was viewed as a moderate in the North, a man known for his eloquent speeches. Self-taught and from humble beginnings, the tall, lanky man from Illinois was a lawyer who'd served in the U.S. House of Representatives.

White Southerners viewed Lincoln as an uneducated roughneck, not the equal of a Southern gentleman. They saw him as a dangerous free-soiler who hated the South—a man who wanted to free black people, though Lincoln had never said this. If the "Black Republican" Lincoln won, some white Southerners asked, would the South be forced to secede—actually leave the United States of America—in order to save its way of life? As the election neared, this volcanic question mono-polized politicians, newspaper editors, and citizens across the Southern states.

Lee stated his solution to the election dilemma in a July letter: "If Judge Douglas would now withdraw & join himself & [the Democratic] party to aid in the election of Breckinridge, he might retrieve himself before the country & Lincoln be defeated." Lee wished Northern Democrats would simply give in to Southern demands.

But Douglas did not withdraw, and in November, with the Democratic vote split among the candidates, Lincoln won the presidency. Although Lincoln said he would not touch slavery in the states where it already existed, Southerners didn't believe him. A Richmond newspaper warned Virginians that "a party founded on the single sentiment . . . of hatred of African slavery, is now the controlling power."

After Lincoln's election, citizens of Savannah, Georgia, raise a flag for Southern independence, November 8, 1860.

"IT IS IDLE TO TALK OF SECESSION"

In mid-December 1860 Senator John J. Crittenden proposed a compromise to address white Southerners' fears. The plan guaranteed the permanent existence of slavery, and it guaranteed the extension of slavery in the West below the old dividing line set by the Missouri Compromise. Lee thought the plan a just one. Its terms "ought to be cheerfully assented to by all the States," he wrote his son Custis. "But I do not think the Northern and Western states will agree to them. It is, however, my only hope for the preservation of the Union, and I will cling to it to the last."

On December 20, 1860, the South Carolina legislature responded to Lincoln's election with defiance, becoming the first state to secede from the Union. At this turn of events, words like *anxious*, *grief*, *fearful*, *sorrow*, and *misery* spilled across the pages of Lee's letters. He couldn't envision a country dissolved, a nation plunged into fiery anarchy and civil war. He believed secession was unconstitutional. States could not just leave the Union as if it was some loosely organized gathering. "Secession is nothing but revolution," he told Rooney. "It is idle to talk of secession."

In January 1861, Mississippi, Florida, Alabama, Georgia, and Louisiana followed South Carolina out of the Union. The legislators in each state noted that they seceded to protect their rights to own and keep black people enslaved. The Mississippi secession document summed up the situation:

[The North] denies the right of property in slaves, and refuses protection to that right. . . .

It refuses the admission of new slave States into the Union, and seeks to extinguish it by confining it within its present limits, denying the power of expansion.

It tramples the original equality of the South under foot.

The states that had seceded quickly seized United States property, like forts and arsenals, within their borders. Lee could not understand how the South could destroy a government built by the blood and wisdom of "our patriot fathers." He wrote Markie, "God alone can save us from our folly, selfishness & short sightedness."

Mary Lee echoed her husband's feelings. She wondered how love for their country had died in the South. In this rush to secession they tore the country to bits. Were there "no rights & privileges but those of negro slavery" that mattered? she asked a friend. She wished the rest of the South had left South Carolina to wither alone in secession.

Lee's loyalties tugged him in all directions. He sympathized with the complaints of the South while also deploring secession. Lee felt angry with the Deep South cotton-growing states like Mississippi and Alabama. He called them selfish and labeled them dictators for threatening Virginia and other states "if they will not join them." At military forts around the country, men felt pressured by one another. Would Southern men go with their states or stay in the U.S. Army? Lee wrote Custis from Texas, "While I wish to do what is right, I am unwilling to do what is wrong, either at the bidding of the South or the North."

"I SHALL GO BACK IN SORROW"
While against secession, Lee lamented to Rooney that a Union "maintained by swords and bayonets, & in which civil war are to take the place of brotherly love and kindness, has no charm for me." Some of his fellow officers from the South began resigning their commissions in the United States Army. "If a disruption takes place," Lee confided to Markie at the end of January 1861, "I shall go back in sorrow to my people & share the misery of my native state, & save in her defence there will be one soldier less in the world than now. I wish for no other flag than the 'Star Spangled banner.'"

Lee watched all this unfold from Texas, which voted in February 1861 to secede from the Union. The Texas Declaration of Causes cited Northern demands for the abolition of slavery as a reason to secede. The North would insist on "the recognition of political equality between the white and negro races, and avow[ed] their determination to press on their crusade against us, so long as a negro slave remains in these States."

111

In mid-February, delegates from six of the states that had seceded met in Alabama and adopted a Provisional Government of the Confederate States of America. They named Jefferson Davis—former West Pointer and soldier, United States senator from Mississippi, and Secretary of War—the provisional president.

Alexander Stephens, vice president of the Confederacy. A small man, barely one hundred pounds, Stephens and Lincoln had been friends who'd served in Congress together.

Alexander Stephens, vice president of the Confederacy, summed up the cornerstone of this new government. It rested, he wrote,

upon the great truth, that the negro is not the equal of the white man; that slavery subordination to the superior race is his natural and normal condition. This, our new Government, is the first, in the history of the world, based upon this great physical, philosophical, and moral truth.

When Texas commissioners pressured Lee to join the newly formed Confederacy, he vehemently rejected the idea. The nation lay "between a state of anarchy & Civil War," he wrote Mary at the end of February. "May God spare us from both." He seemed fatalistic, a victim of events spiraling out of control. "I must try & be patient & await the end for I can do nothing to hasten or retard it."

He talked with his fellow officers. Some of them later recalled Lee saying he would never fight against the United States, but he *would* fight in defense of Virginia. The struggle over these opposing ideas haunted Lee. He prayed that Virginia would not secede, saving him from making a decision. To others, Lee said he would resign and retire from military life to plant corn.

Then he received orders from the War Department—report back to Washington.

* * * * *

By the time Lee reached Alexandria on March 1, 1861, Virginia had organized a convention in Richmond, the state capital, to consider the Old Dominion's future. Just a few days later, Lincoln pledged his inaugural oath in Washington.

Lincoln promised he would "hold, occupy and possess the property and places belonging to the Government." He put the responsibility for war, if it came, upon the South. "You can have no conflict without being yourselves the aggressors," warned Lincoln. "You have no oath registered in heaven to destroy the Government, while I shall have the most solemn one to 'preserve, protect, and defend it.'"

In the end, Lincoln asked Americans to hold tight to their shared past and save the Union. "The mystic chords of memory, stretching from every battlefield and patriot grave to every living heart and hearthstone all over this broad land, will yet swell the chorus of the Union, when again touched, as surely they will be, by the better angels of our nature."

Lee still hoped Virginia would remain in the Union. Many Virginians, like the Lee and Custis families, had fathers and grandfathers who'd fought in the American Revolution and then helped create the U.S. Constitution. To turn their backs on that heritage, to sever Lincoln's "mystic chords of memory," was not taken lightly.

Both sides reached out to Robert. The Confederacy offered him the rank of brigadier general in the Confederate army in mid-March, which he seems to have ignored. He did accept promotion from President Lincoln, however, on March 28, 1861, to full colonel in the 1st Cavalry Regiment. Lee held the command for less than a month.

* * * * *

Life rested on a knife-edge. In April, everything toppled. Fort Sumter was a United States military post in Charleston harbor. The fort's commander, Major Robert Anderson, refused to surrender to the new Confederate government of South Carolina. On April 12 the state unleashed a barrage of cannon fire on Fort Sumter. Anderson, low on food and supplies, surrendered the next day. Lee commented that Anderson "was a determined man, & I know held out to the last." Lincoln responded to this shelling of federal property by calling up 75,000 volunteer soldiers. War seemed unavoidable now.

In light of Lincoln's call for troops to use against the South, the Virginia convention in Richmond voted on April 17, 1861, to join the Confederacy, with 88 votes for joining and 55 votes against. The Virginia Secession Ordinance repealed the state's 1788 ratification of the Constitution of the United States. The convention declared the old federal constitution no longer binding on Virginia's citizens. That constitution had "perverted" its powers, "not only to the injury of the people of Virginia, but to the oppression of the Southern Slaveholding States."

At the War Department in Washington no one knew which way Robert Lee would go—remain or resign. On April 18 Francis Blair, one of Lincoln's advisors, asked Lee to meet with him in Washington. Blair told Lee that Lincoln planned to offer him command of the troops called up to defend the Union. This was a promotion Lee would have rejoiced in at any other time, but now he didn't hesitate to decline the president's offer. Although he saw ruin in secession, he could not lead an army against the Southern states.

Upset, he went to see Winfield Scott, a fellow Virginian and a man Lee had admired greatly since the Mexican War. They talked for several hours. Lee wondered if he might somehow sit out the coming conflict. The old general, whose loyalties never wavered from the Union, told Robert there was no sitting out. If he planned to resign, he'd better do it soon, before he received new orders. Robert returned to Arlington, "worn and harassed," faced with making the biggest decision of his life.

"I HAD TO MEET THE QUESTION"

Loyalty—to the United States? to the United States Army? to Virginia? And what of honor? What was the honorable thing to do?

Robert knew that if he resigned he'd lose the respect of many of his longtime military friends and comrades. His own extended family might not understand, either. Most, from Robert's generation, remained pro-Union. Somber shadows hung over Arlington as if there had been a death in the family. Agnes wrote her sister Mildred that the family talked of nothing but their troubles. The army was home and country to their father.

Robert retired to his private office, where he struggled alone. Time had run out for him. It wasn't Virginia's secession that forced Lee to make a decision—it was his meetings with Blair and Scott two days before.

115

Winfield Scott around 1861

He had to act quickly. New orders might arrive at any moment, orders he "could not conscientiously perform," as he told his brother. Lee considered it dishonorable to resign "under orders"—a soldier should do his duty and follow orders even if he did not like them.

Before the family came down to breakfast on April 20, Robert had written two letters. He had Perry, an enslaved man who personally served Lee, deliver the letters to Washington. One letter went to General Scott; the other was his formal resignation from the United States Army. Lee thanked Scott for his many kindnesses and spoke of "the struggle it has cost me to separate myself from a service to which I have devoted the best years of my life, and all the ability I possessed."

Robert called the family into the office. He sat at his table, spread over with papers. He read aloud a copy of his letter to General Scott. The news stunned them; no one spoke a word. As Daughter (Mary) later recalled the scene, her father finally said, "I suppose you all think I have done very wrong, but it had come to this, & after my last interview with Gen. Scott I felt that I ought to wait no longer." Then Daughter spoke up, saying that she did not think he'd done wrong, but she knew that her family, and her mother especially, were "a conservative, or 'Union' family." Indeed, her mother had said she would lay down her life to save the Union. But whatever their personal feelings, once Robert Lee made his decision, no one in the family looked back.

Later that afternoon, Markie's brother Orton Williams rode over from Washington. The young man served on General Scott's staff. He reported that Scott, overcome by Lee's decision, had lain down on a sofa in his office and said, "D'ont mention Robert Lee's name to me again, I cannot bear it."

In the end, it came down to family and the way of life Lee knew, accepted, and loved. Virginia equaled family to Lee—scores of cousins, aunts, uncles, and friends he would not raise his sword against. He had said so during the past year: he'd only draw his sword in defense of Virginia, and he could not fight against his native state.

"THINK AS KINDLY OF ME AS YOU CAN"

And yet, much of Lee's family aligned against him. Robert wrote other letters that day. The most difficult may have been to Anne Lee Marshall, his sister. "With all my devotion to the Union," Robert wrote her, "and the feeling of loyalty and duty of an American citizen, I have not been able to make up my mind to raise my hand against my relatives, my children, my home." Robert implored her, "I know you will blame me;

Lee's letter to Winfield Scott, delivered April 20, 1861

but you must think as kindly of me as you can, and believe that I have endeavored to do what I thought right."

Anne's family remained solidly pro-Union, and her son, Louis, fought with the armies of the North. She died during the war, having never spoken or written to Robert again. Lee's brother Smith resigned his commission in the U.S. Navy but regretted the decision the rest of his life. A number of Lee's cousins remained pro-Union. In 1861 Markie Williams had one brother, Lawrence, fight for the North; her brother Orton fought for the South. Lee's decision pitted him against many Southerners in the United States Army, too. Of the thirteen other Southern men who shared Lee's rank of full colonel, ten remained with the U.S. Army.

Lee had once said he would sacrifice anything for the Union except his honor. Some Lee cousins wondered how Robert could speak of honor. Where was the honor in breaking thirty-five years of military oaths of allegiance to the United States? Instead, wrote one cousin, Robert Lee headed off "to treat [deal] with Traitors."

Two days after resigning, Lee boarded a train bound for Richmond, where he accepted the commission of major general of the Virginia forces. Lee had said he would not raise his sword and make war against the United States. But he always added he would draw that sword to defend Virginia. Now convinced he fought only for Virginia's defense, Lee aligned himself wholeheartedly with the Confederacy and all it stood for. "I am willing to do anything I can do to help the noble cause we are engaged in," he said a year later. After all, his beliefs were the beliefs of most white Southerners. He, too, complained of Northern aggression against the South over the issue of slavery. He, too, saw black people as inferior and judged slavery to be the best relationship between the two races. He was willing to put his life on the line for it.

CHAPTER TEN

THE FIRST YEAR

*"The Confederate States have now but one great object in view.
The successful issue of their war of independence. Everything
worth their possessing depends on that. Everything should yield
to its accomplishment."*

—Robert E. Lee to Andrew Magrath,
December 24, 1861

Lincoln meant to force the Southern states back into the Union. The Confederate states vowed they'd fight for the independence of a slaveholding republic. As the ugliness of civil war loomed, Lee faced the uncertainty by fretting over tiny details that really didn't matter. He'd forgotten to snip the hook-and-eye fasteners from his old army uniform—the ones that held the epaulettes in place—and he'd meant to take the collar loops. Would Mary send these to him in Richmond? He'd discarded the heavy, dark blue coat, once worn so proudly, for Arlington's slaves to use.

His family weighed heavily on Lee's mind those first weeks of the war, late April and early May of 1861. Custis Lee also resigned his commission in the United States Army; both he and Rooney joined their father to fight for the South. Rob, the youngest son, wanted to leave college and enlist in the army, too, but Lee said no. There were enough men for the army without taking boys out of college. And what if the war lasted ten years? Robert asked Mary, "Where are our ranks to be filled from then," if not with the young men now in college?

Worries about his wife topped Lee's list of concerns. He feared that vandals inflamed with fury against the South would enter Virginia to rob and plunder. As the North now viewed him as a traitor and rebel, Lee thought Arlington might become a special target. But it wasn't for this reason alone that he urged Mary to pry herself and their belongings out of Arlington as soon as possible.

Lee knew that the North could not allow Confederate cannon to line Arlington's hills and bombard the Capitol and the White House, only a few miles away. Sooner rather than later, Federal forces—another name for Union forces—would occupy Arlington. Their home would become the family's first casualty of war. But where should his family and their belongings go? When the fighting started, no place would really be safe.

"COMPLETE YOUR ARRANGEMENTS"

Yellow jasmine bloomed on the hillsides and perfumed the air at Arlington, and it seemed like nothing had really changed. Mary stalled. Leaving the home she'd been born in, the place where her parents lay buried, where she'd been married and given birth to her own children, "could scarcely be endured." But Robert's urgency, and a warning from Orton Williams, finally roused Mary to action. She didn't want to risk losing family treasures that could never be replaced.

Mary shipped family silver, letters and papers, and small valuables to Robert in Richmond, who sent them on to safety. She had family portraits cut from their frames, rolled up, and carted away—along with some Washington relics—to a cousin's home in the country. Carpets, Martha Washington's curtains, and more Washington treasures—china, Revolutionary War tents—were locked in the attic and cellar, books stashed in closets and cupboards.

But Mary did not leave. Robert tried to be understanding. "I grieve at the necessity that drives you from your home," he wrote.

An 1861 drawing of Arlington. The Lees never got over the loss of their home and many of the Washington treasures.

"I can appreciate your feeling." But she had to accept the situation. "Be content & resigned to God's will," Robert told his wife.

Mary heard no sounds drifting from Washington across the river, no signs of excitement or stirring of Northern troops. "This is a lovely morning I never saw the country more beautiful, perfectly *radiant*," she wrote Robert on May 9. Her husband responded sharply two days later: "You had better Complete your arrangements & retire farther from the scene of the war. It may burst upon you at any time." More sympathetically he added, "It is sad to think of the devastation, if not ruin it may bring upon a spot so endeared to us."

Mary finally left Arlington to ease Robert's anxiety. Otherwise, as she explained to Mildred, away at school, "I would not stir from this house, even if the whole Northern army were to surround it." She handed Arlington's keys over to Selina Gray, the home's enslaved housekeeper.

* * * * *

122

As Lee had expected, thirteen thousand Federal troops soon crossed the Potomac from Washington on a moonlit night and took possession of Arlington. The Union general Irvin McDowell, who knew the Lees, replied to an angry letter from Mary. Trying to reassure her, McDowell wrote that he hoped "on your return you will find things as little disturbed as possible."

But the sheer numbers of men, horses, and wagons destroyed the estate. Soldiers pulled down fences for firewood. Grass and gardens lay trampled under boots and hooves. Paths and roads cut through the famous woods till only stumps dotted the hillsides. To protect Washington, Union soldiers built a string of forts along Arlington Heights, dug trenches and rifle pits, and piled up earthworks.

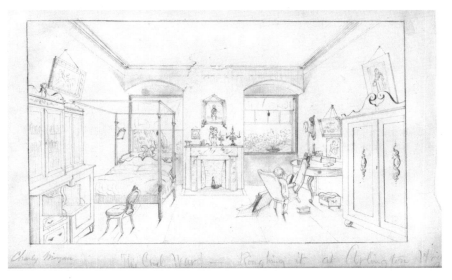

Sketch of the girls' bedroom upstairs at Arlington by Union soldier Charly Miyan. He labeled the drawing "Roughing it at Arlington."

Eventually Union officers and their staff claimed Arlington's rooms as offices and sleeping quarters. People came and went, including curious visitors roaming through the house. Before long Selina Gray discovered

123

the cellar and attic broken into. Heirlooms had gone missing, snatched for souvenirs, including the Washington punch bowl. People thought nothing of swiping the belongings of the traitor Robert Lee. General McDowell sent the remaining Washington treasures to the U.S. Patent Office for safekeeping. They were labeled "Captured from Arlington."

The loss of Arlington and the family's historic treasures marked the Lees for the rest of their lives, filling them—especially Mary—with anger, despair, and hatred for the enemy. Mary clung to the hope that one day her family would return home to Arlington. But Robert knew better.

Once, Lee had written how his heart leapt at the thought of visiting "Dear A----." Arlington held his affection more than "any other place in the World." Now, Robert could not bear to think of its destruction, perhaps because his own decision had played a part. Better it had been "wiped from the earth, its beautiful hill sunk, and its sacred trees buried," he wrote, than have it "degraded" by "those who revel in the ill they do." Arlington's loss was a tragedy Robert could only explain as God's punishment. His family had "not been grateful enough for the happiness there within our reach."

"MORTIFIED AT MY ABSENCE"

Robert Lee began the Civil War behind a desk in Richmond, a general in Virginia's forces, charged with organizing and supplying the state's troops. Jefferson Davis, president of the Confederacy, asked Lee if he minded that his commission in the Virginia state forces left him outranked by those in the Confederate national army. "My commission in Virginia [is] satisfactory to me," Lee replied. This humble answer pleased Davis. The Confederate president spent too much time dealing with ambitious officers, jealous of each other's reputations and jockeying for the best rank.

Jefferson Davis, president of the Confederate States of America

By the end of May the Confederate government had moved to Richmond, making the Virginia city the capital of the Confederacy. Virginia's governor turned over the Army of Virginia, and Robert E. Lee, to the Confederate States. Lee, now a general in the Confederate army, remained at his desk as an advisor to Jefferson Davis.

Another young officer arrived in bustling Richmond: Walter Taylor, a twenty-two-year-old lieutenant, had been assigned to work for Lee.

Slim, youthful in appearance despite his new mustache, Taylor had graduated from the Virginia Military Institute. He was deeply religious, hardworking, and in love with a girl he would woo through letters during the long years of war.

Like nearly everyone who ever met Lee, Taylor noticed how Robert carried himself. Lee's five-foot-eleven-inch frame stood perfectly straight yet graceful; he radiated a sense of dignity and calm. Taylor called Lee strikingly handsome. The dark brown eyes penetrated right through a man. Aside from a mustache, Lee's face was cleanly shaven, though he'd soon grow a beard. Iron gray shot through his dark hair. Only fifty-four years old, Lee's hair and beard would turn completely gray under the strain of war.

Lee had his hands full trying to build an army for the Confederacy. He recommended that soldiers enlist for the duration of the war, however long, but he was overridden by those who felt an enlistment period of one year allowed ample time to whip the Yankees. He advised moving new recruits away from towns. Prepare them for the hardships of military life, said Lee, by isolating recruits in camps for "constant instruction & discipline." In another letter he reminded commanders they must prevent the troops from disturbing citizens' rights and property and enforce "rigid discipline & obedience to orders."

Like Davis, Lee, too, had to deal with small-minded behavior of officers over the issue of rank. He slapped down one man with a terse reminder. "Petty jealousies," wrote Lee, "about slight shades of relative command and bickering about trivial matters are entirely out of place and highly improper." If the bickering interfered with creating a working chain of command, continued Lee, it became "criminal and contemptible."

Lee believed, however, that the sons of Virginia's upper class deserved more attention and honor than others. "I am pained," he wrote Mary, "to see fine young men . . . of education and standing, from all the old and respectable families in the State, serving in the ranks. I hope in time they will receive their reward."

While Jefferson Davis valued Lee's efforts as an advisor, he did not view Lee as a field commander. Instead he saw Lee as an organizer and an engineer. But Lee, tied to his desk job, wanted more. "I am very anxious to get into the field, but am detained by matters beyond my Controul," he wrote Mary in early July. He'd "broken down a little" and fallen ill with the stress of it all. On July 21, 1861, Confederate forces routed the Union army at Manassas outside of Washington, the first major battle of the war, and Lee felt "mortified at my absence."

He soon got his wish to claim the field. In late July, Davis offered him command of military operations in western Virginia. Lee rode along the same road he'd used traveling to St. Louis over twenty years before. If anyone had told him then about his present duty, Lee would have "supposed him insane."

While serving in western Virginia, Lee bought a new horse he named Traveller, a tall, iron-gray animal with a black mane and tail. Strong and muscular with energy to spare, Traveller craved action and fretted if not exercised enough, though under Lee's training the horse "calmed down amazingly."

Buying Traveller was about the only thing that went right for Lee. Troubles plagued him at every turn. His soldiers sickened with measles and typhoid that spread quickly through the camp. A cold, constant rain drenched men and weapons and turned dirt roads impassable. In mid-September the Union general William Rosecrans defeated Lee's troops at Cheat Mountain. Lee had lost western Virginia, which broke off from the Old Dominion and joined the Union as a new state in June 1863.

"DREADFULLY DISAPPOINTED AT THE SPIRIT"

Faced with failure, Robert again suffered the sting of "regret & mortification." Davis recalled Lee from the field, which must have been humiliating. In late November the president sent Robert to strengthen defenses along the coast of Georgia, South Carolina, and Florida. But the Union navy had already built fortifications on South Carolina's Sea Islands, and their overwhelming power easily threatened the South Carolina and Georgia coastline.

Lee considered it impossible to defend the coast itself: the many miles of islands, rivers, and channels provided too many points for Union attacks. He decided his best chance to check any Yankee advance was to build fortifications inland, away from the Union naval guns. His soldiers could defend these fortifications and fight Union troops who had come ashore. But he had little manpower, heavy weapons, or money, and confided to his daughter Mildred that he'd been sent on "another forlorn hope expedition. Worse than Western Virginia."

The enemy threatened everywhere in Lee's region. He received constant reports of Union pillaging, burning, and robbing. At the same time, the Union general Ulysses S. Grant racked up victories in Tennessee and occupied the state capital of Nashville by the end of February 1862. Southerners' morale plummeted, including Lee's. He wrote Agnes that his anxieties drove away sleep. He told the Confederate inspector general, "I am aware that we must fight against great odds, & always trust that the spirit of our soldiers will be an overmatch to the numbers of our opponents."

But Lee worried that Confederate soldiers weren't actually up to the task. They faced setbacks with a lack of "energy & activity" instead of trying even harder, he wrote his family. Lee saw only a continuation of the "same selfishness & carelessness of their duties." Why didn't his men see "the necessity of endurance & labour"? In a perfect world, Lee would have an army filled with men just like him. But even these exasperating soldiers were better than brand-new recruits. What would happen when the men who signed up for a year of military service left in the spring? The Confederates would have to raise, organize, and train

128

a new army in the face of Union strength. "I tremble to think of the consequences," Lee wrote.

Lee also felt let down by the Southern people. He prayed that God might rouse them to a sense of their danger. "I am dreadfully disappointed at the spirit here," he wrote Custis from South Carolina. Citizens did not exert themselves in any way "but are willing to leave that to others." Lee believed that the war would be long and severe and that "the whole country [had] to go through much Suffering," as he told Mary. Southerners needed to be "humbled & taught to be less boastful, less selfish, & more devoted to right & justice to all the world."

"HE NEVER COMPLAINS"

On March 4, 1862, Davis again called Lee back to Richmond and his role of advisor. Lee wrote a short note to his older brother Carter, displaying his lack of confidence. He was willing to do anything Davis wanted, Lee said, "but the lower & more humble the position the more agreeable to me & the better qualified I should feel to fill it." Mary's loyal heart rose on behalf of her husband. "He never gets any credit for what he has done," she wrote a friend. "He never complains or seems to desire anything more than to perform his duty but I may be excused for wishing him to reap the reward of his labors."

Lee may not have been happy, but he gained valuable experience in his advisor role. In March he wrote orders to take more control over the Southern railroads to move troops and supplies. He helped push through Confederate draft laws in April. He worked closely with generals in the field like Joseph E. Johnston and Thomas Jonathan "Stonewall" Jackson, getting to know the abilities of Southern commanders. But most of all, Lee learned how to work with Jefferson Davis.

The two men had known each other since West Point, but never well. Lee, recognizing that Davis carried a heavy burden, willingly subordinated himself to Davis's needs and wishes. Some of the other generals showed less respect. Lee's old friend Johnston, who commanded Confederate troops in Virginia, proved touchy over rank, was unwilling to listen to Davis, and usually failed to communicate with the president at all. Most troubling to Davis, Joseph Johnston showed no will to fight.

Union general George B. McClellan, known as "Little Mac" to his troops

In April 1862, a vast Union army under General George B. McClellan began moving up the Virginia peninsula between the James and York Rivers. A West Pointer who had served in the Mexican War, McClellan was a businessman at the start of the Civil War. After the humiliating Union defeat at Manassas, it was McClellan who trained and organized the fighting force known as the Army of the Potomac. Lincoln demanded action from this army of 100,000 men, and now "Little Mac" marched toward Richmond.

Both Lee and Davis urged Johnston to hold the Virginia peninsula and throw back McClellan's troops. Lee did not want Richmond, the capital of the Confederacy, put at risk. He did something few others in the Confederate army had done—Lee asked Davis what *he* thought. It was a simple thing, but Lee's action, his humility and concern, won Davis's loyalty.

FAMILY WORRIES

Family worries piled on Lee, too, as McClellan's army gathered on the peninsula. Although he'd specifically told his youngest son to remain in school, nineteen-year-old Rob feared that the war would end before he had a chance to fight. In March Rob defied his father, left college, and joined the Rockbridge Artillery, part of Stonewall Jackson's forces. With the deed done, Lee resigned himself and took the newly enlisted Private Lee to get his army overcoat and blankets. "I hope our Son will do his duty & make a good Soldier," he wrote Mary. Now, all three of their sons served in the Confederate army.

Meanwhile, Lee worried about the safety of his wife and daughters. Mrs. Lee, Annie, and Mildred had been visiting Rooney's wife, Charlotte, and her baby son at White House plantation. On May 11 McClellan's advancing army forced the family to flee, a difficulty for Mary, hampered by her painful arthritis. The Union troops burned White House to the ground, despite a note Mary had nailed to the door demanding that they spare the place where George Washington had wed Martha Custis.

Mother and daughters sought refuge with friends but were finally placed under house arrest. An anxious Robert wrote Agnes on May 29 that it was true—her mother and sisters were "in the hands of the enemy. The house was surrounded by a body of the enemy's Cav[alry]."

131

White House, the Custis plantation on the Pamunkey River

By now McClellan's army appeared within sight of Richmond. Confederate and Federal troops clashed just miles from the city. McClellan hoped to lay siege to Richmond, using artillery to pound the capital into submission and perhaps end the war. As people evacuated, wagons piled with boxes and trunks clogged the roads. In battle on May 31, 1862, commanding General Joseph Johnston fell severely wounded.

The next day Jefferson Davis turned to the man who'd quietly earned his respect and trust—Robert E. Lee—and assigned him command of Johnston's army. Lee now had a second chance as a field commander. However much his confidence had wavered in the past year, Lee knew he must make the most of this opportunity.

CHAPTER ELEVEN

"VALOUR FORTITUDE & BOLDNESS"

"Our people are opposed to work. Our troops, officers, community & press. All ridicule & resist it. It is the very means by which McClellan has & is advancing."

—*Lee to Jefferson Davis,*
confidential letter of June 5, 1862

On June 5, 1862, Lee wrote Davis outlining his plans to protect Richmond. "Our position requires you should know everything," said Lee. The two men quickly forged their working relationship. Lee handled Davis's ego gently. He proposed ideas rather than dictating plans to the president. "I shall feel obliged to you for any direction you may think proper to give," Lee told Davis.

Lee earned Davis's loyalty by not challenging him or questioning his judgment. And Davis appreciated how Lee avoided controversy, never running to reporters or whispering with politicians—things the very private Lee avoided at all cost. But for Lee to really serve Davis and the Confederacy he needed to prove himself as a field commander. He needed victories.

Faced with the enemy on his doorstep, Lee had no time to ease into his new job. He began reorganizing the army. He improved food rations and camp sanitation and paid attention to complaints about pay. He renamed his forces the Army of Northern Virginia, though men from throughout the South—not just Virginians—served in it.

McClellan wrote Lincoln about the change in Confederate commanders, noting that he preferred facing Lee rather than Johnston. "TOO cautious & weak under grave responsibility" McClellan labeled Lee, even though "personally brave & energetic to a fault." Lee was, finished McClellan, "likely to be timid & irresolute in action." As it turned out, "Little Mac" could have been describing himself.

The public, "feverish and excited," wanted action. When Lee ordered a ring of trenches and earthworks dug around Richmond, he triggered criticism in the army. The Richmond papers echoed McClellan's words. How could this be considered fighting? People dubbed him timid, called him "Granny Lee" and the "King of Spades." The *Richmond Examiner* told readers Lee misused the army. They were only allowed to dig, for that was West Point's idea of war, and now West Point had command. Lee didn't need guns and bullets when he had spades and shovels. But Rooney Lee confided in a letter to his wife, Charlotte, "Now that Pa has command I feel better satisfied."

Many of the men believed trench digging beneath them and complained. Robert, in turn, griped about the Southern people ridiculing and resisting work. Success required *hard* work combined with "valour fortitude & boldness." Lee rode through the lines of digging men, encouraging them and reminding all of their common goals.

As the protective trenches began encircling Richmond, Lee sent J. E. B. Stuart on a scouting mission to locate McClellan's right flank. Twenty-nine-year-old Stuart, with his luxuriant full beard and plumed hat, became one of the dashing figures of the war. His cavalry included Lee's son Rooney and nephew Fitz Lee. The Confederate cavalry rode clear around the Union army gathering important intelligence on troop positions and supply lines. Lee planned to disrupt those supply lines, especially targeting McClellan's use of the railroad to move his heavy artillery.

James Ewell Brown Stuart, better known as J. E. B. "Jeb" Stuart, cavalry commander

Lee ordered Stonewall Jackson to march his army from Virginia's Shenandoah Valley for support around Richmond. Thirty-eight-year-old Jackson had earned his nickname when his troops held like a stone wall against the Yankees at Manassas. Jackson, like so many other generals, was a West Point graduate and Mexican War veteran. When civil war

Thomas Jonathan "Stonewall" Jackson, the South's most beloved general after Lee

broke out, he had been out of the army for a decade teaching at the Virginia Military Institute. A stern disciplinarian, the deeply religious Jackson had little sympathy for weakness in others. He was a tough and aggressive general and the South's shining star—a hero who'd harassed and defeated larger Union forces in the Shenandoah Valley.

As Lee quickly formed plans to protect Richmond, he also worked to get Mary and the girls back through enemy lines. On June 10 they made it to Richmond, carrying a pass from General McClellan and under a flag of truce. "I have heard with great delight of your arrival in Richmond," he wrote in a quick note to Mary. "I am strongly tempted to go in to see you. My Constant duties here alone prevent, & preparations for the anticipated movement of troops will detain me. . . . Give much love to Annie & Life [Mildred] & tell them I want to see them badly."

The letter was sent from somewhere "Near Richmond." Robert had not seen his wife for fifteen months. Mary had sad news to send her husband. Charlotte and Rooney's little boy, the Lees' only grandchild, had died.

With his wife and daughters safe, Lee prepared for battle. No one expected Lee, the commanding general, to fire a gun or charge the enemy at the head of his troops. Instead, he planned the battle, placed and maneuvered his men, explained what they must do. He remained at the rear of his troops or at an established headquarters where racing messengers could find him as he watched a battle unfold through his field glasses.

Of the 80,000 men under Lee's command, 27,000 stayed behind in the earthworks to defend Richmond; the rest hit McClellan in a series of ferocious battles over seven days. From June 25 to July 1, at places

Alfred Waud, known for his quick, accurate sketches, traveled with the Army of the Potomac for *Harper's Weekly*. Here he shows "the destruction of the Locomotives on the Bridge Over the Chickahominy"—one of Lee's goals during the Seven Days' Battle was cutting McClellan's supply line.

like Mechanicsville, Gaines' Mill, and Malvern Hill, Confederate forces battled the Army of the Potomac. Jackson's famous troops performed sluggishly, leaving the brunt of the fighting to commanders A. P. Hill and James Longstreet; Lee called Longstreet "the Staff of my right hand." Union troops inflicted heavy casualties on Lee's men, but in the end the Army of Northern Virginia drove McClellan's troops away from Richmond and back down the peninsula. Lee's victory, coming after only a few weeks in command, guaranteed life to the Confederacy.

Still, the Army of the Potomac had survived to fight another day, and critics asked why Lee hadn't finished McClellan off. Lee wrote Davis, "I fear all was not done that might have been done to harass and destroy our enemies, but I blame nobody but myself." With the Confederate capital safe from Union forces, however, most praised Lee. The victory had "imbued every man of ours with a determination to fight like demons," said one soldier.

While Lee quickly reorganized his forces into two corps under Jackson and Longstreet, Lincoln put General John Pope in charge of 50,000 Union soldiers in northern Virginia. McClellan still hunkered down with his massive army on the peninsula. Lee figured the best way to nudge McClellan from the peninsula was for Lee's army to threaten Washington D.C. Walter Taylor, Lee's young adjutant, called it a bold move by "our so-called *timid?* General."

Lee sent Jackson, soon joined by A. P. Hill's division, ahead to engage Pope. McClellan started his withdrawal toward Washington, an immense task involving some four hundred ships and barges. In late August, Pope and Jackson clashed along the old Manassas battlefield. Jackson's 20,000 men hung on like bulldogs, repulsing the larger Union force. They knew that Lee and Longstreet, with 30,000 reinforcements, should arrive the next day. On August 30, 1862, Longstreet punished the weary Yankees, raking their lines with artillery and throwing his divisions against Pope's flank. Only a heroic stand by Pope's army allowed them to retreat under cover of darkness. Robert Lee's army decisively defeated Pope at the Second Battle of Manassas. Lee's men cheered as he rode along the lines, a dashing figure sitting tall on Traveller.

Young Rob Lee later recalled an encounter with his father at Second Manassas. Lee was conferring with a group of officers just fifteen feet away from his son. Rob leaned on his cannon, sponge-staff in hand, tired and breathless. The teenager had gone into battle after marching day and night for four days. His father glanced at him, seeing only an unwashed and ragged young man, with gunpowder-sweat blackening his face and grime covering him from head to toe.

"Well, my man, what can I do for you?" Lee asked.

"Why, General, don't you know me?" exclaimed Rob.

Lee then recognized his son and was "much amused at my appearance and most glad to see that I was safe and well," Rob later remembered.

"This Army achieved today on the plains of Manassas a signal victory," Lee wrote Davis. "We mourn the loss of our gallant dead . . . yet our gratitude to Almighty God for his mercies rises higher and higher each day, to Him and to the valour of our troops a nations gratitude is due." Both McClellan and Pope retreated to the fortifications around Washington. The image of timid "Granny Lee" vanished from the public mind. They had clamored for action. Lee had not only delivered action, he'd won victories and offered hope to the Confederacy.

Lee wanted to "change the character of the war." He would not simply defend Richmond. Lee pushed to take the war north out of Virginia. With two victories under his belt that summer of 1862 and his army's morale high as September opened, Lee and Davis decided the time had come to try something bold.

CHAPTER TWELVE

"WE CANNOT AFFORD TO BE IDLE"

Hark!—the artillery massing on the right,
Hark!—the black squadrons wheeling down to Death!
—From "Fredericksburg,"
a poem by Thomas Bailey Aldrich (1836–1907)

Entrenched Union troops, 140,000 strong, dug in around Washington D.C. Lee had no intention of attacking this stronghold. Two months of unending hard marches and fighting had left his men exhausted, ragged, and hungry. Miles of farmland stripped of food and supplies surrounded the Army of Northern Virginia's camps. They'd been living on unripe green apples and green corn.

They could head back to Richmond. But Lee favored offense over defense. If he crossed the Potomac River and moved north into Maryland, maybe even into Pennsylvania, the Union armies would have to come to him and leave Virginia alone. In Maryland, his army could feed off the state's bounty and rest a bit while waiting for the notoriously slow McClellan to move.

There were political reasons, too, for Lee's decision to march into Maryland. The North would hold midterm elections that November. A Confederate victory on Northern soil, Lee wrote Davis, might push Peace Democrats to vote for men who'd end the war. A victory might also spur European recognition of the Confederacy. Lee's victories

140

that summer had nearly convinced French and British politicians that Lincoln could never force the South back into the Union through war.

Lee recognized that he faced problems invading the North. His army lacked equipment, and thousands of his soldiers didn't have shoes. Battle casualties, hunger, and disease had decimated his numbers. "Stragglers"—or deserters—plagued Lee, too. He estimated that nearly 10,000 men had vanished from the ranks, reducing his army to about 51,000 soldiers. He ordered brigade commanders to post guards in the rear to arrest stragglers, and he promised severe punishment for these "cowards of the army" who deserted their comrades in times of danger.

"Still, we cannot afford to be idle," he wrote Jefferson Davis, "and though weaker than our opponents in men and military equipments, must endeavor to harass if we cannot destroy them." What Lee *did* have were men buoyed by their victories, battle-hardened veterans who knew how to fight, and the same leaders—himself, Jackson, and Longstreet— who had whipped the Yankees at Second Manassas. On September 4 his army splashed across the Potomac River into Maryland. A few days later McClellan advanced out of Washington.

A freak accident nearly knocked Lee out of commission. He'd dismounted one day and sat down on a fallen log with Traveller's reins looped over his arm. Something spooked Traveller and he bolted, dragging Lee to the ground. Lee sprained both his wrists and broke some small bones in one of his hands.

The swollen, painful injuries improved slowly. Six weeks later he wrote Mary that the bandages had been removed and he'd discarded his sling. He'd progressed to dressing and undressing himself—"which is a great comfort"—and could also sign his name. But he still couldn't hold the reins to ride; an aide had to lead Traveller as Lee sat on the horse. Sometimes, he rumbled alongside his marching troops sitting in an army ambulance wagon. And so Lee forged ahead into Maryland.

Though a slaveholding state, Maryland had not joined the

Confederacy. Citizens met Lee's soldiers unmoved, silent, or hostile. One woman described Lee's men crowding her doorway begging with faces of "gaunt starvation that looked from their cavernous eyes." A man described the soldiers as the filthiest creatures he'd ever seen, their clothes not changed for weeks.

No civilian rejoiced at the sight of an advancing army. Soldiers carried sickness. They all had empty bellies and expected food from local farms. As enemy armies converged upon one another, citizens fled before the threat of battle, death, and destruction. Shot and shell shattered homes into kindling. Famished soldiers killed or carried off livestock; crops in the fields vanished, razed by bullets, trampled by tens of thousands of feet. Afterward, the rotting carcasses of men and horses ruined people's drinking water and bred disease. A war of this magnitude couldn't help but touch the lives of thousands of civilians.

ANTIETAM

As he'd done during the Seven Days' Battle and Manassas, Lee once more divided his army in the face of McClellan's larger forces, a move not advised by most military men. Big, burly James Longstreet tried to talk Lee out of it. Nicknamed "The Old War Horse," Longstreet was a fierce fighter and one of the men Lee relied on most. Longstreet was another West Pointer and a close friend of Ulysses S. Grant from their academy days. A man of caution, he preferred fighting from a defensive stronghold; let the enemy destroy themselves trying to take his fortified position, a view that often differed from his commanding general's plans.

Lee had successfully divided his army before and saw no reason not to do so again. Now, he sent Stonewall Jackson to seize the Baltimore & Ohio Railroad and then help General Lafayette McLaws secure Harpers Ferry, held by 12,000 Union soldiers. Lee wanted the area cleared for his supply lines and communications back to Virginia. The rest of Lee's army moved north and west.

Lee outlined his plans in Special Orders No. 191, and a copy somehow fell into McClellan's hands as the Confederates left Frederick, Maryland. This should have been a great advantage for McClellan. Luckily for Lee, the orders made no mention of troop numbers. McClellan assumed Lee had far greater numbers than he actually did, and it hampered the Union general's strategy. But knowing that Lee had divided his army, and that those armies were marching miles apart from one another, spurred McClellan to move faster than Lee expected.

On September 14 an outnumbered force of Confederates failed to block the Union's advance over South Mountain. Lee considered returning to Virginia, but when he got word that Jackson had been successful, he decided instead to make a stand near the little town of Sharpsburg. Lee had no more than 30,000 troops with him when McClellan's army of some 60,000, with 15,000 reinforcements a few miles away, arrived along Antietam Creek. But McClellan made no move to attack. This allowed some of Lee's other divisions—the men marched forward at a frantic pace—to rejoin the main command.

Lee concentrated his army on the western side of Antietam Creek. He used the woods and rocks, the stone walls, dips, and valleys of the farmland, to place his troops. Longstreet's command held the center and right, while Jackson moved up to cover the left. Lee sent word to A. P. Hill, still at Harpers Ferry, to hurry up with his forces.

On September 17, 1862, guns and cannon roared along the lines as dawn broke over the fields and woods outside Sharpsburg. McClellan planned to attack Lee's left, then the right. If successful, he would advance on the Confederate center with troops he'd held back in reserve.

McClellan threw his men in three major waves of attack against the Confederate left. Bullets shredded stalks of corn once high as a man's head. Blue-clad soldiers toppled and died in the rows where they'd stood seconds before. Savage fighting broke out in the woods on the left and right. Lee managed the battle on foot or from Traveller's back, with a courier leading the horse. All that day, he expertly shifted his troops around the battlefield from points of inaction to spots of fierce fighting to hold against Union assaults.

Alfred Waud's sketch of hand-to-hand fighting at Antietam, September 17, 1862

Toward the center of Lee's line, Confederate troops positioned themselves in an old country lane called the Sunken Road. Standing in this ready-made earthwork, they mowed down the first advances of Union forces. But as the hours passed, the Federals circled the Sunken Road and the ditch became a deathtrap. Rebel soldiers fell under a rain of bullets until 2,000 Confederate dead and wounded lay in the road, known ever after as Bloody Lane.

In late afternoon the timely arrival of A. P. Hill from Harpers Ferry saved the Confederate right for Lee. As the light failed that evening,

Alexander Gardner photographed Confederate dead in the Bloody Lane at Antietam.

Lee and McClellan were both largely holding the same ground they'd started with that morning. The battle had ended as a stalemate. But it had been a terrible day, twelve hours of often close-range combat, the bloodiest single day in American history. Nearly 23,000 men were dead, wounded, captured, or missing. As the exhausted commanders gathered at Lee's headquarters that night, some reported losses of half their men.

The next day the armies tended to their wounded, buried their dead, and burned the corpses of slain horses. As night fell, Lee retreated to Virginia. Taking the war north had failed. Walter Taylor wrote his sister that one of the bands began playing the popular tune "My Maryland" but was silenced by "the groans & hisses of the soldiers." Lee's losses at Antietam, especially when added to the slaughter from the Seven Days' Battle and Second Manassas, were staggering.

The Army of Northern Virginia had fought bravely, but it had fallen short of a convincing Southern victory. This gave Lincoln an opening he'd been waiting for since July. He declared Antietam a Union victory and issued the preliminary Emancipation Proclamation on September 22. It declared that, effective January 1, 1863, "all persons held as slaves" within any state where the people "shall then be in rebellion against the United States, shall be then, thenceforward, and forever free."

Though his Democratic opponents denounced the proclamation, Lincoln offered the North a dual purpose for the war: they were fighting not only to save the Union but also for a higher moral cause—the eventual end of slavery. Lincoln's proclamation, and Lee's failure to once more defeat the Union forces, also helped deny the South its hope of European recognition. Both France and Great Britain had already abolished slavery.

"IN THE QUIET HOURS OF THE NIGHT"

Lee spent the autumn months after Antietam recruiting, rebuilding, and supplying his army—he even assigned several hundred men to the Quartermaster's Department to make shoes. The army moved between several camps north of Richmond at places like Winchester and Culpeper. Rob wrote his mother that the army "is doing nothing at all now but drill! drill!" and reported to his sister Mildred that "Pa is looking very well & is in very good spirits."

Several weeks after Antietam, Custis visited his father in camp. The young man served as a military aide to Jefferson Davis and hated being stuck in Richmond instead of fighting in the field alongside his father and brothers. Lee, his writing hand still injured, took advantage of this chance to write Mary a scolding letter about private family business. He dictated while Custis wrote:

I do not like your establishing yourselves in Richmond. It is a bad place for six unprotected women, and I think your visit

146

had better be made as short as possible. . . . Mildred, I think, had better go to school; and I know no better one than that at Raleigh [North Carolina]; you had better fix her there at once. After that, you had better endeavor to fix yourself at some place more permanently until the war is over, as I see no benefit of your being constantly on the move and in peril, and as I am so situated that I can not either see you or counsel you or help you, it adds to my anxiety and trouble.

He told Mary about financial arrangements, shared the news that Rooney had been made a general, and finished the letter with love and longing for his wife and daughters.

Against this advice, Mary decided to remain in Richmond. She eventually moved into a narrow brick house nicknamed "The Mess," rented by Custis and some other officers. By staying in Richmond, Mary stole moments to see her husband when he came to the capital on war business. Mary saw Custis nearly every day, and this somewhat eased Robert's fears for her. Never idle, she worked for the cause knitting quantities of socks and gloves and sewing shirts that Lee distributed to his men.

In early October Lee received word that his daughter Annie, in North Carolina with her sister Agnes, had taken sick. She suffered chills and headaches and developed a fever and stomach troubles. Within a few days her condition worsened with a spiking fever and weakness. Agnes called a doctor, who diagnosed typhoid.

There was little for Agnes to do besides apply cold cloths to her sister's burning skin and offer fluids. She also treated Annie with a commonly used blue pill, known today to contain dangerous amounts of mercury. Mary traveled to North Carolina to help nurse her daughter and wrote family members on October 18 that Annie was in much pain and so deaf she could scarcely hear a word. Around seven in the morning on October 20 Annie Lee died quietly and peacefully at the age

147

Portrait thought to be of Anne Carter "Annie" Lee, by an unknown artist

of twenty-three. "O Mildred," Agnes wrote her little sister, "I can not realize it, it is too strange, too unnatural. I never had an idea of it, never felt she was even seriously ill until yesterday morning nor until last night that she was to die." Mary wrote Daughter, "My darling Annie I never had expected to weave a funeral wreath for her." Agnes wanted to take Annie's body back to Richmond, where she might find comfort visiting her grave. But Mary arranged for Annie's burial in North Carolina.

Meanwhile, at headquarters, Walter Taylor and Lee spent their mornings penning numerous letters and reports. A few days after Annie's death, Taylor left Lee alone in his tent after going through the paperwork. But Taylor forgot something and ducked back inside.

Shocked, he found his chief "overcome with grief, an open letter in his hands" telling him Annie had died.

"I Cannot express my dear Mary," Robert wrote, "the anguish I feel at the death of our sweet Annie. To know that I shall never see her again on earth, that her place in our circle which I always hope one day to rejoin is forever vacant is agonizing in the extreme." God had taken "the purest and the best. May you be able to join me in saying His will be done! . . . I Can write no more. The rest is pent up in my troubled thoughts." The family already grieved for Rooney's little boy, who had died in June.

A month after Annie's death, Lee confided to Daughter, "In the quiet hours of the night, when there is nothing to lighten the full weight of my grief, I feel as if I should be overwhelmed."

FREDERICKSBURG

Lincoln, disappointed in his general's performance one time too many, relieved George McClellan of command in early November and appointed Ambrose Burnside in his place. Burnside hoped to move his troops across the Rappahannock River before Lee blocked his path. He'd take the town of Fredericksburg, Virginia, and then march on the Confederate capital at Richmond.

The November weather turned cold and wet as Lee arrived at Fredericksburg. Burnside's forces massed opposite the town on the north bank of the Rappahannock. Under miserable conditions the Army of Northern Virginia, about 75,000 men strong, dug into the surrounding hills and positioned their artillery. Soldiers' tin plates and mugs froze to their fingers. Lee wrote Mary that he'd seen Rob, who had "picked up on the last battle field a soldiers overcoat (yankee) which kept him tolerably dry." But their son had no blanket, so Lee had shared his.

With a battle looming, Lee ordered the use of military wagons and ambulances to evacuate people from Fredericksburg. "It was a pitious sight," Robert told Mary. "But they have brave hearts. What is to become of them God only knows." Many people camped in the open fields and awaited Burnside's move: he soon shelled, burned, and unleashed soldiers to loot the town.

During the night of December 12 Union forces crossed the river on five floating pontoon bridges. When the fog lifted the next morning, Lee's men looked out over the imposing lines of the Army of the Potomac, a solid blue wall of nearly 100,000 men. The Union troops advanced, bayonets glittering. Their regimental flags unfurled as vivid splashes of color against the deep blue. They moved forward to the thunderous boom of artillery fire. The Confederates, wrote Walter Taylor, held their breath at the sight, "as glorious as it is terrible."

Protected by their earthworks, the Rebel guns thundered, and waves of shot and shell swept the advancing Union columns. The Union divisions fell in heaps of mangled bodies ripped by heavy Confederate volleys. It was a lopsided win, Lee's easiest victory of the war. The Union suffered 13,000 casualties; Lee thought he'd lost no more than 2,000 men. All the next day he willed Burnside to renew the attack, confident he could smash the Army of the Potomac, but nothing happened. "They suffered heavily as far as the battle went," Lee wrote Mary, "but it did not go far enough to satisfy me."

The Army of the Potomac retreated back across the river and scurried into winter quarters around Washington. The carnage at Fredericksburg, on top of Lee's other victories, had many in the North wondering if they'd paid too much in blood with nothing in return. Was this war worth it? The following month a frustrated Lincoln removed Burnside from command. Where was a general, Lincoln wondered, who would pursue Robert Lee's Army of Northern Virginia into oblivion?

Jefferson Davis also had problems with generals. Lee's Army of Northern Virginia was the bright spot of the Confederate military. Southern losses in places like Tennessee and Mississippi plagued Davis.

Gen. Robt. E. Lee at Fredericksburg, Dec. 13, 1862.

Lee watches his troops defeat a much larger Union army at the Battle of
Fredericksburg, December 13, 1862.

These western armies seemed in disarray, and his generals bickered among themselves. In November he put Joseph E. Johnston—who'd failed to drive McClellan back from Richmond—in charge of a new Department of the West, overseeing Confederate armies from Mississippi to the Appalachian Mountains. But Johnston wanted his old Virginia command back, and the situation in the west did not improve.

"THEY ARE ALREADY FREE"

As the end of the year neared, unfinished business from before the war required Lee's attention. The Virginia courts had given their final ruling and ordered him to free the Custis slaves. Lee told Mary that he wished "to liberate all of them" on December 31.

In numerous letters Lee had complained about Perry Parks, the personal enslaved servant he had taken to war. He called the man weak, slow, inefficient, and too "fond of his blankets" in the morning. "I hope he will do well when he leaves me," Lee wrote now to Mary, "& get in the service of some good person who will take care of him." The idea that Perry Parks could or would take care of himself seems not to have occurred to Lee.

The slaves he'd hired out in Richmond "can be furnished with their free papers & hire themselves out," wrote Lee. He'd wait and see if those left on the farms could take care of themselves or if they needed to continue as they were—working on the Lee properties. "Any who wish to leave can do so," he noted. "The men could no doubt find homes, but what are the women & children to do?"

Lee desired "to do what is right & best for the people," he told Mary. He'd paid G. W. Custis's legacies and debts and wished "to close the whole affair, but whether I can do so during the war I cannot say." The slaves they'd left at Arlington, now living behind the Union army lines, "are already free," Lee pointed out.

As 1862 drew to a close, Robert felt the satisfaction of having foiled Burnside's plan to enjoy the Union army's Christmas dinner in Richmond. But success didn't change the fact that many of his men were dressed in rags and suffered in the snow and ice without shoes. And there were the terrible numbers of casualties. His heart bled "at the death of every one of our gallant men." Once more he questioned the faith and resolve of the Southern people. Where was their gratitude to God for his mercies? "Oh if our people would only recognize it & cease from their vain self boasting . . . how strong would be my belief in final success & happiness to our Country," he wrote Mary.

Faced with spending Christmas without his family, Lee took stock. His soldier sons were safe and well, and so were Agnes and Mildred. Daughter Mary remained safe, though trapped behind enemy lines while visiting friends. He could only send her verbal messages through his scouts, afraid that his letters might be intercepted. The family's darkest cloud was the death of Rooney and Charlotte's second child, a baby girl. Lee grieved for "that little child of so many hopes & so much affection, & in whose life so much of the future was centered." And he still mourned for Annie.

In a melancholy spirit Robert wrote Mary on Christmas Day: "What a cruel thing is war. To separate & separate & destroy families & friends & mar the purest joys & happiness God has granted us in this world. To fill our hearts with hatred instead of love for our neighbours & to devastate the fair face of this beautiful world."

CHAPTER THIRTEEN

VICTORY AND DEFEAT

"I am more than usually anxious about the supplies of the army, as it will be impossible to keep it together without food."

—Lee to James Seddon, Confederate Secretary of War, January 26, 1863

The opening months of 1863 arrived with knee-deep snow, rain, and rivers of mud. Horses and mules struggled on the nearly impassible roads around Fredericksburg. In the cold and gloom Lee worried over his army. He'd put his men on half rations. At the end of January he wrote to the Secretary of War, James Seddon, that only a week's supply of food remained. "After that is exhausted," said Lee, "I know not whence further supplies can be drawn. . . . The country north of us is pretty well drained of everything the people are willing to part with." The government should appeal to the people to cut their own food rations "and furnish what they have to the army."

Two months later the situation had worsened. Lee wrote Seddon that while his men remained cheerful and he heard few complaints, "I do not think it is enough to continue them in health and vigor, and I fear they will be unable to endure the hardships of the approaching campaign." With his men showing signs of scurvy, Lee sent out daily work parties to gather sassafras buds, wild onions, and garlic for them to eat in place of vegetables. Lee ended one letter to Seddon on a bitter

154

note—he had heard that the Army of the West and armies in Georgia and South Carolina were "more bountifully supplied with provisions." Every soldier in North Carolina received half a pound of bacon each day. "I think this army deserves as much consideration," wrote Lee.

The camp flatware Lee used during the war

Provisioning his army remained a constant thorn for Lee. War had decimated farmlands across the South, and Union armies controlled areas that could have supplied food for the Confederacy. The capture, destruction, or deterioration of Southern railroads made it hard to move provisions. One place might have abundant food while people starved eighty miles away. By late 1862, with inflation raging through the South, people could buy less with the money they had. Flour had risen to $70 a barrel, and the cost of salt skyrocketed from $1.25 a bag to $60. Women rioted in cities like Mobile, Alabama, and Richmond, demanding food for their children. Civilians and soldiers competed for shrinking supplies of food.

"DIMINISHED AND EXHAUSTED TROOPS"

Lee worried about his shrinking army also, its ranks thinned by battle, disease, and daily desertions. Something had to be done to recruit new soldiers, he wrote Seddon. Otherwise, there would be no way to resist the ever-increasing numbers of the Union army. Didn't people understand this danger? Lee asked. The War Department needed to make it clear to the state governors. The successes of the Army of Northern Virginia, Lee said, lulled people into thinking everything was fine.

With fewer numbers, his men needed to fight even harder. They'd achieved victories only through

> a terrible expenditure of the most precious blood of the country. This blood will be upon the heads of the thousands of able-bodied men who remain at home in safety and ease, while their fellow-citizens are bravely confronting the enemy in the field, or enduring with noble fortitude the hardships and privations of the march and camp.

Promising opportunities had already been lost by the lack of men to take advantage of them. What could he do with such "diminished and exhausted troops"? Lee once more felt let down by the people of the Confederacy. The state governments should see that no man able to shoulder a gun "be allowed to evade his duty," he wrote.

Lee also felt physically unwell during those bleak winter weeks. "Old age & sorrow is wearing me away," he told Mary. He caught a heavy cold, and then in April he experienced pain in his chest, back, and arms. Lee had suffered a heart attack, and though he pushed on, it sapped his strength for months.

He wrote Agnes, "I am so cross now that I am not worth seeing anywhere." Still, he wished his daughter could visit. Agnes would have to sit by the little stove that warmed Lee's tent, look out at the rain, and keep herself dry.

Meanwhile, his army waited. The new Union commander, Joseph Hooker, "is obliged to do something," Lee told Agnes. "I do not know what it will be."

WORKING WITH GENERAL LEE

As the commanding general, Lee carried a heavy weight. He digested huge quantities of information, anything dealing with the Army of Northern Virginia, no matter how small or large. He wrote, or dictated to one of the men on his small staff, hundreds of orders and letters—to his officers, to the War Department, to President Davis, to his troops. His poor health, mixed with his anxieties, his sense of duty, and his very private nature, made him a tough taskmaster. He expected complete obedience. He expected people to be on time. He expected an all-out effort.

Lee wasn't the sort to lounge around the campfire and enjoy a drink with his officers. When he had a rare moment to himself, he usually retreated to his tent to write personal letters, seek strength in his Bible, or read the works of Marcus Aurelius, the Roman emperor and general.

Walter Taylor had served as one of Lee's aides since the first days of the war. His experiences offer a peek at what many faced working with Lee. Taylor quickly learned to read his commander's moods. Lee seldom bellowed at those around him; his anger shone forth as sarcasm, silent coldness, and a glare that chilled. A nervous twist or jerk of his head and neck was usually followed by "some harshness of manner," said Taylor. One of Lee's artillery officers called this telltale sign Lee's "snapping at his ear." At one point during the war Taylor vented to his fiancée that he'd never worked harder in his life to please someone, with so little effect: "He is so *unappreciative*. . . . I do want to hear that I please *my general*. . . . I want *him* to tell me, then I'll be satisfied."

Though Lee usually camped in a field tent, one time Taylor found a house where Lee could sleep, had it cleaned, and moved everything in, including all the boxes of army paperwork. Thinking he'd done Lee a good service, Taylor even started "a cheerful fire." Lee came, he slept—and a few days later he moved out to camp in the woods. The house, Taylor exploded in irritation, "was entirely *too* pleasant for him, for he is never so uncomfortable as when comfortable." Lee probably did feel bad having comforts while so many of his men suffered.

Taylor usually seethed silently when angry with Lee or purged his feelings in letters to his fiancée. But a few times things grew heated between them. Taylor then felt guilty, and Lee must have felt a twinge of regret, too. Lee seldom apologized for anything, but he once tried to make up for some angry barbs at Taylor by offering the adjutant a fresh peach an admirer had sent him, which he knew was Taylor's favorite fruit.

The never-ending stream of work overwhelmed both men. Taylor lived in fear of Lee finding fault, and Lee was too busy or distracted—or simply unable—to give Taylor the praise he deserved and craved.

CHANCELLORSVILLE

As the spring of 1863 approached, Lee looked forward to the campaigns ahead and what they might mean. To Mary he expressed his confidence:

> If we can baffle them in their various designs this year & our
> people are true to our cause & not so devoted to themselves . . .
> I think our success will be certain. We will have to suffer & must
> suffer to the end. But it will all come right. This year I hope will
> establish our supplies on a firm basis. On every other point we
> are strong. If successful this year, next Fall there will be a great
> change in public opinion at the North. The Republicans will be
> destroyed & I think the friends of peace will become so strong
> as that the next administration will go in on that basis.

Could he drive Northern public feeling against the war through great victories?

In an effort to improve rations, Lee sent General James Longstreet and two divisions into southeastern Virginia and North Carolina to gather food and supplies. This meant he had even fewer soldiers for whatever lay ahead. And across the Rappahannock River, "Fighting Joe" Hooker, the Union general, had 120,000 men to Lee's 60,000.

As the weather warmed and roads improved, Hooker began to show his hand. He meant to force Lee out of the trenches above Fredericksburg. He sent 10,000 men to cut off Lee's supply lines, and moved the bulk of his army about nine miles west, beyond Lee's left flank, to a place called Chancellorsville. The Chancellor family's sprawling home sat at this intersection of five roads, a place sometimes used as a tavern and inn for travelers. Hooker took over the house as his headquarters. He left 40,000 Union men at Fredericksburg to pin Lee down. Meanwhile the troops at Chancellorsville would sweep around and hit Lee on his left and rear. Hooker sent a message to his troops: "Our enemy must ingloriously fly [flee] or come out from behind his defenses and give us battle on our own ground, where certain destruction awaits him."

Lee, however, did not cooperate with Hooker's plans. He did not retreat to Richmond or wait for Hooker to attack him at Fredericksburg. Instead, he left 10,000 men at Fredericksburg and marched the rest of his men toward Chancellorsville. They beat some of Hooker's advance troops along the way, throwing Hooker back onto defense. Lee then made the aggressive decision to take the offense, even though Hooker's men outnumbered his two to one.

Lee met with Jackson on the night of May 1 to make plans. Of all Lee's generals, Lee consulted Jackson the most and trusted him the most to carry out his orders, no matter the odds. The prickly and aggressive Jackson, who didn't get along with many, called Lee "the only man whom I would follow blindfold."

Fitz Lee's cavalry provided valuable information for his uncle—Hooker's right side was weak. The Union left, on the Rappahannock, couldn't be turned. In the center Hooker had entrenched on a high ground too strong to attack. A forest with dense underbrush claimed most of the area; local people called this place the Wilderness.

Hooker's exposed right side was the opportunity Lee needed. He determined to send Jackson with 30,000 men plus artillery to attack Hooker's weak side while Lee distracted the Union army in the front with about 15,000 infantry. It was a bold plan that required timing and secrecy.

This 1879 print shows a popular theme in Civil War art: the last meeting of Lee and Jackson.

Early on May 2, Jackson led his men out for a twelve-mile march around Hooker's flank. They were noticed. Union soldiers fired on the rear of Jackson's long marching line, but the main body progressed without trouble. They struck the Yankees about five fifteen that evening, catching them by surprise. Lee heard the sound of the guns and began his own attack. Jackson's troops swept forward and broke the Union lines. By nightfall, Jackson's men had rolled back Hooker's right flank. Jackson sent Lee word that all had gone well.

In the early hours of May 3, Lee lay down to catch a bit of sleep. At three in the morning one of his captains woke him—Jackson had been wounded. He'd led a scouting mission, and as they returned to camp in the darkness, his own soldiers fired on them, mistaking the riders for Union scouts. Three bullets hit Jackson—one in his hand, two shattering his left arm. The arm had to be amputated at a field hospital.

Lee couldn't take in the news. "Ah: don't talk about it," he said. "Thank God it is no worse." He sent Jackson congratulations on his victory, on his skill and energy, and said if he could have arranged things, he wished he'd been the one disabled instead of Jackson.

Lee still had a battle to fight that day. He placed J. E. B. Stuart in command of Jackson's troops and sent orders:

May 3, 1863—3 a.m.

General: It is necessary that the glorious victory thus far achieved be prosecuted with the utmost vigor, and the enemy given no time to rally. As soon, therefore, as it is possible, they must be pressed, so that we can unite the two wings of the army. . . .

Let nothing delay the completion of the plan of driving the enemy from his rear and from his positions.

I shall give orders that every effort be made on this side at daylight to aid in the junction.

That morning Lee and J. E. B. Stuart fought their way through and joined the two wings of the Army of Northern Virginia. Lee rode at the back of his troops, watched the action through field glasses, rallied his men, and saw the Confederate lines meet. The Confederates captured the best artillery position on the field and bombarded the Union lines. Chance even seemed on Lee's side—a Confederate cannonball hit a column on the Chancellor house where Hooker stood and knocked him unconscious for a time. The Union pulled back.

By ten o'clock that morning the Army of Northern Virginia stood victorious. As Lee rode through his men, with the Chancellor house ablaze behind him, wild cheers erupted over the roar of flames. Men pushed forward waving their hats, calling Lee's name. He looked so grand and majestic, noted one Virginia soldier, that even some of their Yankee prisoners cheered.

Lee at Chancellorsville, mistakenly shown on a dark horse, encourages his men to victory, May 3, 1863.

But the victory at Chancellorsville proved costly. At first Jackson's injury did not seem life-threatening, but he developed pneumonia and died in the afternoon on May 10. The next day Lee announced the news "with deep grief" to his soldiers, a stirring message meant to encourage his troops. "But while we mourn his death, we feel that his Spirit Still lives, & will inspire the whole army with his indomitable courage. . . . Let his name be a watchword to his Corps, who have followed him to victory on So many fields. Let his officers & Soldiers emulate his invincible determination to do every thing in defense of our beloved Country." The depth of the blow showed more in his simple words to Mary: "Any victory would be dear at such a price. His remains go to Richmond to-day. I know not how to replace him."

The victory—considered Lee's most brilliant—cost more than Jackson. The Army of Northern Virginia suffered 13,000 casualties, about 20 percent of his force. Lee wrote his brother Carter that facing 100,000 men "is fearful odds." He desperately needed more soldiers. "Our ranks are constantly thinning by battle and disease—We get no recruits You can judge therefore of our prospect of disposing of Hooker's Army."

Unlike the generals of the North, Lee couldn't replace all the men he lost. Eventually this would hurt his chances for victory and the Southern war effort. But Lee didn't change his aggressive strategy, though outmanned and outsupplied. He didn't fall back on defense. He didn't back off hurling his forces against the larger Union army.

FAMILY SORROWS

A month after the Army of Northern Virginia's impressive victory, the Lee family suffered a double blow of sorrow. Markie's brother Orton Williams had been a handsome young officer on General Scott's staff before resigning to join the Confederacy. On June 8, 1863, Union officials in Franklin, Tennessee, arrested Orton and another Custis cousin. It was unclear what the cousins' intentions had been, but both were wearing stolen Union uniforms at the time of their arrest. They claimed to be army inspectors. The Union commander sentenced them to death for being spies, and with astonishing haste, had them hanged the next day. Orton Williams was twenty-four.

Lee was livid. Spies were usually imprisoned. The speed of the executions showed "the spirit of our enemies," he exploded to Mary. "I see no necessity for his death except to gratify the evil passions of those whom he offended by leaving Genl Scott." Even years later, Lee wrote that his blood still boiled at the "atrocious outrage," and Mary recalled her "young cousin . . . cruelly murdered."

Markie, whose loyalties had remained with the Union, now became a Southern sympathizer. Orton's brother, Lawrence, a promising officer in the Union army, deserted later that year. And Lee's daughter Agnes, who had shared a close—even romantic—bond with Orton, grew quiet, sad, and withdrawn. "I do not recall hearing her laugh," one friend said of Agnes after Orton's death.

Eleanor Agnes Lee, called Agnes; William Henry Fitzhugh "Rooney" Lee

On the same day that Orton Williams was hanged, Rooney Lee was shot in the thigh during a battle with Union cavalry at Brandy Station, a crossroads between Culpeper and the Rappahannock River. Rooney was lucky—no bones shattered, no artery severed. Lee saw his son that night as he was carried from the field. He quickly wrote Mary assuring her that Rooney, young and healthy, would soon mend.

With White House destroyed, Rob took his brother to Hickory Hill, the home of Charlotte's family, about twenty miles from Richmond. Mary, Agnes, and Mildred arrived to help Charlotte nurse her husband. "As some good is always mixed with the evil in this world, you will now have him with you for a time," Lee wrote comfortingly to Charlotte.

But Rooney's time recuperating with family proved short. Toward the end of June, Rob spied a small group of blue-coated horsemen galloping up the road. He reported to his brother, who told him to run. Rob escaped, jumped a fence, flopped on his stomach behind a hedge, and watched the house.

The Union soldiers had been sent to capture Rooney and hold him hostage to ensure the safety of some Union prisoners. With his wife, mother, and sisters as witnesses, the soldiers carried Rooney out the door on his mattress, shoved him in the Hickory Hill carriage, and drove away. Charlotte broke down in grief. She had lost two children in the past year, and now this. The Federals first locked Rooney up at Fort Monroe in Virginia and later transferred him to a fort in New York Harbor. In all, he spent nine months as a prisoner of war.

NORTH TO GETTYSBURG

Robert Lee knew none of this as he planned his follow-up campaign against the Union army. After Jackson's death at Chancellorsville, he had reorganized his forces into three corps, each of which had three divisions. James Longstreet commanded the first corps, Richard Ewell the second, and A. P. Hill the third. Lee had confidence in his troops and believed he could crush the will of the North to fight. Throughout the war, he never wavered in this, even as the odds were stacked against him. "If we can defeat or drive the armies of the enemy from the field, we shall have peace," he wrote Davis.

With this in mind, Lee once more planned to invade Northern soil. His forces were better prepared and better supplied than when he'd invaded Maryland ten months earlier. Once more Lee led the Army of

Northern Virginia across the Potomac River; they crossed unchallenged into Pennsylvania.

Lincoln had asked Hooker and the Army of the Potomac to follow Lee and "fight him when opportunity offers." Take the chance that McClellan lost last fall, Lincoln urged. But Hooker seemed reluctant to engage Lee's army again. As Lee advanced in Pennsylvania, Lincoln replaced Joe Hooker with General George Gordon Meade.

Union general George Gordon Meade

On June 27 Lee issued General Orders No. 73. He reminded his men that there must be no actions to tarnish the reputation of the army:

> The commanding general considers that no greater disgrace could befall the army, and through it our whole people, than . . . the barbarous outrages upon the unarmed and defenseless and the wanton destruction of private property, that have marked the course of the enemy in our own country. . . . We make war

only upon armed men, and . . . we cannot take vengeance for the wrongs our people have suffered without lowering ourselves.

No reference was made to the Confederate Congress's authorization for captured black people to be returned to slavery. It was not considered a mark of "disgrace" when some of his soldiers seized African Americans, both free people and runaway slaves, and tied them to wagons or drove them like cattle alongside the army.

* * * * *

Lee had sent J. E. B. Stuart's cavalry out a week before with a list of tasks—scout for information, collect supplies, protect the flank of Ewell's corps, and damage the enemy if he met them. Lee had not given Stuart a timetable for reporting back. It was a lot for Stuart to do, and collecting supplies or fighting Union forces distracted from what should have been the most important item—getting Lee the information he needed. Now, Lee didn't know exactly where Stuart was.

Lee didn't know the landscape; he didn't know the number of Union forces. Still feeling the effects of his spring heart attack, he wasn't up to doing reconnaissance himself. "Making use of the eyes of others" embarrassed him. And for the first time he would be going into battle without the general he trusted most, Stonewall Jackson.

On July 1 advance troops under the command of A. P. Hill met several brigades of Union cavalry outside a prosperous little town called Gettysburg, ten miles north of the Pennsylvania state line. Couriers from both sides galloped away to say that fighting had begun and to ask for reinforcements. Ewell's forces arrived, Lee arrived, and the Confederates attacked, sweeping the Union soldiers yard by yard back through town to Cemetery Hill. The Union hung on to this formidable high ground of hills and ridges south of the town. Lee told Ewell to attack Cemetery Hill "if he found it practicable." Ewell, his men spent from hours of hard fighting earlier in the day, decided it was not "practicable" for his soldiers to drive up the slopes carved with hollows and ravines beneath the blazing Union guns.

As the first day of battle ended, Longstreet's corps arrived. Longstreet urged Lee to move the army south and get between Meade's army and Washington—make Meade come fight them on ground of the Confederates' choosing. Lee disagreed, and said, according to Longstreet, "If the enemy is there to-morrow, we must attack him." Lee seemed "under a subdued excitement, which occasionally took possession of him when 'the hunt was up.' . . . The sharp battle fought by Hill and Ewell on that day had given him a taste of victory," Longstreet reported.

James Longstreet disagreed with Lee's plans at Gettysburg.

Lee spent the night planning his attack for July 2. He'd decided to gamble and take the offense, knowing it would come at great cost. But his men had faced huge odds before and won. James Longstreet, unhappy with Lee's decision to attack, would lead his 1st Corps in the main assault on the Union left. A. P. Hill's and Ewell's corps would support him with attacks on the right at Cemetery Hill and Culp's Hill.

By morning, Meade had reinforced his troops; 90,000 Union soldiers held strong along a stretch called Cemetery Ridge. Cemetery Hill, near the town, was on the right, and Big Round Top and Little Round Top anchored the left end of the ridge, where Longstreet would attack. The area around Little Round Top included a rocky fortress of boulders called Devil's Den. The high positions looked over a peach orchard and a wheat field.

On the afternoon of July 2 Lee unleashed heavy assaults on the Union's left flank. Fighting raged at Devil's Den, at Little Round Top, across the wheat field and the peach orchard. On the Union right, he launched his men against Culp's Hill and Cemetery Hill. The fighting was vicious, often hand-to-hand with bayonets. The Rebels came within mere yards of forcing the Union troops from their positions in several places, but by nightfall Meade's men still held their ground. Lee felt his soldiers had come close, and another push might lead to victory. Meade must have weakened his center to reinforce his right and left, Lee thought. Determined to fight again on July 3, Lee ordered an assault on the Union center.

The major action of the day began around one o'clock in the afternoon. Nearly 250 Union and Confederate cannon, facing each other across a wide field, opened fire. The deafening roar, the pounding, the belching gray smoke and shot, the guns blazing hot beneath the July heat, resounded and maimed for nearly two hours. Then the Union cannon fell silent. Meade held back, still ready with more ammunition, but Lee's artillery shells were nearly spent.

As the guns quieted, 12,000 infantrymen of Longstreet's corps commanded by General George Pickett emerged from the Confederate side. They began marching across the open field toward the Union center. The Yankee cannon awakened and fired; rifle bullets sprayed Pickett's men. Soldiers fell in rows. Some managed to reach the Union guns along Cemetery Ridge, but the charge ended in slaughter, chaos, and retreat. Pickett lost two-thirds of his division.

Lee, who had watched the carnage unfold, rode among his men, offering words of calm and encouragement. Lee told one tearful commander, "Never mind, General, *all this has been my fault*—it is I that have lost this fight, and you must help me out of it in the best way you can."

Over three days at Gettysburg, the dead, wounded, missing, and captured totaled over 51,000 Union and Confederate soldiers. Lee's decisions cost him over 28,000 men, nearly a third of his army. A pounding storm pummeled the Army of Northern Virginia as it retreated out of Pennsylvania. Miles of horse-drawn artillery and wagons carrying the wounded rumbled along as exhausted men marched back through Maryland and across the rain-swollen Potomac River into Virginia. All the time Lee feared Meade would attack his vulnerable army in retreat.

One New Yorker wrote in his diary, "The charm of Robert Lee's invincibility is broken." Lincoln, however, wondered how Lee and his army had once again escaped. The Union quartermaster Montgomery Meigs had worked with Lee years before in St. Louis. He voiced Northern frustration: "That rebel army fights so hard that every time it is touched it is like touching a hot iron. Whoever touches it gets hurt."

* * * * *

On July 7, in the midst of his retreat, Lee wrote, "I have heard with great grief my dear Mary that F [Fitzhugh/Rooney] has been captured by the enemy. I had not expected that he would have been taken from his bed & Carried off. . . . But I must bear this as I have to bear other things." In another letter he told Mary that his army should not have been expected to perform impossibilities at Gettysburg. Had he asked too much? Taken too much for granted?

A month later, he wrote a lengthy letter to Jefferson Davis. "We must expect reverses, even defeats," Lee wrote. One should learn from a defeat and try even harder in the future. "The general remedy for the want of success in a military commander," he acknowledged, "is his removal." Lee had thought about it—it was time for Davis to "take measures to supply my place." He had heard the discontent from the public over Gettysburg:

> I do not know how far this feeling extends in the army. My brother officers have been too kind to report it, and so far the troops have been too generous to exhibit it. . . . No one is more aware than myself of my inability for the duties of my position. I cannot even accomplish what I myself desire. How can I fulfill the expectations of others?

Davis declined to replace Lee as commander of the Army of Northern Virginia. To find a man more fit to lead, a man the troops had more confidence in, is to "demand an impossibility," Davis replied.

In Mississippi, on the war's western front, the Confederacy suffered another calamity. On July 4, the day Lee began his retreat from Gettysburg, the Confederate army at Vicksburg surrendered to Union general Ulysses S. Grant after a seven-week siege. This gave the Union control of the important Mississippi River and divided the Confederacy in two, with states on either side of the river. Lee's focus remained fixed on the war in Virginia, but Grant was the star of the Union army, and soon Lincoln would call him east.

CHAPTER FOURTEEN
"A MERE QUESTION OF TIME"

"I . . . feel the growing failure of my bodily strength. I have not
yet recovered from the [heart] attack I experienced the past spring."

—Lee to Jefferson Davis,
August 8, 1863

ollowing defeat at Gettysburg, Lee worked to rebuild his wounded
army. But in September 1863 the government transported two of
Longstreet's three divisions to Tennessee as reinforcements, where the
Confederate army had evacuated Chattanooga. This left Lee without
nearly one third of his force. "I want you badly," he wrote Longstreet,
"and you cannot get back too soon." But the 1st Corps didn't return
until April 1864.

Lee's official letters rang with praise for his soldiers' bravery. In
private letters he reflected more on the death and carnage surrounding
him. Lee coped by embracing his deep faith and focusing on the peace
and joys of the afterlife. He wrote his daughter-in-law Charlotte that the
terrible loss of his officers and men "causes me to weep tears of blood
and to wish that I never could hear the sound of a gun again. My only
consolation is that they are happier and we are left to be pitied."

The family suffered another personal blow when Charlotte died
in late 1863, having never seen her husband again: Rooney remained
a prisoner of war. Lee's grief deepened at the thought of Rooney—at

172

"the anguish her death will cause our dear son," he wrote Mary. And to his brother Carter, Robert wrote that Charlotte's death "has caused an aching void in my heart, that Merciful God alone in his good time can remove."

Lee faced continuing poor health and may have suffered a second heart attack during the fall of 1863. His army fought some small-scale clashes with Union forces, but mostly he watched as the Northern army swelled with reinforcements across the Rapidan River. "Our enemies are very strong at all points," he told a friend, and prayed that God might release the South from the "grevious punishment" he'd inflicted upon them.

Two images of Lee by photographer Julian Vannerson, taken in March 1864

"EVERY MAN AT HIS PLACE"

As 1864 opened, Lee wondered how far his hungry, barefoot men could go. Bitter cold set in, the ground froze hard, beards and mustaches dripped with icicles. He lacked everything—beef, shoes, weapons, even soap for the basic comfort of cleanliness. Lee believed citizens should sacrifice for the good of the army and their Southern cause. It angered him that farmers hoarded grain, only to have it stolen by Union soldiers, and railroads raised rates to move supplies. Inflation raged in the South, and shortages of everything loomed. A pound of bacon cost $10, a turkey $60, a barrel of flour $300.

Anxiety over provisions never left Lee. How could he keep the army together without food? He warned Jefferson Davis that he might have to retreat from war-torn Virginia to seek supplies in North Carolina. In the meantime, "every exertion should be made to supply the [train] depots at Richmond and at other points," Lee wrote. Everything, he warned, must be "*devoted to necessary* wants."

The lack of supplies contributed to an even greater problem for Lee—soldier desertions that decimated his army. Nearly 5,500 men left in March 1864, Lee reported to Davis. He blamed harsh conditions and letters from home begging the men to leave. Lee had stragglers and shirkers shot as examples to keep the other men in line. When Davis urged Lee to pardon some men, Lee did it, but it went against every belief at Lee's core about duty and discipline. He let men off for their youth or for past bravery, but it set a bad precedent, he thought, and encouraged others to hope for a pardon. And he hated the unjustness to the men who remained, suffering for their country.

He offered those who returned a chance to use the upcoming spring campaign to "redeem themselves from the stigma of cowardice, desertion etc. now attached to them." Let their future conduct erase their "past crimes."

Robert wrote Rooney, who'd been released that spring and had rejoined his father, that the Confederacy "demands all our thoughts, all our energies." A huge army had formed against them, and he required "every man at his place. If victorious we have everything to hope for in the future. If defeated nothing will be left us to live for."

* * * * *

In March 1864 Lincoln named forty-two-year-old Ulysses S. Grant commander of all Northern armies. Grant had graduated at the middle of his class at West Point and served in the Mexican War. He'd left the army in 1854 and spent the following years struggling to provide for his family, failing as a farmer and businessman. When the war broke out, Grant was unhappily working in his father's leather tanning shop in Galena, Illinois. Grant rose rapidly in the Union army, despite a reputation for drinking, by smashing Confederate forces in the west— his most recent victory at Chattanooga, Tennessee, in November 1863.

Grant could have remained in Tennessee and still run the war in Virginia, but Lincoln wanted his proven winner to meet Robert Lee head on. Losses in the west had gravely wounded the Confederacy, but most people, Northerners and Southerners, focused on the war in Virginia. Many agreed with Lincoln's Secretary of War: "Peace can be had only when Lee's army is beaten, captured or dispersed."

While Northerners looked upon Lee as a dangerous and slippery foe, people in the South idolized him. A North Carolina woman wrote about Lee in her diary: "What a position does he occupy, the idol, the point of trust, of confidence & repose of thousands! How nobly has he won the confidence, the admiration of the nation." A soldier described the scene when Lee reviewed the troops in April 1864. The men caught sight of him—easily recognized on Traveller—and a wild cheer erupted along the lines. Men tossed their hats, "and many persons became almost frantic with emotion. . . . One heard on all sides such expressions as: 'What a splendid figure!' 'What a noble face and head!' 'Our destiny is in his hands!' 'He is the best and greatest man on this continent!'" A

Charleston newspaper noted that Grant had won many victories, but he was "now opposed [by] a General who stands in the foremost ranks of Captains, and his army is confronted with men accustomed to victory."

Lee remained hopeful that spring could bring victory. He could not take the offensive—Grant outnumbered him two to one—but he could offer a hard-fought defensive war against Grant. "We can alarm & embarrass him to some extent," Lee wrote Davis, "& thus prevent his undertaking anything of magnitude against us." To Rooney he wrote, "We must strike fast & strong. My whole trust is in God, & I am ready for whatever he may ordain. May he guide guard & Strengthen us is my Constant prayer."

Ulysses S. Grant, photographed in June 1864. After a string of Union generals, Lincoln hoped Grant was the man who would finally defeat Lee's army.

Grant arrived at his headquarters in Virginia in late March 1864. He'd put plans in motion to beat the Confederate armies for good. Grant sent General Philip Sheridan's cavalry to wreak havoc in the Shenandoah Valley. He ordered General William T. Sherman to break up Johnston's western army, to march from Tennessee to Georgia—first to Atlanta, then on to Savannah—and up through South Carolina, destroying all he could. Meanwhile, Union naval forces would attack Mobile, Alabama. For himself, Grant planned not a battle against Lee but an entire campaign to destroy the Army of Northern Virginia and capture Richmond. He told General George Meade, "Wherever Lee goes, there will you go also."

THE OVERLAND CAMPAIGN

Despite the odds against him, Lee and his men felt confident. "It never occurred to me," wrote Rob, "and to thousands and thousands like me, that there was any occasion for uneasiness." They trusted that Lee "would bring us out of this trouble all right."

Lee told Walter Taylor, "We have got to whip them, we must whip them and it has already made me better to think of it." He still hoped his battlefield performance might pressure Northern Peace Democrats to oust Lincoln in the November 1864 election. As one Georgia newspaper put it, "If the tyrant at Washington be defeated, his infamous policy will be defeated with him."

The Army of the Potomac crossed the Rapidan on May 4. The two armies met the next day in that densely wooded area near Chancellorsville called the Wilderness. Littering the ground were the skulls and bones of men lost exactly a year before, washed from their shallow graves. That first day in the Wilderness, Lee fought Grant for two roads the Union army needed to continue their march southward. Union forces held the position, and both commanders ordered fresh attacks for early the next morning.

Lee meant to spearhead his attack with Longstreet's corps, marching double time to reach the battle. Grant had 115,000 men to Lee's force of 64,000. Grant attacked first that morning. Union troops drove the Confederates, fighting all the way, back through the woods for nearly a mile, to a small clearing where Lee's headquarters stood.

In the chaos around him, Lee spurred Traveller to the front of a Texas brigade of Longstreet's that had just arrived. He stood in his stirrups and waved his hat and urged the Texans on. No one who saw Lee at that moment would ever forget how he looked—his eyes flashing fire, his face determined, his lips set in a firm line. The sight of their general endangered at the front of the battle rallied the men. One of Lee's generals galloped up and tugged on Traveller's reins. The men cried, "General Lee, go to the rear!" The Texans' counterattack swept forward. Lee drifted back to the rear of his troops. More of Longstreet's men poured into the battle, halted the Union advance, and almost drove Grant's soldiers back to where they'd started that morning.

Later that day, James Longstreet was nearly killed, and energy drained out of the Confederate attack like air from a balloon. Like Jackson a year before, he'd been shot accidentally by one of his own men; he would be out of action for months. Lee continued fighting into the evening but couldn't dislodge Grant's army. During that hellish night dry brush in the forest caught fire. Many of the wounded were burned alive, their screams punctuated by small explosions as the fire ignited the cartridges in their belts.

The battle at the Wilderness ended in a slight victory for Lee. This first clash set the stage for the entire seven weeks that became known as the Overland Campaign—brutal fighting and horrific losses on both sides. Grant suffered nearly 17,500 casualties and Lee lost over 11,000 men in the Wilderness.

Unlike previous Union generals Lee had faced, Grant did not retreat after the hard-fought battle to recover in safety. Instead, giving Lee's soldiers no time to catch their breath, Grant marched his men south around Lee's right flank and tried to plant his army between Lee and Richmond. Lee shadowed Grant's movements, and just days later the two armies clashed again.

Alfred Waud's sketch "Wounded Escaping from the Burning Woods of the Wilderness"

Grant meant to maneuver Lee into open battle, where his greater forces could destroy the Army of Northern Virginia. But Lee's troops dug in near Spotsylvania Court House—Grant would have to go around him or smash his way through. Grant tried both options. On May 9 he failed to turn Lee's flank as Lee moved two divisions to counter the Union attack. The next day Grant hit Lee's left center across a mile-long front. Lee had entrenched along a prominence called the Mule Shoe, which jutted out as half a mile of high ground. Union troops failed to take this and fell back.

The day after that, one Union corps fought through and split Lee's army in two. As he'd done at the Wilderness, Lee answered the threat by charging to the front to lead a counterattack. Once more his soldiers begged him to fall back. His troops swept forward and engaged the Yankees in fierce, close-quarters fighting. Meanwhile, a second Union assault on the Mule Shoe—at a spot known afterward as the Bloody Angle—resulted in some of the most brutal carnage of the war. For hours the armies clashed in the pouring rain. Men slipped in the blood-drenched trenches as the fighting intensified into a frenzy of hand-to-hand combat with gun and bayonet. Walter Taylor would describe the "hissing fire, an incessant, terrific hail of deadly missiles. No living man nor thing could stand in the doomed space embraced within those angry lines; even large trees were felled—their trunks cut in twain [two] by the bullets of small-arms."

Grant couldn't break Lee, so southward he went, the Army of the Potomac edging toward a railroad juncture near the North Anna River. Lee followed, his army marching only a few miles to the west of Grant's men. Walter Taylor, noting Grant's "terrible record of killed & wounded," called him "such a brute"—but, he acknowledged, Grant "holds on longer than any of them." Lee's casualties were terrible as well. Grant had lost 18,000 men, but from his much smaller army Lee had lost 13,000 at Spotsylvania. He'd also lost twenty of his fifty-seven commanders. Lee called in men from the Shenandoah Valley and Richmond to bolster his forces.

One of those killed was Lee's dashing general J. E. B. Stuart, mortally wounded in a cavalry battle at Yellow Tavern on May 11. "A more zealous, ardent, brave & devoted soldier, than Stuart, the Confederacy cannot have," Lee wrote Mary. He added, "I have thought of you very often in these last eventful days & have wished to write to you, but have found it impossible."

Lee sent a sober letter to Davis, detailing Grant's strengths—even the Union's cannon were "superior in weight of metal and range to our own." Lee reported that Grant had called for reinforcements. "The importance of this campaign to . . . Mr. Lincoln and to General Grant leaves no doubt that every effort and every sacrifice will be made to secure its success."

The armies clashed for four days along the North Anna River, from May 23 to May 26. Grant once more failed to break Lee and headed south toward Cold Harbor. This relentless, bruising, exhausting style of warfare, which decimated the ranks, took more than just a physical toll. With Longstreet still recovering from his injuries, Lee's remaining corps commanders, Richard Ewell and A. P. Hill, suffered mental breakdowns. Lee had to replace Ewell with General Jubal Early.

Reinforcements swelled Grant's forces to about 109,000 men. Lee could counter with 59,000 Confederate troops. The last week of May, Lee was so sick he couldn't even leave his bed. "It is the more aggravating [because of] the work I have to do," he agonized to Mary.

But Lee was at the front when he had to be. It was this determination, said one of his generals, that made Lee "the head and front, the very life and soul of the army." Another soldier wrote home that Lee and the army were "full of fight and unconquerable."

Lee had his men dig intricate lines of zigzagging earthworks and trenches at Cold Harbor. Grant believed he could finish Lee's army off since the Confederates couldn't fight outside of their protective lines and attack him.

Grant ordered a frontal assault on Lee's dug-in forces for the morning of June 3. The Confederates repulsed Union troops all along the line, shattering the blue-clad ranks. Union dead and wounded piled up in front of the Confederate earthworks. Grant lost 7,000 men within minutes in a single assault on the Rebel lines. He called off the attack. General Meade wrote his wife, "I think Grant has had his eyes opened and is willing to admit now that Virginia and Lee's army is not Tennessee."

Grant didn't stop; once more he moved south, and the Army of Northern Virginia had to follow. The saddle rarely left Traveller's back. Lee told General Jubal Early, "We must destroy this army of Grant's before he gets to the James River." From there Grant could set up a base and protect a water route for a steady stream of reinforcements and supplies. "If he gets there, it will become a siege," said Lee, "and then it will be a mere question of time."

As Lee had feared, Grant moved nearly his entire army south to the James River. In mid-June Grant failed to seize the town of Petersburg, sitting on the Appomattox River twenty-three miles south of Richmond. The town was an important railroad center, with five different rail lines, and served as a main supply base for Richmond and Lee's army. Lee had to protect both Petersburg and Richmond.

The two armies dug in around Petersburg. It was the last thing Lee wanted. Grant could harass and starve Lee's troops, waiting months if need be. While Lee's army withered away, Grant could tighten the Union's noose around Petersburg, Richmond, and the Army of Northern Virginia.

CHAPTER FIFTEEN

SIEGE AND SURRENDER

"Our numbers are daily decreasing, and the time has arrived in my opinion when no man should be excused from [military] service."

—Lee to James Seddon,
Confederate Secretary of War,
August 23, 1864

Lee fortified his position around Petersburg—a semicircle twenty-six miles long of earthworks, trenches, and forts of logs and dirt. His men stretched along the earthworks in a thin gray line. Federal troops also built earthworks and prepared for siege. They brought cannon to shell the town and squat mortar artillery to lob missiles against the Confederate lines. Grant, with his superior supplies and superior numbers, had options: he could wait Lee out, break Lee's line, or move around his flank.

"The enemy has a strong position, & is able to deal us more injury than from any other point he has ever taken," Lee wrote Jefferson Davis. "Still we must try & defeat them. I fear he will not attack us but advance by regular approaches. He is so situated that I cannot attack him." All Lee could do was order limited strikes to defend railroad lines, his main hope for getting supplies.

Grant was under pressure to do something that summer of 1864. He'd pinned down the Army of Northern Virginia, at great cost in blood,

Confederate trenches at Petersburg

but had not destroyed Lee's army. On July 30, the Union launched an attempt to break the Confederate line at Petersburg. They'd dug a 500-foot-long tunnel under the Rebel fortifications and blasted it with gunpowder at 4:45 in the morning. Union troops meant to dash through the hole, break Lee's line, and capture Petersburg.

The earth exploded. Heavy Confederate cannon were thrown thirty or forty yards away. Southern soldiers lay tumbled and buried beneath the dirt. The blast formed a crater about 120 feet long and deep enough to hold a house. But the Union soldiers charging down into the crater made easy targets for the Confederate counterattack; the gaping hole filled with a jumble of dead and wounded.

The Union assault included African American soldiers. The advancing wave of black faces shook the Confederate soldiers to murderous fury. How dare these black men, many of them escaped slaves, fight racially superior white men? The Confederates slaughtered many of the black

Union soldiers, not allowing them a chance to surrender. "No doubt the majority of them . . . once owned masters in happy Virginia homes," wrote Walter Taylor. "There was but little mercy shown them in the engagement." The Confederates had once more frustrated Grant's plans to break Lee's line.

As the months ticked away at Petersburg, the strain of siege showed on Lee. He felt old; his temper flared. Walter Taylor found him "unreasonable and provoking." Lee was in the saddle most of the day and working at his desk long into the night. He never failed to write Mary, though, and from the trenches at besieged Petersburg he sent her well-wishes on their wedding anniversary. "Do you recollect what a happy day thirty-three years ago this was. How many hopes & pleasures it gave truth to?"

"THE STRUGGLE NOW"

At Petersburg, Lee faced an army of contrasts. On one hand, he inspired great personal loyalty in men who saw him as fatherly and approachable. But on the other hand, in the harsh conditions of the trenches, with little food or comfort, soldiers deserted Lee and the Army of Northern Virginia in record numbers. As one soldier noted, it was "hard to maintain one's patriotism" on a supper consisting of cornmeal cake cooked in ashes, washed down with water. And if they themselves were hungry and burdened, how must their families be suffering back home without them?

"The struggle now," Lee wrote the Secretary of War, "is to keep the army fed and clothed. Only fifty men in some regiments have shoes, and bacon is only issued once in a few days." And unless something could be done to replace the men he lost, "the consequences may be disastrous," Lee told Seddon in August. "There must be more men in the country liable to military duty than the small number of recruits received would

185

seem to indicate. . . . Without some increase of strength, I cannot see how we are to escape the natural military consequences of the enemy's numerical superiority."

Even though desperate for more soldiers, the duty-and-obedience-driven Lee drummed an entire battalion out of his army that fall for "cowardly conduct." He marched the men to headquarters, where they surrendered their colors (flags), then marched them to the rear in disgrace. He regretted that "some brave officers and men" in the battalion must share that dishonor, "but the good of the Service requires it, and they must bear it as brave soldiers."

He responded to desertions by demanding even more discipline from his army. He denounced officers who failed to set a good example for their men. Disciplining the troops, he told Davis, "is a painful tedious process, & is not apt to win popular favor. Many officers have too many selfish views to promote to induce them to undertake the task of instructing & disciplining their Commands."

Lee also sought another way to retrieve more soldiers. He wrote Grant on October 1 proposing an exchange of prisoners, man for man. Grant responded, asking if Lee proposed delivering black Union soldiers "the same as white soldiers." Lee said he intended to include "all captured soldiers of the United States of whatever nation and color under my control." However, "negroes belonging to our citizens are not considered subject of exchange and were not included in my proposition." Escaped slaves wearing Union uniforms "cannot be returned."

Grant replied that all persons in the United States military had the same rights as soldiers. "This being denied by you" to those men who'd "escaped from Southern masters induces me to decline making the exchanges you ask." Grant knew Lee needed the prisoner exchange more than he did. The breakdown of exchanges over African American soldiers doomed thousands of men on both sides to suffering and death in prisoner-of-war camps.

THIS "WILL BRING US CALAMITY"

Lee still hoped the political situation in the North would change Southern fortunes. Get rid of Lincoln, halt the war, and let the South negotiate its independence. The presidential election of 1864 pitted Lee's old foe, General George B. McClellan, as the Democratic candidate against Lincoln. The Democratic Party's platform demanded an immediate end to the fighting—peace was the first priority; reunifying the country would come later. This platform "must lead to peace and our independence," an editorial in the *Charleston Mercury* proclaimed. Until the election, Confederate armies must hold their own "*and prevent military success by our foes.*"

But Confederate armies did not hold. Sherman captured Atlanta on September 2, 1864, a huge blow to the South. Sheridan and his Union cavalry unleashed destruction in the Shenandoah Valley, where Lee had sent Jubal Early to try and stop him. Grant, twice, hit Lee on both flanks. He couldn't break Lee's lines, but it forced Lee to stretch his defenses further, into a thirty-five-mile semicircle extending from east of Richmond to southwest of Petersburg. His already thin gray line grew even thinner.

The fall of Atlanta secured Lincoln's re-election in November. "We must . . . make up our minds for another four years of war," Robert wrote Mary sadly. God meant, said Lee, "to cleanse us of our sins & make us worthy to become his servants." Lee steeled himself with such thoughts, the only way he could face more years of unending war.

Union successes continued. In December, Sherman captured Savannah, Georgia, a Christmas gift for Lincoln. He now marched into South Carolina, where he meant to brutally punish the state that had started the war. In January 1865 the Confederacy lost its last port to the outside world when Fort Fisher fell at Wilmington, North Carolina.

Lincoln's re-election led to a piece of historic legislation in the North. On January 31, 1865, the U.S. House of Representatives—by a vote of 119 to 56—passed the 13th Amendment to the Constitution, abolishing slavery. If the South was defeated or if they surrendered, they'd be forced to accept the end of slavery, the very thing they'd gone to war to protect back in 1860–1861.

Lee's collapsible camp cup and holder

The weather turned as bitter as the course of events for the South. Trying to make light of things, Lee joked with Mary that he and his men were "enjoying ice water in abundance," and added, "Our neighbors also possess the same luxury." But with Lincoln returned to the White House and the bad military news, desertions again rose in Lee's ranks. Even troops who had "acted so nobly and borne so much" had vanished, Lee told the Secretary of War. This, he said, "will bring us calamity."

Lee desperately needed soldiers. But where was he going to get them?

"EMPLOY THEM WITHOUT DELAY"

The situation had become so grave for the South that Lee warned he might have to abandon Petersburg and Richmond. He urged the

Secretary of War to prepare for this. If things grew worse, uniting his army with the remnants of Johnston's bruised forces, then in North Carolina, seemed a last-ditch solution. Separately, neither army could "make headway against the enemy."

In January 1865 Lee addressed the question of using slaves to fight for the Confederate army. Lee had not changed his mind about the inferiority of black people or whether they should remain enslaved. He firmly believed that "at present in this Country" the relation of master and slave was "the best that can exist between the white & black races."

Southern armies were already using enslaved laborers as trench diggers, wagon drivers, and cooks. Enslaved black men rebuilt damaged bridges and roads, and acted as personal servants for officers such as Lee. Masters leased or volunteered their slaves' services to the Confederate armies. But the idea of arming an enslaved man, turning him into a soldier, was nightmarish to most white Southerners, and it called into question the accepted notions of the racial inferiority of black people. "If slaves will make good soldiers," noted a Georgia politician, "our whole theory of slavery is wrong. But they won't make soldiers. As a class they are wanting of every qualification of a soldier."

But across the trenches, dressed in Union blue, *were* African American soldiers, many of them escaped slaves. Not only did these black men fight against their former masters, but in escaping they'd robbed the South of its labor force.

Lee explained his thoughts about using slaves in a letter to a Virginia state senator. Northern armies, said Lee, had "access to a large part of our negro population." They meant to "convert the able bodied men among them into soldiers." The North would put white Southerners under the control of their former slaves, said Lee. "I think therefore we must decide whether slavery shall be extinguished by our enemies and the slaves be used against us, or to use them ourselves," even if this meant risking the "social institutions" of the South. "My own opinion,"

189

Lee continued, "is that we should employ them without delay."

Because the enslaved were used to following orders and being under the "moral influence" of white people, Lee thought he could turn them into efficient soldiers. But the South needed to secure the slaves' loyalty. This was trickier, and it was the point at which slave owners balked.

Giving "our negroes" immediate freedom when they enlisted, said Lee, and freedom to their families at the end of the war, was the surest way to gain their loyalty. They could not be expected to fight for a *promise* of freedom; they could *gain* their freedom at any time by running away to the Yankees. By taking this action, the Confederates would deprive the North of using slaves as soldiers. "It would disappoint the hopes which our enemies have upon our exhaustion," he wrote. But whatever measures the government adopted, they must be undertaken at once: "Every day's delay increases the difficulty; much time will be required to organize & discipline the men & action may be deferred until it is too late."

Within the ranks, Lee's men debated this question. Some went along with the idea of using black soldiers because Lee said he needed them, and they believed in Lee. Most greeted the idea less warmly. One North Carolina soldier summed up his feelings in a letter to his mother: "I did not volunteer to fight for a free negroes country but to fight for a free white mans free country & I do not think I love my country well enough to fight with black soldiers." Walter Taylor, too, was against the use of black soldiers in the Confederate army but resigned himself to the reality. "It makes me sad however to reflect that the time honoured institution [of slavery] will be no more," he wrote his fiancée, "that the whole social organization of the South is to be revolutionized. But I suppose it is all right and we will have to be reconciled."

The plan to use black men as Confederate soldiers, a last-minute act of Southern desperation, came too late in the war to matter.

"FIGHT TO THE LAST"

On February 6 Jefferson Davis named Lee commander of all the Confederate forces, a hollow promotion, perhaps meant to offer a spark of hope to the Confederacy. Many still believed Lee could win and save the South from Northern domination. Lee was seen as the great Christian gentleman and general, the victor against long odds.

But when he wrote Mary in late February 1865, Lee didn't sound like someone who thought he could win the war. He talked of Grant moving against him soon, of Sherman's 60,000-man army having everything go its way in South Carolina. "I pray we may not be overwhelmed," Lee wrote. "I shall however endeavour to do my duty & fight to the last." But if it did become necessary to abandon his position to keep Grant from surrounding him, what would Mary do? "Will you remain or leave the city? You must consider the question & make up your mind. You will be able to retain nothing in the house, & I do not see how you can live, or where go. It is a fearful condition." They must place their faith in God, "who does not always give the battle to the strong." A demoralized Robert, who always had answers, now had none to offer his wife.

In early March, Lee reached out to Grant. Could they meet? He wanted to leave "nothing untried which may put an end to the calamities of war." He made no mention of surrendering his army, though. Grant noted this and declined to meet.

The siege had dragged on for over nine months. Something had to happen. Rations, if available, did not reach most of his troops. He had around 55,000 soldiers, the numbers shrinking each day. Grant's Army of the Potomac had 120,000 men. Lee knew Grant would soon break through his poorly manned lines or cut around his flank.

On March 25 Lee made a desperate move to break Grant's hold with a surprise attack against the Union position just east of Petersburg at Fort Steadman. The Union's counterpunch pushed Lee's forces back and won some of the Confederate trenches. On April 1, Philip Sheridan's Union cavalry defeated George Pickett's divisions at a place called Five Forks about ten miles southwest of Petersburg. Pickett, who'd never forgiven Lee for the destruction of his troops at Gettysburg. The loss of Five Forks cut off Lee's last rail supply line.

Grant ordered Union assaults all along the Confederate line on April 2. Corps commander A. P. Hill was one of the soldiers killed that day. Lee knew he could no longer hold off the Union advance. He had to retreat. He sent word to Jefferson Davis and ordered his men to evacuate Petersburg and Richmond that night. The Siege of Petersburg was over.

Jefferson Davis and other members of the Confederate government dispersed and fled south. Union shells exploded in the capital. People tried to escape the city, wagons and carts clogging the streets. Citizens sobbed as they handed bits of food to the retreating soldiers, men so ragged and hungry it seemed cruel "bidding them do their duty and come home victorious," one woman recalled. Not knowing what his future held, Walter Taylor, with Lee's consent, galloped to Richmond. Sometime after midnight Taylor married his fiancée, Bettie Saunders, at a friend's house before hurriedly rejoining the retreating Army of Northern Virginia.

After sunrise on April 3, Custis Lee, who had not served in the field the entire war, led Confederate supply wagons out of Richmond and went to join his father. The retreating Confederates left much of Richmond in flames, burning anything the Yankees might find of value.

APPOMATTOX

Lee's army headed west from Petersburg and Richmond in four separate columns, which he planned to unite at Amelia Courthouse. Lee hoped to put time and distance between himself and Grant's pursuing army and find rations for his men, many of whom had had nothing to eat for three or four days. Finally, he planned to turn south in an attempt to link up with Johnston's army in North Carolina.

About 35,000 men remained in Lee's depleted ranks. Huge numbers had left at the end of the siege, and now, all along the retreat route, exhausted and starved men vanished. Some wandered off, some surrendered to Union forces, and others simply lay down and waited for the Yankees to collect them. Horses, bone thin, also lay down, too weak to go on.

The hungry Confederates found no rations at Amelia Courthouse. Lee appeared anxious and haggard; some of the columns were tardy. As they waited, a strong Union force caught up with them and blocked Lee's route south toward Johnston.

He kept pressing westward. "Tired and hungry we push on," wrote a Confederate soldier from New Orleans. "It is now a race for life or death. We seldom receive orders now." Whatever he felt inside, Lee continued to ride among his men and give them encouragement. On April 6, Union troops cut off a third of Lee's army in a battle one Rebel described as butchery. Six thousand Confederates were captured, including Custis Lee.

* * * * *

On April 7 Grant sent Lee a note. Further resistance on Lee's part was hopeless, and surely Lee knew it, said Grant. He felt it his duty "to shift from myself the responsibility of any further effusion of blood by asking of you the surrender of that portion of the Confederate States Army known as the Army of Northern Virginia." Lee replied that he wasn't sure his situation was hopeless. But what terms did Grant offer if the Army of Northern Virginia surrendered? Grant answered that there was only one condition: Lee's men must lay down their arms and not fight again against the government of the United States.

Some, including Jefferson Davis, wished Lee to fight on, even breaking up his army into small bands of soldiers for guerrilla warfare.

But Lee refused to do this. He believed guerrilla bands lacked any sense of military order or discipline. As lawless men, they supported themselves by raiding and pillaging. To Lee's mind this meant only more suffering for the country. If the young men wanted to go "bushwhacking, the only proper & dignified course for me would be to surrender myself & take the consequences of my actions," Lee told one of his officers.

On April 8, Lee camped just east of the little village of Appomattox Court House. He knew his army was trapped, but he would make one more attempt on the morning of April 9 to clear the road so he could head south to meet up with Johnston. One of Lee's generals noted, "If there is any hope for the Confederacy it is in delay. For if the Army of Northern Va. surrenders every other army will surrender as fast as the news reaches it. For it is the morale of this army that has supported the whole Confederacy." The Federal soldiers, sensing the finish at long last, circled the Confederates and threw back Lee's attempt to break free, ending his hope of escape. Lee knew there was nothing to be done but meet with Grant, "and I would rather die a thousand deaths," he said.

The two generals met on April 9, 1865, in Appomattox Court House at the home of Wilbur McLean. Lee dressed carefully in his dress uniform with polished boots and sword. Always punctual, he arrived at the house at the appointed time, one o'clock, in the company of one of his secretaries, Charles Marshall. Walter Taylor made excuses not to go, for he couldn't bear to "accompany my chief in this trying ordeal."

For an hour, which must have seemed like forever, Lee and Marshall waited. Grant had to ride over twenty miles that day to reach Appomattox Court House, and when he arrived in an old uniform, his boots and clothes spattered in red Virginia mud, he looked quite unlike the spit-and-polished Lee. Other blue-coated officers crammed into the McLean parlor. Lincoln had told Grant at the end of March, "Let them surrender and go home. . . . Give them the most liberal and honorable terms."

The two men talked briefly, mentioning their shared service in the

Mexican War. Then Lee broke off and asked Grant to put his terms in writing. Grant said that Confederate officers must sign paroles promising not to fight again. They would also sign paroles covering the men under their commands. Officers could keep their side arms, horses, and personal baggage. All soldiers would simply be allowed to return home.

"We the undersigned prisoners of war . . ." Parole signed by Lee (top name) and his staff at Appomattox.

As Lincoln had wanted, the terms were generous. Lee pointed out that cavalrymen and some of the artillery men also owned their own horses. Could they keep them? Grant said anyone who claimed to own a horse or mule could take the animal home. This would have a good effect on his men, Lee replied. Grant signed two copies of the surrender terms and Lee signed the letter of acceptance Charles Marshall had written out for him. Union general Philip Sheridan noted that Lee's face betrayed no emotion. Grant offered rations to the hungry Confederates, and with that, Robert E. Lee's famed force, the Army of Northern Virginia, ceased to exist.

Alfred Waud's sketch of Lee leaving the McLean house on Traveller after the surrender. Charles Marshall rides behind him.

"I felt . . . sad and depressed," Grant later wrote, "at the downfall of a foe who had fought so long and valiantly, and had suffered so much for a cause, though that cause was, I believe, one of the worst for which a people ever fought."

Lee left the house and mounted Traveller. Union officers in the yard raised their hats as a show of respect as he rode by. Word of his surrender spread like an electric current through the ranks on both sides. When he reached his camp, hundreds of ragged, loyal men broke their lines and engulfed Traveller, reaching out to touch Lee, touch his horse. Tears streamed down Lee's cheeks and men cried at this, the end, the loss. But there was also a numb sense of relief that the blood and carnage was over. Lee tried to speak but failed, so overcome with emotion.

The next day Lee issued General Orders No. 9, his last words to the army. He praised the courage and steadfastness of his men. He told them they'd been forced "to yield to overwhelming numbers and resources." He had determined to "avoid the useless sacrifice of those whose past services have endeared them to their Countrymen." Go home, Lee told them, knowing that they'd faithfully performed their duty.

While the men waited to stack their arms before Union troops, while they waited for printing presses set up in haste to spit out thousands of paroles, Lee left Appomattox. A paroled prisoner of war, he turned Traveller east toward Richmond, toward Mary and his daughters.

CHAPTER SIXTEEN

"THE COWARD LOOKS BACK"

"I shall be very sorry if your presence be lost to Virginia. She has now need for all her sons, & can ill afford to spare you."

—*Lee to Captain Matthew F. Maury,*
in exile in Mexico,
September 8, 1865

Ｎews of Lee's surrender at Appomattox stunned white Southerners. One woman scribbled in her diary, "How can I write it? How find words to tell what has befallen us? *Gen Lee has surrendered!* . . . We stand appalled at our disaster! . . . *Lee*, Lee upon whom hung the hopes of the whole country." A Florida woman wrote, "[We] wish we were all dead. It is as if the very earth had crumbled beneath our feet."

Lee arrived in Richmond on April 15. "We have all been here very quiet since the sad event that has so darkened our souls," Mary wrote a friend. Her husband needed simple things—sleep, food, peace, the chance to deal with his own grief. Custis, captured just days before his father's surrender, had been paroled through "the courtesy of some old friends among the Federal officers," Mary reported. They'd allowed him to join his parents on the excuse that Mary was very ill. Rooney and Walter Taylor had ridden to Richmond with Lee, and Rob soon arrived.

As word spread that Lee was in Richmond, throngs of people showed up at the house on Franklin Street. Mothers knocked on the door, wanting to know the fate of their sons. Politicians and clergymen

"The Mess," the home in Richmond where Lee joined his family after Appomattox, photographed in 1865

Ruins of Richmond, Virginia, 1865, the former capital of the Confederacy

The photographer Mathew Brady took a series of photos behind the Franklin Street house a week after the surrender. In the seated portrait, son Custis stands on the left, with Walter Taylor on the right.

appeared; soldiers heading home stopped for a word. It wore Lee out even more, keeping up polite courtesies. His sons and daughters began turning visitors away. Lee paced on the veranda behind the house or went out at night under cover of darkness, alone or with Mildred, to walk the streets.

Letters poured in from well-wishers, heaping gratitude on Lee for his service, lamenting what would soon be called the "Lost Cause." A Petersburg clergyman summed up for many: "The greatful [*sic*] hearts of millions will ever bless you for struggling so long and so nobly for their right of self government. . . . The Powers of the world, misunderstanding us, coldly left us to expire. Our confederate nationality is gone, but not the glory of its brief existence and history. Whatever we have lost, our honour is safe."

Glory and honor didn't conceal the stripped and burned ruins of farms, factories, bridges, railroads, and cities across the South. Confederate money was worthless. No one knew the number of civilian dead. In this tattered world loomed the most frightening change of all for Southern whites—the new freedom of the former enslaved.

To Mary, the future seemed so dark they were "tempted to think God has forsaken us." When Lincoln died from an assassin's bullet, Mary claimed he now had to stand before God and account "for the misery he has wrought in our unhappy Country." Her heart burned at the "savage cruelty" that had destroyed the South. "Future generations may forget but we never can," she wrote, pouring out her feelings in a letter to a friend. "We are all unsettled now & know not what our future may be."

AN INTERVIEW

One of the people turned away from the Richmond house was Thomas Cook, a reporter from the *New York Herald*. Cook then wrote to say that he hoped Lee's "sense of justice" and a desire to present "the truth of history" would lead him to grant Cook an interview. Lee agreed to talk with him after all. At that point, Lee did not know if he'd be sent to prison or tried for treason; Confederate armies still held on in the field, and Jefferson Davis remained on the run. Lee hoped the interview would soften Northern views of himself and the South. But bitterness, and a twisted version of events, laced Lee's words, perhaps reflecting his uncertainties and fears.

Lee excused the war as something that *had* to happen. The question of states' rights versus the power of the federal government had not been ironed out since the time the Constitution was written, Lee said. "It is unfortunate that it was not settled at the outset," he told Cook, "but, as it was not settled then, and had to be settled sometime, then the war raised on this issue cannot be considered treason. If the South is forced to submission in this contest, it of course can only be looked upon as the triumph of Federal power over State rights."

Lee made the astounding statement that peace could have been achieved two years before. During all that time, said Lee, the South had "been ready and anxious for peace. They have been looking for some word or expression of compromise . . . from the North upon which they might base a return to the Union."

When asked about slavery, Lee answered, untruthfully, "The best men of the South have long been anxious to do away with this institution, and were quite willing today to see it abolished. They consider slavery for ever dead." As to the freed slaves, Lee's view was that "unless some humane course is adopted, based on wisdom and Christian principles, you do a gross wrong and injustice to the whole negro race in setting them free."

Lee hoped Northern policies would bring "immediate peace." But if the North used revengeful policies, Lee threatened, the South could continue the struggle "until the whole country would be impoverished and ruined." He then claimed that "the South was never more than half in earnest in this war."

202

"A man should not be judged harshly," Lee told Cook, "for contending for that which he honestly believes to be right. Such was the position of the vast majority of the Southern people." They had fought for freedom and states' rights, "sacrificed home, friends, property, health, all on this issue. Men do not make such sacrifices for nothing. They have made the sacrifice from honest convictions."

Lee believed that unless "moderation and liberality" be shown the South, all the best people would flee to foreign lands. The country needed these men; they were the hope for the future. Lee also promoted the belief that Southern political leaders should not be held accountable for the war. "What has Mr. Davis done more than any other Southerner that he should be punished?" Lee asked. "His acts were the acts of the whole people." Davis was not accountable for the beginning of the war. Why should he suffer more than others?

Lee stated that his only desire was to retire to private life and end his days in seclusion. "It was, I thought," wrote Cook, "an evidence of painful sadness" that had prompted Lee to say he would have been happy to die on the battlefield. Cook told Lee that "he was greatly respected by a very large body of good men at the North, and that as a soldier he was universally admired."

Lee's justifications for the war, for the South, and for his own actions enraged many in the North. They wanted the South to show remorse for dragging the country into war. They wanted the dreadful slaughter acknowledged. Instead, Lee talked about the sufferings of the South and offered no word of sorrow that Northern families suffered, too. He talked of how the North must be generous and not provoke the South; he declared that Southern leaders should not be prosecuted for treason.

Just days before the interview appeared on April 29, Joseph E. Johnston surrendered his Confederate army to General Sherman. Smaller scattered forces in the Deep South and west of the Mississippi River surrendered in May and June. Meanwhile, Union soldiers captured Jefferson Davis in Georgia on May 10 and imprisoned the former president of the Confederacy.

"MY DEAR HOME"

At age fifty-eight, Robert Lee had no job and few resources. He still held some Northern railroad bonds from before the war, which gave him something to help settle his family once more. But they had no permanent home. Mary still believed they might return to Arlington, but her hopes hung only by a thread.

Back in January 1864 the United States government had levied taxes on Rebel-owned property within Federal army lines. Arlington's taxes were set at $92.07, payable only by the owner. Government commissioners knew that neither Robert nor Mary Lee could show up to make the payment. The Lees asked a cousin to pay for them, but tax commissioners refused the money.

Arlington, 1864, with Union soldiers

On January 11 the auctioneer's gavel punctuated the sale: the government bought Arlington—the house along with 1,100 acres of land—for $26,800. There was a chance, however, that after the war the Lees could sue to regain their property. Mrs. Lee was not paid any money for the estate after the taxes she owed were subtracted, and if challenged in court, the tax might be declared unconstitutional.

But in the spring of 1864, as Lee and Grant squared off in the Overland Campaign, U.S. Secretary of War Edwin Stanton and Quartermaster Montgomery Meigs, Lee's old friend from St. Louis, approved a plan to ensure that the Lees couldn't return to their home. Stanton ordered the creation of a new national military cemetery at Arlington. Meigs carried out Stanton's vision, personally seeing that gravediggers buried the bodies of Union soldiers "up to the very door" of the house. "My heart will never know rest or peace while my dear home is so used," Mary raged. "If *justice & law* are not utterly extinct in the U.S. I *will have* it back."

Montgomery Meigs, who'd known Lee since the 1830s, turned the Arlington estate into a national cemetery to prevent the Lees from returning home. Meigs and his family are buried there, not far from the graves of Mary Lee's parents.

Rooney still had the White House plantation, though the home lay in ashes, and Rob still had his land at Romancoke. The sons soon left Richmond to try farming. Lee envisioned buying a little farm for himself, too. He ached for seclusion, for "some humble but quiet abode for your mother & sisters," he wrote Rooney, "[where] I hope they can be happy." But he wasn't sure what sort of life would be "permitted by the victor."

Robert E. Lee Jr., called Rob

"THE DUTY OF ITS CITIZENS"

As president of the victorious North, Andrew Johnson made plans for the reconstruction of the country that included a pardon for nearly all Confederates. New state governments in the South would be put in place with constitutions abolishing slavery. Each state's secession ordinance would be declared invalid. Johnson issued a general amnesty on May 29 to those Confederates who had signed an oath of allegiance to the United States.

Robert Lee approved of Johnson's "conciliatory manner" and thought the president's plan "would go far to promote confidence, and to calm feelings which have too long existed." But he himself was excluded from Johnson's amnesty for two reasons—he'd been a leader in the Confederacy, and he'd broken his previous army oaths of allegiance to the United States.

On June 7, Lee heard that a judge in Norfolk, Virginia, had recommended his indictment by a jury on charges of treason. "I shall avoid no prosecution the Govt thinks proper," he wrote Markie. "I am aware of having done nothing wrong & cannot flee." He resolved to be patient. But Lee thought the parole granted him at Appomattox protected him from charges of treason. He wrote Grant, asking for clarification and requesting an application for amnesty. While he waited, Lee drew strength from his faith. "I can do but little but am resigned to what is ordered by our Merciful God," he wrote Markie, "who will I know do all that is good for us."

Some of Lee's fellow officers fled to Mexico or other countries. They feared treason charges or were unwilling to take an oath of allegiance to the United States. They wrote Lee from exile expecting words of encouragement, but Lee responded differently. "The thought of abandoning the Country & all that must be left in it," he told one of them, "is abhorrent to my feelings; & I *prefer* to struggle for its restoration, & share its fate, than to give up all as lost." He offered similar words to Walter Taylor: Virginia wanted all her sons, "all their support . . . to sustain and recuperate her."

Lee grappled with his wish for seclusion and the reality that others wished to hear his opinion and looked to him for advice. What would help the South most, Lee wondered, and especially Virginia? What would most quickly turn the corner from war to the future?

Lee stepped back from the denials and accusations of his interview with Cook. He charted a new course, one more suited to his dignity.

Publicly, Robert E. Lee turned his voice toward peace and rebuilding. He wrote Virginia's former governor:

> The duty of its citizens, then, appears to me too plain to admit of doubt. All should unite in honest efforts to obliterate the effects of war, and to restore the blessings of peace. They should remain, if possible, in the country; promote harmony and good feeling; qualify themselves to vote; and elect to the State and general Legislatures wise and patriotic men, who will devote their abilities to the interests of the country, and the healing of all dissensions.

Lee believed only this behavior would advance Southern prosperity. Only this behavior would regain what the South had lost. Lee counseled patience. He advised Jefferson Davis and Jubal Early to silence their angry responses to Northern jabs. Southerners must submit to civil authority, said Lee, keep order, avoid controversy, and "give full scope to reason and to every kindly feeling."

An 1865 tobacco package label bearing Lee's image reminded Southerners that "Defeat is not Dishonor."

When asked if he'd return to Gettysburg for placement of granite monuments commemorating the battle, Lee declined. "I think it wiser not to keep open the sores of war," he replied, "but to follow the examples of those nations who . . . obliterate the marks of civil strife." Admiration for Lee rose even higher among white Southerners—their general stood above the fear, uncertainty, and anger of the country "in this trying hour," lighting the way toward self-respect in defeat. It was a balm that only Lee, revered for his character and leadership, could bestow.

A JOB OFFER

While Lee recovered and waited for his future to unfold, he accepted a friend's loan of a four-room country house away from the demands of Richmond. Robert, Mary, Agnes, and Mildred moved there in July. Lee spent the weeks writing letters, visiting family, and riding Traveller. He thought about writing a history of the Army of Northern Virginia, but unlike many other Confederate generals, Lee would never write anything. He had "little desire to recall the events of war."

In early August a visitor arrived at Lee's cottage. Judge John Brockenbrough, wearing a borrowed suit and traveling with borrowed funds, had a proposal for Lee. He was a trustee at Washington College in Lexington, Virginia. Most of the students had gone to fight, Brockenbrough told Lee, and the war prevented others from coming. In June 1864 the Union general David Hunter had looted the school and nearly burned it down. The Yankees had stolen or destroyed the school's lab equipment, furniture, and books. About forty students remained now, most under the age of eighteen, and only four professors. There were just a few buildings, plus two dormitories the students dubbed Hell and Purgatory. Yet the school's trustees were determined to stay open. Would General Lee be interested in becoming the new president of Washington College?

It was a bold request of the most famous man in Virginia. Brockenbrough appealed to Lee's sense of duty toward the South and the state. Lee could cast off his role of soldier and be seen in a new light, as an educator. By taking the job he'd show confidence in Virginia's future, be useful to the state, and guide young men toward productive futures. Lee alone, said Brockenbrough, could fill the college's halls and attract students not just from Virginia but from all the Southern states, and even from the North. Washington College offered him a $1,500 salary for the year, free housing, and 15 percent of the tuition fees.

Lee pondered the offer for a few weeks. He considered educating the youth of the South "one of the most important objects now to be attained." On August 24 he wrote the trustees an awkward acceptance letter. He feared he didn't possess enough physical strength or good health for the job. He feared that his abilities would fall short of satisfying the trustees and that his work might not benefit the country. His future remained undecided regarding charges of treason. Since he was "an object of censure" to some people, his involvement might bring "injury" to the college. However, Lee wrote, if the trustees took a different view and thought his services "advantageous to the College & Country," he would yield to their judgment and take the position. The trustees assured Lee they wanted him.

As Lee had warned, some Northerners reacted angrily because "the arch traitor Lee" could now instruct students "in more treason," or because "the bloodiest and guiltiest traitor in all the South" was being made president of a college. But others applauded Lee's undertaking. One paper noted that in accepting the job Lee had earned anew the love of his countrymen.

In mid-September Lee saddled Traveller and set out alone on the four-day ride to Lexington. He wore his Confederate gray uniform stripped of military insignia. Mary and his daughters would stay behind until he had established a home for them.

The gloom that had settled over Lee the last year of the war had not lifted. He shared his feelings with Mary that fall, writing that "life is indeed gliding away and I have nothing of good to show for mine. . . . I pray I may accomplish something for the benefit of mankind and the honour of God."

Michael Miley (1841–1918) shot this photo of Lee on his beloved horse, Traveller, in 1866. Lee still wears his Confederate officer's coat with the emblems of rank cut off.

Traveller proved the greatest escape and pleasure for Lee. "You know the comfort he is to me," Lee told Markie. On horseback Lee sought release in the mountains around Lexington, flat-out galloping up long hills or picking his way up rocky slopes. Rob noted that his father craved "the quiet and rest, the freedom of mind and body, the close sympathy of his old war-horse, and the beauties of Nature." Traveller's fame rivaled Lee's own. People yanked so many hairs from Traveller's tail for souvenirs that Lee compared his poor animal to a plucked chicken.

Lee had accepted the presidency of Washington College with the hope that he "might be of service . . . and not from any preference of my own," he wrote Rooney. He still longed for that little farm and quiet life, but his deep sense of duty mercilessly drove him on. As he'd once told his son, "The coward looks back, the brave ahead."

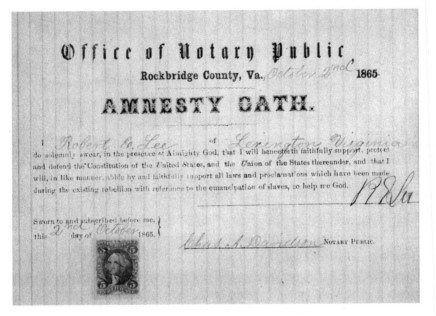

The Amnesty Oath that Lee signed and submitted in October 1865. The October 17 issue of the *New York Times* announced that the State Department had just filed Lee's oath and printed it out in its entirety so that "all the world may know what this man promises for the future."

CHAPTER SEVENTEEN

"GENERAL LEE'S COLLEGE"

"We have but one rule here, and that is, that every student must be a gentleman."

—*Lee to an unnamed student*

Classes began at Washington College on October 2, 1865, and Lee buckled down to work. He surprised everyone by tackling a much larger role than just serving as a famous figurehead and fundraiser for the school. Within weeks he outlined plans to transform the college; within six months he'd set changes in place. He considered it "of prime importance to adapt this plan to the wants of our people at the present time."

Lee felt that the young men of the South, "looking forward to an early entrance into the practical pursuits of life," needed training not provided by the common classical education, which emphasized Latin, Greek, math, and English. Lee intended to immediately add five new professorships in five new courses of study. First, he wanted "practical chemistry" taught—chemistry as it applied to farming, mining, and manufacturing. A second professorship, this one in "experimental philosophy," would include classes on drawing, architecture, and the use of building materials in railroads, canals, and bridges. The third professorship, in "applied mathematics," would cover civil and mechanical engineering. The fourth professorship would be in modern languages such as French, German, and Spanish, and the fifth in history and literature.

Lee reorganized the college into ten independent schools. Instead of having students take a prescribed set of courses, he allowed them to pick their own classes. He raised academic standards, which included testing the student body in December and June.

The Colonnade at Washington College, built between 1823 and 1842, survived the Civil War with damage. It is shown here in 1867.

Over time, Lee expanded and tweaked the coursework. Because farming was "the most important interest of the Southern people and must continue so for years to come," Lee added agriculture classes. He added classes in commerce, mining engineering, applied chemistry, astronomy, and geology. He added to his original courses in engineering and math. He incorporated Judge Brockenbrough's Lexington School of Law into Washington College. He proposed a journalism school, the first of its kind, and hoped to endow it with fifty scholarships and a printing shop. Lee wanted the shop because most Southern newspapers were published from printing offices, with the same man serving as both editor and printer.

In 1867 Lee purchased this orrery for the college—a mechanical model of the solar system. Designed by Thomas Barlow, it can be seen today in the Lee Chapel and Museum at Washington and Lee University. Lee had once written about astronomy, "I think it afforded me more pleasure than any other branch of study."

Lee, the hater of debt, took on the college's financial woes as well. At first he borrowed money to pay professors and repair buildings. He began improving the college grounds, adding walkways, planting grass and trees. He ordered new books and lab equipment. But to really secure the future of Washington College, Lee needed to raise large sums of money.

His name both helped and hurt fundraising. People started calling the school "General Lee's College." Some Northerners protested the idea of donations being made to a rebel institution. The *Chicago Daily Tribune* claimed that the school encouraged "hatred to the Union." One man wrote that Lee, his hands stained with "the blood of tens of thousands of his country's noblest men, for the purpose of perpetuating human slavery," was unfit to teach young men. He warned against contributing money to Washington College.

215

But others saw Lee as an honorable man who wished to ease the tensions of a war-torn country and help the South rebuild. Lee secured large donations from the inventor and businessman Cyrus McCormick, a Virginian who'd lived in the North for many years, and the wealthy Massachusetts banker George Peabody. The abolitionist and orator Henry Ward Beecher donated to Lee's college and urged others to do so, too. Within two years the school's endowment reached nearly $235,000.

Lee's name, coupled with school improvements, attracted students. At first, many of them were former Confederate soldiers. By the 1867–68 school year Washington College had grown significantly—from forty students and four faculty members to 410 students studying under a faculty of twenty-one professors, assistant professors, and instructors.

Lee's first building project at Washington College was a large red-brick building filled with light from rows of tall windows. The space, which served as both an auditorium and a chapel, could hold the entire student body. Here the college hosted events like musicals, debates, meetings, and graduation ceremonies. The building was never consecrated as a church. But Lee attended daily morning prayers there, an imposing figure sitting in a front pew, and he expected students to attend also. The lower level held Lee's office, the library, and the bursar's office.

DEALING WITH STUDENTS

Instead of copying West Point's list of rules and the demerits that came from breaking them, Lee had only one rule at Washington College— the students must behave like gentlemen. Lee asked students to pledge to an honor code, each man taking responsibility for his own actions. "You should not force young men to do their duty, but let them do it voluntarily and thereby develop their characters," Lee wrote a newly hired professor.

He tried to get to know his students and kept a sharp eye on their performance. A dip in grades or poor conduct meant a meeting in Lee's office. "I wished he had whipped me," one student said, "but he talked to me about my mother and the sacrifices she is making to send me to college." The student ended up "blubbering like a baby." In another case, Lee determined that the student was deeply homesick and asked the mother to visit. "I think every boy," he wrote her, "can be persuaded & led to do what is right by an affectionate mother."

A much tougher Lee cracked down on students who displayed bad attitudes or fondness for vices like drinking and gambling. Lee wrote to the parents and asked them to address their offspring's shortcomings. When this failed, he took action. In some cases he recommended that the family withdraw their son from college and save the money. The worst cases he expelled, like the three students who neglected their studies for the pleasures of Lexington's public billiard room. For another youth, he wrote the father: "I hope this severe lesson will teach him the self-command he so much needs, and enable him to refrain from the indulgence of a vice, which, if it becomes a habit, may prove his ruin."

FAMILY LIFE AGAIN

Lee's hard work for Washington College paid off. The trustees, thrilled with what Lee accomplished, raised his salary to $3,000 a year. They also earmarked funds for Lee to build a president's residence for the college. While most Southerners suffered during the lean years after the Civil War, the Lee family ended up very comfortably off. Mary and the daughters joined Lee in Lexington in early 1866. Custis taught engineering next door at the Virginia Military Institute and saw his family often.

Before the president's house was built, the family used a smaller home that Stonewall Jackson had once lived in. Local women supplied the house with donated furniture. The family looked forward to having some of their own belongings about them, items Mary had saved from

Arlington in 1861. As they waited for things to arrive, they dug out Robert's utensils and dishes from his camp chest for dining and used his camp stools for extra seating. The old Arlington rugs, when they came, proved too large for the cramped rooms and had to be folded over, which made it hard for Mary to navigate in her wheelchair.

Robert described Mary—whom he often called "the Mims" in letters to their children—as "very busy, and full of work." She filled her days sewing and knitting, writing, reading, and keeping up on the news—which usually roused her fury at what she saw as injustice toward white Southerners. She began painting again. She tinted prints of George and Martha Washington with watercolors, which sold briskly, raising money for their church. She also handled a steady pile of requests for signed photographs of her famous husband. And she never backed off from talking politics. As Lee remarked, "We are all as usual—the women of the family very fierce and the men very mild."

* * * * *

His steady salary afforded Lee the chance to help his children. He offered Rooney and Rob money to revitalize their farms and barraged them with letters of advice about building homes, choosing breeds of cows, and growing wheat, oats, and corn. "A farmer's motto," he told them, "should be *toil and trust*." They must be patient; they should add lime to enrich the soil; they should buy mules. "I can help you in these items," he wrote Rob, "and, if you need, can advance you $500. Then, as regards a house, I can help you in that too." He urged his sons to work hard—words they'd heard their whole lives—and learn from their mistakes.

The Lee daughters took turns keeping house for their parents and spent time traveling to visit friends, staying away for months at a time. Travel did not spare the daughters from fatherly advice. They must be useful, Lee told them, and remember that it was not "becoming in a Virginia girl now to be fine or fashionable, and that gentility as well as self-respect requires moderation in dress and gaiety." They should go to bed early and enjoy only "rational amusements." Lee often tired of their traipsing about and wanted them home.

Lee constantly badgered his sons to marry. He wrote Agnes, visiting in Maryland, to ask if she could not "persuade some of those pretty girls in Baltimore to take compassion" on her bachelor brothers. But Lee never pushed Mary, Agnes, or Mildred to wed; instead, he wanted their attention fixed at home. None of the Lee daughters ever did marry, which was very unusual for a time when a woman's main role in life was that of wife and mother. Perhaps they never married because so many young men of their generation were lost in the war. Perhaps no man measured up to their famous father. Mildred wrote years later in her diary, "To me he seems a Hero—& all other men small in comparison."

The youngest Lee daughter, Mildred Childe Lee, was named for Robert's sister. She was called Milly or Precious Life within the family circle.

When Rooney remarried in 1867, Lee traveled to Richmond for the wedding, though he didn't want to go. He knew it would be exhausting, filled with scores of people he'd be forced to meet and talk with. Two thousand guests packed the church while another thousand well-wishers waited outside. For the people of Richmond, the marriage of

219

Fitzhugh Lee and Miss Mary Tabb Bolling was like a royal wedding. Robert wrote Mary, who was unable to go, that their son "shone in his happiness."

Lee visited nearby Petersburg, which reminded him of those final months of war. "There was a great crowd at the Richmond depot to see Genl. Lee . . . ," a friend observed, "but when we got to the bridge at Petersburg, it was like a triumphal procession. . . . Music greeted the arrival of the General. There was a great multitude on the bridge, & all the way to Jarratt's hotel, & filling the large area between the Railroad & the hotel a sea of heads. . . . General Lee had a seat in an open carriage . . . & drove off amid the deafening cheers of the people."

Within a small circle of friends, Lee told amusing stories "as his custom is," one friend noted. But he thought Lee had "an air of sadness about him," though he talked a great deal "both in a playful & serious strain & we all enjoyed the visit exceedingly." Since the war, memories of the people of Petersburg haunted Lee, especially of that "gloomy night when I was forced to abandon them," he told Rooney. But the townspeople seemed cheerful and hardworking, and seeing these signs of recovery lifted "a load of sorrow" from his heart.

As he resettled into family life, Lee spent months designing and then overseeing work on the new President's House at Washington College. He added every comfort he could for Mary, making their home accessible for her wheelchair. The doorways were wide, and Robert installed a low bell pull in the wall that she could reach and use to summon help. She had three rooms on the main floor—a bedroom, a family parlor, and a dressing room. Lee built a large, wraparound porch on the house, for his wife loved to sit outdoors. At one end of the porch, outside Mary's parlor, he built a little glassed-in room where she could sit in bad weather or tend potted flowers. The floor of Mary's parlor and the glass room were level, without a door sill or step, so she could move her wheelchair onto the porch.

The President's House that Lee designed and built at Washington College is still used today.

The Lees' parlor, looking into the dining room, at the President's House. Custis family portraits saved from Arlington hang on the walls.

Across the wide front hall from Mary's rooms was another parlor, opening into the dining room beyond. A large folding door and red plush curtains made it possible to separate the two spaces. In these spacious rooms the Lees entertained guests. After one of Mary's parties, Lee joked to daughter Mildred, "You know how agreeable I am on such occasions, but on this, I am told, I surpassed myself." He liked to sit in the dining room's bay window and look out over the fields of grass and grain to the mountains beyond. A roomy breezeway attached the stable to the house, prompting Lee to tease that he and Traveller finally lived together under one roof. He and Mary encouraged friends and relatives to visit, and the new president's house often filled with company.

Lee worked hard to heal at least a small corner of the South. He'd put Washington College on the map. He'd established anew his own family circle. But political changes in the country awakened harsher feelings in Lee. The calming words he spoke in public would soon contrast with an anger he mostly revealed in private.

CHAPTER EIGHTEEN

"PEACE IS NOT RESTORED"

Question: "Do you think the State of Virginia is absolutely injured and its future impaired by the presence of the black population there?"

Robert E. Lee: "I think it is."

— *Lee testifying before the Joint Committee on Reconstruction, February 17, 1866*

By December 1865, all states of the former Confederacy except Texas had complied with President Andrew Johnson's provisions for Reconstruction, which Lee had admired as "conciliatory" and promoting "confidence." The states held conventions to write new constitutions and elected new governors, senators, and representatives.

But Johnson had carried out his plan without consulting the Republicans in Congress. This set up a battle between the president and that wing of the Republican Party known as the Radical Republicans, who wanted to grant full civil rights for newly freed African Americans.

When Congress reconvened in December 1865, members of the House and Senate said "Not so fast!" to Johnson's plan. They wanted to see how the South behaved before welcoming the states back into the Union, and they wanted a closer examination of conditions in the South. They refused to seat the Southerners elected to Congress, most of them prominent former Confederates—a fact that angered the Radicals.

Reports from the South troubled members of Congress. Some

Southern states balked at ratifying the 13th Amendment, which would abolish slavery. Others hedged on renouncing their secession. The new legislatures enacted "black codes" meant to control freed African Americans. Northern visitors to the South reported hostility. "They hate us and despise us," one newsman wrote. "They call us cut-throats, liars, vandals, cowards, and the very scum of the earth. . . . They won't even allow that we won our own battles." Another man noted that "although the freedman is no longer considered the property to the individual master, he is considered the slave of society, and all independent State legislation will share the tendency to make him such." Most troubling were accounts of violence against the former enslaved and whites who had opposed secession.

Congress set up a Joint Committee on Reconstruction in December 1865 to further investigate conditions in the South and plan legislation to address problems. One of the key men they summoned to Washington to testify was Robert E. Lee.

"AS FAR AS I HAVE HEARD"

Lee arrived in Washington, a city he'd once known well, in February 1866. As he stood in the train station, he looked into the distance toward a familiar spot and saw Arlington sitting like a Greek temple above the Potomac. He wished he could stop the burials at his former home and find some way to get Arlington back. But he still waited, as he told his brother Smith, "for the action of President Johnson upon my application to him, to be embraced in his proclamation of Amnesty." Without a restoration of his citizenship rights, Lee didn't feel he could do anything about Arlington. Any appeal having to do with the house would "excite the Radicals, with whom I do not appear to be in favour."

He visited some friends, but "I am considered now such a monster," he wrote Markie afterward, "that I hesitate to darken with my shadow the doors of those I love lest I should bring upon them misfortune."

On February 17 he entered the Capitol building, draped inside with captured Confederate regimental flags.

Lee told the committee he lived quietly, avoided discussions about politics, and never read the newspapers. During questioning, he walked a careful line as Congressmen asked him about conditions in Virginia and the mindset of its people. He painted a picture of a state that was poor and dealing with difficult times, but of people who were cheerful and anxious to cooperate with federal authority. The committee had many questions about freed African Americans. Lee defined the former enslaved as lesser people than whites and a threat to Virginia. He qualified many of his answers, often starting his sentence with a phrase like "As far as I have heard . . ." Sometimes he answered that he didn't know or couldn't recall.

The committee posed ninety-five questions and follow-up questions to Lee on a range of topics, including:

Q: "How do the people in Virginia, the secessionists more particularly, feel toward the freedmen?"

A: "Every one with whom I associate expresses kind feelings towards the freedmen. They wish to see them get on in the world, and particularly to take up some occupation for a living and to turn their hands to some work. . . ."

Q: "Are you aware of the existence of any combination [collusion] among the whites to keep down the wages of the negroes?"

A: "I am not. I have heard that, in several counties, land owners have met in order to establish a uniform rate of wages; but I never heard, nor do I know, of any combination to keep down wages, or establish any rate which they did not think fair. The means of paying wages in Virginia are very limited now. . . ."

Q: "General, you are very competent to judge of the capacity of black men for acquiring knowledge: I want your opinion on that capacity, as compared with the capacity of white men?"

A: "I do not know that I am particularly qualified to speak on that subject, as you seem to intimate; but I do not think that he is as capable of acquiring knowledge as the white man is. There are some more apt than others. I have known some to acquire knowledge and skill in their trade and profession. I have had servants of my own who learned to read and write very well."

Q: "Has the colored race generally as great a love of money and property as the white race possesses?"

A: "I do not think it has. The blacks with whom I am acquainted look more to the present time than to the future."

Q: "Does that absence of a lust of money and property arise more from the nature of the negro than from his former servile condition?"

A: "Well, it may be, in some measure, attributable to his former condition. They are an amiable, social race. They like their ease and comfort, and, I think, look more to their present than to their future condition."

Q: "Is there not a general dislike of northern men among secessionists?"

A: "I suppose they would prefer not to associate with them. . . ."

Q: "What is the position of the colored men in Virginia with reference to the persons they work for? Do you think they would prefer to work for northern men or southern men?"

A: "I think it is very probable that they would prefer the northern man, although I have no facts to go upon."

Q: "You do not feel down there that while you accept the result [of the war], that we are as generous as we ought to be under the circumstances?"

A: "They think that the north can afford to be generous."

Q: "If the 'once rebel States' had 'the opportunity again to secede from the Union, would they or not, in your opinion, avail themselves of that opportunity . . . ?'"

A: "I suppose it would depend upon the circumstances existing at the time. If their feelings should remain embittered, and their affections alienated from the rest of the States, I think it very probable they might do so, provided they thought it was to their interest."

Q: "Would a Virginia jury convict Jefferson Davis for having levied war upon the United States, and thus having committed the crime of treason?"

A: "I think it is very probable that they would not consider he had committed treason."

Lee told the committee that Virginia's act of withdrawing from the United States "carried me along as a citizen of Virginia, and that her laws and her acts were binding on me."

The committee clarified this statement: "And that you felt to be your justification in taking the course you did?"

"Yes, sir," Lee replied.

Q: "How would an amendment to the Constitution be received by the secessionists, or by the people at large, allowing the colored people . . . to exercise the right of voting at elections?"

A: "I think, so far as I can form an opinion, in such an event they would object."

Lee answered several more questions about voting rights for African Americans:

> I think it would excite unfriendly feelings between the two races. . . . In a good many States in the south, and in a good many counties in Virginia, if the black people now were allowed to vote, . . . proper, intelligent people would not be elected, and rather than suffer that injury they would not let them vote at all. . . . My own opinion is, that, at this time, they cannot vote intelligently. . . . What the future may prove, how intelligent they may become, . . . I cannot say more than you can.

Lee was asked what he knew about the "cruelties practiced towards the Union prisoners of war," where soldiers died of "cold and starvation"— "those scenes have created a sad feeling in the hearts of the people at the north."

Lee answered: "I never knew that cruelty was practiced, and I have no reason to believe that it was practiced. I can believe . . . that privations may have been experienced among the prisoners, because I know that provisions and shelter could not be provided them."

> Q: "Do you not think that Virginia would be better off if the colored people were to go to Alabama, Louisiana, and the other southern States?"
>
> A: "I think it would be better for Virginia if she could get rid of them. That is no new opinion with me. I have always thought so, and have always been in favor of emancipation— gradual emancipation."

Congress added Lee's testimony to the information it collected.

A NEW RECONSTRUCTION

Based on conditions in the South, Radical Republicans drew up new Reconstruction legislation. In February 1866 they extended the life of the Freedmen's Bureau, an agency whose mission included helping former slaves find food and shelter and receive an education. In March they passed a Civil Rights Act, granting citizenship rights to African Americans. The act protected civil liberties for black people like the right to hold property and equal rights before the law, liberties that Southern whites had continually violated.

This Thomas Nast illustration, titled "Shall I Trust These Men," appeared in *Harper's Weekly*, August 5, 1865. "Columbia" (representing the United States) wonders who is more deserving of civil rights—former Confederates like Lee (shown kneeling) or the African American soldier wounded in the Union's cause.

President Johnson vetoed the Civil Rights Act and the Freedmen's Bureau Bill. He felt Congress had no authority to legislate any matters for the former eleven Confederate states, since those states were not represented in Congress. Johnson also thought that the new laws favored the freed slaves over Southern whites. The president's veto galvanized

229

Andrew Johnson, the first president to be impeached, clashed with Radical Republican leaders over Reconstruction.

moderate Republicans to join the Radicals, and together they overrode Johnson's vetoes. When the Radical Republicans triumphed in midterm elections, it set up a change of course for Reconstruction.

In March 1867 Congress passed the first of four new Reconstruction Acts. The legislation swept away the Johnson state governments in place since December 1865 and now treated the South like a conquered territory. Only Johnson's home state of Tennessee, long under Union control, had been readmitted to the Union with its rights restored. The Reconstruction Act divided the ten remaining rebel states into five military districts, each governed by a former Union general with soldiers to enforce his authority. District commanders should protect "all persons in their rights, . . . to suppress insurrection, disorder, and violence and to punish, . . . all disturbers of the public peace." They could use military courts instead of civilian courts to try offenders, removing the justice system from the hands of white Southerners. Virginia became district number 1, the only district made up of a single state.

Under the Reconstruction Act, the duties of a district commander included registering male citizens, age twenty-one and older, to vote. This included men "of whatever race, color, or previous condition [enslaved]. . . except such as may be disfranchised for participation in the rebellion."

Former Confederates could be registered only if they'd sworn an oath of allegiance, been pardoned, offered proof of their pardon, been examined under oath, and been approved by a board of commissioners. The act prohibited any man who'd broken previous oaths to the United States, or engaged in rebellion, from holding public office.

Eligible voters would elect delegates to write new state constitutions. These state constitutions had to adopt the newly proposed 14th Amendment guaranteeing African American civil rights, and they had to include voting rights for black men. Once the constitution had been approved by qualified voters in the state and "declared by Congress to be in conformity with the provisions of the act . . . the State shall be declared entitled to representation, and senators and representatives shall be admitted therefrom."

As Virginia began organizing a constitutional convention to recognize Radical Republican requirements, many urged protests and even violence. Lee publicly stood against this. He urged "all persons entitled to vote should attend the polls & endeavour to elect the best available men to represent them in the convention, to whose decision every one should submit."

"WHEREVER YOU FIND THE NEGRO"

Lee submitted because he believed in law and order, but he hated this swiftly shifting world around him. His vision of a restored Union was a return to how things had always been in the South. Slavery would be gone, but Southern white men, superior in work ethic and intelligence, would still control black lives. Instead, "the South is to be placed under the dominion of the negroes," he complained to his nephew, Edward Childe.

For Lee, everything had changed. "The purpose for which the North went to war has been perverted by the radical party," he told his nephew. The North had said they fought to preserve the Union, but now everything was about rights for the black man, including the right to vote, while that right was denied to many former Confederates. If the "present policy" had been announced before the war, Lee said, he doubted that it "would have been tolerated by the country."

Robert E. Lee, photographed by Michael Miley, 1870. Miley, a war veteran, studied photography after the surrender and opened a gallery and studio in Lexington, Virginia.

Complaints about the Radicals ran through Lee's letters to Edward. "The Conservatives," he wrote, "are too weak to resist successfully the radicals, who have every thing their own way." He believed the Radical Republicans gave the vote to African Americans only to "counterbalance the Conservative votes of the whites at the north." He worried that "the party in power are determined to retain its possession even at the risk of destroying the country." In February 1868 the House of Representatives impeached President Johnson. Only the difference of a single vote in the Senate saved Johnson from removal.

The North had promised, Lee believed, that the Union would be restored "with all the dignity, equality & rights of the states *unimpaired*." But now, with the South facing military occupation and a new standing for black people, Lee felt that dignity, equality, and rights for white Southerners had been tossed aside. "The certain fact seems to be that though the war has ended, peace is not restored to the Country," said Lee.

Publicly, Lee said he wished the former slaves no evil and that he would do them "every good in my power." Privately, he advised friends and family to get rid of black workers and hire whites. Lee supported the Virginia Emigration Company, which encouraged European whites to come work in America. "I have always observed," he wrote, "that wherever you find the negro, everything is going down around him, and wherever you find the white man, you see everything around him improving." Remember, Lee told Rob, "our material, social, and political interests are naturally with the whites."

While Lee spoke his racism and white supremacy in subdued words, Mary seldom reined herself in. Her anger overflowed at her changed world, and reflected the thoughts of many white people in the South. The hard work of white Southerners, she wrote, was "stolen by a set of lazy idle negroes who roam about by day marking what they may steal at night & are kept attending political harangues of which they understand about as much as the African gorilla."

She wished the blacks "no greater evil than a safe landing in their Father land"—Africa—or that "their Northern friends would take them to their bosoms, as it is hard that we as the South who have already done so much for them more than their labor has ever repayed." She called radical members of Congress "malignant enemies" and cowards, and added, "The country that allows such scum to rule them must be fast going to destruction."

In July 1868 the nation had ratified the 14th Amendment to the Constitution, guaranteeing civil rights to African Americans. White Southerners resented having been forced to accept this amendment as part of the Reconstruction Act. As Congress prepared to pass the 15th Amendment, which would guarantee voting rights to black men, Lee took a public political stand for the first time. He met with other conservative Southern leaders at White Sulphur Springs, West Virginia. On August 26, 1868, they released a letter known as the White Sulphur Springs Manifesto.

In the letter, Lee and the other conservative leaders presented "a candid statement of what we believe to be the sentiment of the Southern people." The letter acknowledged that questions of African slavery and the right of the South to secede had been decided by the war. Southerners meant "in good faith to abide by that decision," and they had done as asked—their state conventions had abolished slavery and nullified the ordinances of secession. But their actions had not "been met in a spirit of frankness and cordiality," which would have helped heal the wounds of war.

"The idea that the Southern people are hostile to the negroes, and would oppress them if it were in their power to do so, is entirely unfounded," the writers declared. "They have grown up in our midst, and we have been accustomed from childhood to look upon them with kindness. The change in the relations of the two races has brought no change in our feeling towards them."

African Americans, the letter stated, made up an important part of the South's workforce. "Self-interest, even if there were no higher motive, would therefore prompt the whites of the South to extend to the negroes care and protection." Both sides needed the other and would soon adjust to conditions "but for the influences exerted to stir up the passions of the negroes."

As to African American men voting, the letter continued, "It is true that the people of the South, together with the people of the North and West, are, for obvious reasons, opposed to any system of laws which will place the political power of the country in the hands of the negro race." But this feeling was not born of hatred; it came from "a deep seated conviction that at present the negroes have neither the intelligence nor other qualifications which are necessary to make them safe depositories of political power."

The people of the South wanted peace and the restoration of the Union, the letter said; "they desire relief from oppressive misrule." They wanted the rights of every American—"the right of self-government." Give this to the South, and the signers of the letter promised on behalf of the Southern people to "faithfully obey the Constitution and laws of the United States, treat the negro with kindness and humanity, and fulfill every duty incumbent on peaceful citizens loyal to the Constitution of the country."

Lee signed his name first at the bottom of the letter. Newspapers across the South blazoned the manifesto on their pages. A Virginia newspaper responded enthusiastically: "The whole people of the South, with possibly the exception of mangy scallawags diseased with the leprosy of Radicalism, will heartily endorse the able and patriotic letter of Gen. Lee and the other distinguished men whose signatures are attached."

The letter painted a reflection of the past that had never existed, one in which white Southerners treated black people with kindness, and had been raised to do so. The letter echoed arguments from before the war, that blacks and whites had good relations, that black people were contented—if only the outsiders who "stirred up their passions" had left things alone.

As for Lee's signature ensuring that blacks would be treated with "kindness and humanity," he had his hands full just keeping his own students from responding to Reconstruction with violence.

"OUTRAGE AGAINST LAW & ORDER"

While Lee opposed Republican policies, including the Northern military occupation of the South, he still believed in law and order. Many resentful white Southerners, however, funneled their hate of Reconstruction into violence. They joined organizations like the Ku Klux Klan, formed in 1866, to terrorize and intimidate African Americans and white people who supported Radical Republican programs. Washington College students engaged in several violent incidents under Lee's watch in the late 1860s.

In November 1866 students marched through the streets of Lexington after tense exchanges with the local military garrison. Lee urged them to remember their "honor and self-respect." Given their duty to themselves, their parents, and the college, they must suspend further marches. Their behavior only gave others in Lexington the chance to "commit outrages for which you will have to bear the blame."

A few months later, in January 1867, four students were arrested for attacking a Freedmen's Bureau school for African Americans, breaking windows and pistol-whipping a black man who tried to stop them. Lee expelled the student who took the blame for the incident and put the other three on probation.

An event a year later made national news. In February 1868, students threatened a white man named Erastus Johnston—a former Union soldier—who taught black children and ran a store for African

236

Americans. A mob pelted Johnston with sticks and stones and tried to break into his store. Lee quickly expelled three students. But as he'd feared, a New York newspaper reported on the incident and commented that "every Northern man who has given a cent to General Lee's College" must feel that "his money has been worse than thrown away." A white woman teacher at the Freedmen's Bureau also spoke to the papers, recounting how college students spit upon her and called her a "Damn Yankee bitch of a nigger teacher."

Lee quashed several other student attempts to stop black people from exercising their rights. But in May 1868 a student mob nearly lynched a young black man named Caesar Griffen. Griffen had wounded a white youth who'd shoved him off the sidewalk into the road. A Washington College professor, who was also a former Confederate captain, prevented the hanging, pushing his way into the mob and ordering the students in the name of General Lee to turn Griffen over to authorities. Lee chose to think that none of his students would have carried out such a violent act as a lynching, that "none would countenance such outrage against law & order." This time, no students faced expulsion.

In November 1868 Lee told the commander of the local military garrison that he was doing everything he could to prevent students from breaking up a black political meeting. But he couldn't stop the pattern of violence. He expelled another student in January 1869 for wounding a black man on the streets of Lexington.

Lee did not speak out publicly against the violence toward African Americans spreading across the South, especially lynching. His response to such incidents at Washington College focused more on how events affected the school than on the fact that such violence was wrong. Lee implored his students to do nothing that might "disturb the public peace, or bring discredit upon themselves or the institution to which they belong." Lee feared that the Northern press, politicians, or military authorities would target the college.

Treason charges against Lee had come to nothing, and on Christmas Day of 1868 his citizenship was restored. President Johnson issued a proclamation of "universal amnesty and pardon . . . for the offense of treason against the United States or of adhering to their enemies during the late civil war, with restoration of all rights, privileges, and immunities under the Constitution."

A few months later Lee wrote his nephew that the pardon had saved men like Jefferson Davis from charges of treason and restored the rights of those who'd fled the country. But the laws of the Congress and the Republican state legislatures still "imposed disfranchisement upon the late Confederates & their property that was sold by the Government is still withheld." He wished the American people would one day be worthy of a great republic, as the founding fathers had hoped—"though I shall never see it," he wrote sadly.

CHAPTER NINETEEN

"ONLY THE HERO OF A LOST CAUSE"

"The toils of his crowded & eventful life are ended, & had he succeeded in gaining the cause which cost him so much labor & sacrifice, he could not have been more beloved & lamented than he is now only the Hero of a lost cause."

—*Mary Lee to Letitia Burwell,*
November 15, 1870

Robert Lee knew he suffered from a serious heart condition. His health had steadily worsened since the middle of the war. Rob thought his father now looked upon himself as an invalid—he tired easily, ached with rheumatism, and experienced chest pains and difficulty breathing. He labored under "great weariness and depression," wrote Rob.

On his way to visit doctors in Baltimore in 1869 Lee stopped in Alexandria. He searched out his boyhood home. He visited the cousin's estate outside of town where his mother had died. Lee stood in the doorway of her room, remembering her death, remembering himself as that young man fresh out of West Point. It seemed more like yesterday than forty years ago, Lee said. On the trip he also visited with his dear brother Smith, who would die a few months later.

The Lee family spent summers at hot springs near Lexington, seeking medicinal relief. "I take no pleasure in these fashionable resorts," Lee wrote his nephew Edward Childe, "& would much prefer mounting 'Traveller' & taking a solitary ride through the mountains. . . .

239

But the hope of benefiting your poor Aunt [Mary] would induce me to go anywhere." Letters overflowed with woes of illness, family members feeble, hurting, and often stricken with colds. In the summer of 1868 Lee and Agnes nursed Mildred through typhoid fever, which must have raised fearful memories of Annie's death.

Lee, photographed by Michael Miley, 1870. Late in life, Miley patented a process to color film but abandoned it as too expensive and time consuming.

A CHANGE OF SCENERY

At the end of March 1870, Lee reluctantly gave in to pressure from doctors and family that he relax in warmer temperatures. With Agnes as his companion, Lee set off for a six-week trip to parts of South Carolina, Georgia, and Florida.

As he had in Alexandria the year before, Lee again sought out touchstones from his life. He wrote Mildred that he wished "to visit my dear Annie's grave before I die. . . . I wish to see how calmly she sleeps away from us all." Afterward, he wrote Mary that the visit was "mournful, yet soothing to my feelings." He and Agnes also visited the grave of Light Horse Harry Lee, which Agnes decorated with flowers.

Wherever he went, people crowded train depots and way stations, even in pouring rain, craning their necks to catch sight of him, chanting "Lee! Lee!" Old ladies poked their heads into the train windows, drew back, and reported, "He is mightily like his pictures." Lee complained in a letter to Mary, "I do not think travelling in this way procures me much quiet and repose."

Doctors in various cities along the route examined Lee and prescribed medicines. Landlords invited them in or delivered food to their train compartment; former soldiers sent fruit, till Agnes thought they might "die of eating." Mayors whisked them away to receptions and small children named after Lee pushed forward to press flowers into his hands. Agnes wished her mother might see "the affection and feeling shown toward him everywhere. . . . Papa has borne the journey and the crowds far better than I thought he would."

On the return trip through Virginia, Lee visited Shirley plantation, his mother's childhood home and the place of his parents' marriage. He joked in a letter to Mildred that after weeks of being cooped up with him, "Agnes threatens to abandon me" at the ancestral home.

Mary met her husband and daughter at White House, where they enjoyed time with their baby grandson—"the most pleasant part of my journey," Lee told his nephew Edward. He traveled the few miles to visit Rob's farm at Romancoke. He couldn't hide his shock upon seeing Rob's bachelor quarters: an old overseer's cabin, nearly a ruin beneath a sagging roof. How would Rob entice a wife with this mess? When Lee returned to Lexington he immediately sent advice on picking a home site, creating house plans, and so forth.

The trip also saddened Lee. He and Agnes had traveled to places he'd visited before, but had not seen since the devastation of the war. Those ravages were nothing compared to "the depression & stagnation it has undergone since from the evil legislation of Congress," he wrote his nephew. "Nor did I witness anywhere I went devastation equal to that felt by Virginia."

Whatever his inner struggles with his failing body and with the nation's political turmoil, whatever scars of war he carried inside, to those who flocked to see him Lee appeared a man of dignity and courtly manners. "He kept his suffering locked up in his great heart," wrote Mildred, "and it did not show in his face."

"A TRUE HISTORY"

Publicly, Robert E. Lee refused to relive the war. He would not give speeches; he published no words about it. He had lost in the greatest undertaking of his life at an unspeakable cost in lives, and perhaps for that reason, Lee began rethinking the past as he aged.

In several private conversations he shifted blame from himself onto others for failures during the war, including his generals and Jefferson Davis. Lee claimed he'd wanted to free the slaves early in the war, "to remove a weakness at home and to get sympathy abroad, and to divide our enemies, but Davis would not hear of it." He claimed he would willingly have freed his own slaves before the war in exchange for peace. The most haunting defeat of all, Gettysburg, had not been his fault but happened because J. E. B. Stuart failed to carry out his orders and "the imperfect, halting way" his corps commanders fought "gave victory finally to the foe."

Lee hoped to shape "the opinion which posterity may form of the motives which governed the South in their late struggle." For Lee those "motives" became something lofty, a cause worthy of so much bloodshed and sacrifice. The war had been a political quarrel. The North had departed from the ideals of the Constitution, while the men of the

242

South had laid down their lives "for the maintenance of the principles of the Constitution."

Southerners had not been traitors, Lee wrote, but had fought for freedom, a second American Revolution. They'd fought for states' rights and equality against an aggressive, sprawling federal government. As for his own actions, "I had no other guide," Lee claimed, "nor had I any other object than the defense of those principles of American liberty upon which the constitutions of the several States were originally founded." Lee hoped that "a true history will be written & justice be done" to the people of the South.

Lee forgot his own words about secession. He ignored the fact that the "American liberty" for which they shattered the Union was the liberty to own slaves. He disregarded the reality that the states' rights insisted on in 1860 and 1861 had been the right to spread slavery into the western territories. Those were the rights Southerners feared the North would trample, and they had expressed that fear in their secession documents.

Lee bristled when people said the war had been about slavery. He had always hated slavery. He also insisted he'd always been for emancipation, which stretched the truth. He'd been for *gradual* emancipation—the kind of emancipation that meant waiting for God to decide when slavery would end. He had not freed the enslaved under his own control until a court ordered him to do so. And when he talked of freeing slaves at the end of the war, it was only to use them as soldiers for a gasping and devastated Confederacy.

During the war Lee repeatedly prayed that he might accept God's will. He'd prayed that the blood, destruction, and suffering would cleanse his sins and the sins of the South. But he never saw God's hand in the Civil War's deathblow to slavery.

In the final years of his life, Lee tried to validate his decisions, smooth over his failings, and mold how history might judge him. He said the greatest mistake of his life was becoming a soldier. When his nephew asked for his thoughts on the war being fought between France and Germany (July 1870–May 1871), Lee said he wished they had submitted their differences to judges from friendly powers. But that would be "expecting too much from present civilization. . . . We are not yet ready for such an elevated act," Lee wrote, "& must butcher & slaughter each other I fear for years to Come."

"GOD TOOK HIM"

The college year began in mid-September and Lee returned to work. One night at the end of the month, Mary prepared for their evening tea. A steady rain poured down and Lee still hadn't come home from a meeting at their church. She bent over her sewing while Custis relaxed on the sofa. At seven thirty Mary heard Lee shut the front door and take off his hat and old military cloak. He entered the dining room and stood at the head of the table as if to say grace, but no words came out. He sank down onto his chair. "You look very tired," said Mary. "Let me give you some tea." Again Lee tried to speak but failed. Mary sent for doctors. Her husband had suffered a stroke.

They undressed him—Lee told the doctors they hurt his arm—and applied cold cloths to his head and a warm bath to his feet. The family set up a camp bed in the dining room bay window, Lee's favorite spot in the house. For the next two weeks Lee slept, uttered few words, and ate little, as his family clung to hope. Doctors prescribed a dozen different medicines, including castor oil and tiny amounts of strychnine, morphine, and turpentine.

He "looked so beseechingly at us," Mildred later wrote, "always those glorious dark eyes from the little bed." By October 11, "he was so much worse that the Dr. advised us not to retire," Mary wrote Robert's brother Carter. "During the early part of the night I sat up with all of us around his hand in mine. . . . He was breathing heavily & the Dr. said utterly unconscious of all around him but might live 10 or 12 hours longer."

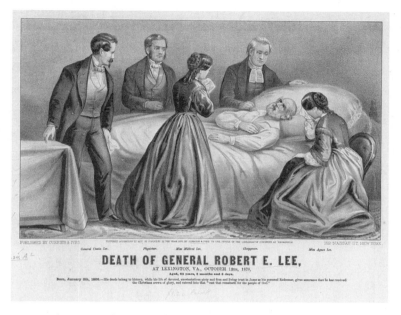

A Currier and Ives print shows Lee's family and doctors at his deathbed.

The stroke had not paralyzed Lee, but it had affected his cough reflex and now fluid filled his lungs. He remained unconscious. His hands grew cold, said Mary, "& the struggles for breath much more intense at last ended in a continuous moan. Still the Dr. assured us he was perfectly insensible to all suffering, we silently & sorrowing all sat round." At about nine thirty in the morning on October 12, 1870, Robert Lee passed away as Mary held his hand, with Custis, Agnes, and Mildred surrounding their father's bedside. He did not suffer long, Agnes wrote a friend. "In the midst of his energy and usefulness God took him." Lee was only sixty-three years old.

Within minutes of Lee's death Washington College canceled classes to mourn his loss. Heavy rains had flooded the Lexington area, washing out bridges, sweeping away houses. The undertaker's coffins, stored in a waterfront warehouse, had floated away. Three men fished a coffin out of the river to use for Lee. It was a bit too short, so they placed Lee inside without his shoes on. A student at the nearby Virginia Military Institute described how mourning black covered everything—people wore armbands of black crepe, and draped houses and buildings with so much black fabric that they had to send to a nearby town for more.

Students sit with Lee's body inside the chapel, draped in mourning black.

Students watched over Lee's body as he lay in state within the chapel he'd built, "no one speaking except in a low whisper." One young man who'd seen Lee a few days before his stroke was astounded on viewing the body, as he "looked to be reduced to half his original size, and desperately thin."

Though flooding made it difficult for mourners to reach the college, thousands attended Lee's funeral on October 15. His family laid his body to rest in the crypt below the chapel.

Mourners line up outside the chapel for Lee's funeral, October 15, 1870.

The trustees honored Robert Lee by changing the school's name to Washington and Lee University. Lee's office was left untouched; it remained exactly as when he'd closed the door on the day of his stroke, his papers scattered on the round table, library books Lee had borrowed, never returned.

In Richmond, businesses closed for two days as the city mourned. An editorial in the *Charleston Daily News* expressed feelings across the South:

> The mournful tidings of the death of General Lee will
> awaken in every Southern heart a grief second only to that

247

which bowed in anguish the heads of our people when the Great Captain yielded up his knightly sword on the field of Appomattox. . . . Lee lived on to show himself as great in peace as in the turmoil and carnage of war. . . . The kindly beaming eye is closed forever; the patriot heart has ceased to beat. And of him who was all in all to the South, there remains naught but a memory and a name—a memory cherished . . . by eight million souls; a name which shall live while virtue and valor are reverenced and loved.

Lee's office as he left it the day of his stroke. It has remained virtually untouched to the present day.

The *New York Times* ran a lengthy obituary for Lee on October 13. They regretted that one "so rarely gifted" had cast his lot with traitors and devoted "his splendid talents to the execution of a wicked plot to tear asunder and ruin the Republic in whose service his life had hitherto been spent." But the *Times* also praised Lee's service at Washington College. Lee had kept himself as much as possible from public notice, said the *Times*, "and by his unobtrusive modesty and purity of life, has won the respect even of those who most bitterly deplore . . . his course in the rebellion."

Julia Ward Howe, a Northern woman, had written a poem after visiting Arlington early in the war. It became one of the most famous songs of the Union war effort—"The Battle Hymn of the Republic." In the years after his death, Howe turned her pen to praise him in a poem called "Robert E. Lee":

> *A gallant foeman in the fight,*
> *A brother when the fight was o'er,*
> *The hand that led the host with might*
> *The blessed torch of learning bore.*
>
> *No shriek of shells nor roll of drums,*
> *No challenge fierce, resounding far,*
> *When reconciling Wisdom comes*
> *To heal the cruel wounds of war.*
>
> *Thought may the minds of men divide,*
> *Love makes the heart of nations one,*
> *And so, thy soldier grave beside,*
> *We honor thee, Virginia's son.*

EPILOGUE: MYTH BUILDING

His family crowded around Lee's camp bed. Though unconscious, Lee spoke clearly. "Tell Hill he must come up," he said, his thoughts drifting back to the battlefield. He lapsed into silence, but then, at the very end, Lee uttered the perfect words: "Strike the tent." It was over; the old soldier prepared to leave, and Robert Lee breathed his last.

These final deathbed words, never spoken, are a shining example of the mythology that shrouded Lee soon after his death. The story appears as fact in dozens of biographies and books describing Robert E. Lee's poignant end. But why does he need this heroic ending? Why did Lee the man need to become Lee the myth? The people of the South needed a hero. Who else but Lee offered them greatness in defeat? Who else enveloped them in dignity and Christian values? Who else was more loved than Robert Lee?

People scrubbed away Lee's humanity and imperfections till he became saint-like. One woman described him as "bathed in the white light which falls directly upon him from the smile of an approving . . . God." A Northern historian likened Lee to "the sun as it rises and sets"; Lee was simply "beyond description." For Jubal Early, protecting and burnishing the memory of his former commander became a "sacred duty" and "pious work." Early pushed for a monument of Lee "at the Confederate Capital, in defence of which his wondrous talents and sublime virtues were displayed."

Any fellow officer who questioned Lee's generalship—like James Longstreet—was attacked and silenced. Jubal Early, calling such men "renegade to their comrades and our holy cause," was blunt: "Let them go out from among us with the brand of Cain upon them!" Mistakes Lee made on the battlefield were erased until he loomed as the foremost military genius in American history, the perfect general. And though people called Grant a butcher for how he used his soldiers, Lee, who'd done the same, received a pass on criticism.

An 1896 colored lithograph titled "Our Heroes and Our Flags" depicts Lee (center right) with generals Stonewall Jackson (center left) and G. T. Beauregard (center middle).

The myth included the idea that Lee was such a gentleman, he referred to his Union opponents politely as "those people"; he never even called them "the enemy." In truth, Lee called the North "the enemy" in hundreds of letters. He labeled them pillagers, robbers, people who burned, plundered, and destroyed. He talked of their dirty work, done with malice and revenge in their hearts. Why create the myth that he didn't use those words? It was war, after all, and war breeds hatred. But the hero Lee had to rise above such things.

Most of all, the ugliness of slavery could not tarnish the mythical Lee. People claimed—and still do today—that Lee hated slavery, that he did not own slaves, that he believed in emancipation. But the historical record tells a different story. Lee did believe in slavery. He believed in white supremacy. Though Lee didn't like the messy burden of slaveholding—slaves were not worth the trouble they caused—he owned enslaved people, and he benefited from their work and care. He expressed his racism in words and actions both before and after the war.

Lee was a man of his time. Most white Southerners, and many white Northerners, shared his views about African Americans. But the myths about Lee and slavery, repeated by historians, ordinary citizens, orators, and writers, haunt us today. Because Lee was seen as a good man of pure Christian values, he became a symbol that hid racism. He stood as an example of a righteous South, and that image masked the political and economic suppression of African Americans, the violence, lynching, and racial segregation. The myth of Lee allowed an untruthful version of history that the Civil War was not about slavery. At its simplest, without slavery there would have been no need for decades of consuming political battles and failed compromises, for raging sectionalism, for secession, for war.

Lee had hoped that "a true history" of the Confederacy might be written, meaning a history from the South's perspective. And that was done, using some of the arguments Lee himself used after the war. In many ways, the South—defeated in battle—won the war of history with words. Those words shaped how the South was viewed, shaped what became part of our historical memory of the Civil War. Words led to actions that stripped away the freedoms African Americans gained after the war.

Groups like the United Confederate Veterans (founded in 1889) and the United Daughters of the Confederacy (formed in 1894) took steps to defend, honor, and vindicate the Old South. They advanced certain points: Lee had not been defeated. He fought heroically for the just cause of states' rights and surrendered only because the North had more men. Slavery was a kind institution, the slaves themselves faithful to their masters, and happy. Reconstruction, bringing with it voting rights for African American men, was "a crime against the white people of the South." Most importantly, these groups hammered home the belief that slavery had not been the cause of the Civil War. Lee, too, believed that.

The United Daughters of the Confederacy distributed a booklet nationwide called *A Measuring Rod to Test Text Books, and Reference Books in Schools, Colleges and Libraries*, to ensure the "truths of Confederate history." The Daughters meant the booklet for "all scholastic and library authorities in all parts of the country, in justice and fairness to their fellow citizens of the South." Among the reasons listed to condemn a book:

> Reject a book that speaks of the Constitution other than a Compact between Sovereign States. Reject a book that says the South fought to hold her slaves. Reject a book that speaks of the slaveholder of the South as cruel and unjust to his slaves. Reject a text-book that glorifies Abraham Lincoln and vilifies Jefferson Davis. . . .

This "measuring rod" affected what was taught and read in white public schools across the South for decades. For white Southern schoolchildren, the Civil War and Reconstruction lived on and felt personal, even years after the last war veterans had died. The United Daughters of the Confederacy placed thousands of portraits of Robert E. Lee in Southern classrooms and insisted that children "[be] instructed as to his life and character." Some Southerners celebrated Lee's birthday.

Outside of school, white children joined groups like the Children of the Confederacy. Here they sang Confederate songs, wrote essays on Confederate history, and learned *The Confederate Catechism*, the first version of which was published in 1904. The Catechism offered questions and answers for children to memorize and recite, again shaping perceptions of the South and the Civil War. Some examples include:

> *What was the cause of secession in 1861?*
> It was the fact that the Union consisted from the first of two jarring nations having different interests, which were brought to the breaking point in 1861 by the intemperate agitation in the North against everything Southern.
> *Was secession the cause of the war?*
> No, secession is a mere civil process having no necessary connection with war.
> *Did the South fight for slavery or the extension of slavery?*
> No, for had Lincoln not sent armies to the South, that country would have done no fighting at all.
> *What did the South fight for?*
> IT FOUGHT TO REPEL INVASION AND FOR SELF-GOVERNMENT, JUST AS THE FATHERS OF THE AMERICAN REVOLUTION HAD DONE.
> *Did Lincoln, by his conquest of the South, save the Union?*
> No; the old Union was a union of consent; the present Union is a great Northern nation based on force.

The United Daughters of the Confederacy raised tens of thousands of dollars to fund Confederate monuments meant to reinforce Southern pride in the past and romanticize the Old South of master and slave. Most were unveiled between 1894 and 1920 with lavish parades, speeches, and ceremonies. The celebrations often included hundreds of children, dressed in red and white, arranged to form "living" Confederate battle flags. In June 1914 the United Daughters of the Confederacy dedicated a monument to Confederate soldiers at Arlington National Cemetery on land once belonging to the Custis-Lee family. Veterans from both armies attended alongside President Woodrow Wilson and 4,000 other guests, including a grandson of Robert and Mary Lee.

By this time, conservative Democrats had regained control of Southern legislatures, securing white supremacy once more. They'd swept aside the civil rights gained by black people during Reconstruction. The rise in Confederate monuments coincided with the passage of "Jim Crow" legislation that enforced brutal racial segregation.

The myth building worked. Within sixty years of the Civil War's end, Robert Lee emerged as a national hero, not just a Southern one. He earned praise as a rebuilder after the war, a man who sought peace and justice. President Theodore Roosevelt said Lee's surrender at Appomattox had actually saved the Union. Woodrow Wilson, a Virginian, claimed that Lee's star shone so bright, he couldn't "be lifted to any new place of distinction by any man's words of praise." A Southern biographer in 1895 stated simply, "Perhaps no man ever lived that was so great, so good, and so unselfish as Lee." Lee, the perfect man, had completely overshadowed Robert Lee, the human being, and the whole nation embraced the perfect version.

Even though historians have re-examined Lee's life since the 1970s, myths about the war and Reconstruction still resonate. We need to look more closely than ever at Lee, read his words, question the myths so easily accepted and repeated. In Lee's case, the myths hurt us as a nation and in how we see one another. Robert Lee, the flawed man, the husband, the father, the soldier, the white supremacist, fixed in his own time and place, is the Lee we should remember—not the vision of a myth cast in a bronze statue forever riding Traveller.

A Mathew Brady photograph taken of Lee in April 1865.

AUTHOR'S NOTE

When you write a book, you start with questions. Long ago, as a nerdy history girl, I climbed around Devil's Den at Gettysburg, stood by Lee's and Meade's statues, and looked across the field where Pickett made his charge. But what did I really know about Robert Lee?

What mattered to him? What were his feelings about slavery, the terrible institution that divided the country? How had he come to resign his army commission? With so many myths swirling about Lee, what was the truth—or how close could we get to a truth? And what had been his life beyond those four years of the Civil War that define him in history? What of his family, his years of work?

I started my research by reading biographies of Lee and combed through their bibliographies and source notes for other references. I found the Lee Family Digital Archive, an online repository of documents at Stratford Hall, Lee's birthplace. Here were thousands of Lee family letters and documents I could read for myself. What did Lee have to say? What did the people who knew him have to say? What little details of his life and personality would the letters reveal?

If I'm lucky, I get to go and see things for myself. This time I was lucky enough to visit Virginia. I spent a day with historian Tom Clemens at Antietam and driving country roads past John Brown's cabin and into Harpers Ferry. I spent an amazing day at the Custis-Lee home— Arlington. With National Park Ranger Matt Penrod, I explored the house and listened to his incredible store of Lee and Custis family knowledge. One of the other rangers told me they all wished they had Matt's brain—and I could see why. I visited the battlefield of Second Manassas. I walked through the rooms at Stratford, and I contemplated that dangerous set of stone steps. I visited Petersburg, a beautiful place today, a far cry from the stripped landscape of entrenchments and

257

hardship. At Appomattox I stood in the room where Lee surrendered and thought about how incredibly difficult and moving that day must have been. And at Washington and Lee University I got to sit in Lee's pew in the chapel and listen to the fascinating Lucy Wilkins talk about Lee's years as president of Washington College. Most thrilling, she took me through the president's house that Lee designed for his family, and we even climbed up into the hayloft above Traveller's stall.

It's been a fascinating journey. We can never truly know another person, especially someone who lived in such a different time. I hope readers take away new knowledge about Robert Lee and the times he lived in, and how our westward expansion, slavery, the Civil War, and Reconstruction still affect us today. I thank the people who've made this journey with me.

—*Brandon Marie Miller*

TIMELINE

January 19, 1807—born at Stratford, Westmoreland County, Virginia.

June 1825–June 1829—attends the United States Military Academy at West Point, New York, and earns a place in the prestigious Army Corps of Engineers upon graduation.

June 30, 1831—marries Mary Anna Randolph Custis, at Arlington.

September 16, 1832—son George Washington Custis Lee born.

July 12, 1835—daughter Mary Custis Lee born.

May 31, 1837—son William Henry Fitzhugh Lee born.

August 1838—begins engineering work on the Mississippi River at St. Louis; promoted to captain.

June 18, 1839—daughter Anne Carter Lee born.

February 27, 1841—daughter Eleanor Agnes Lee born.

April 1841—reports to Fort Hamilton, New York.

October 27, 1843—son Robert E. Lee Jr. born.

February 10, 1846—daughter Mildred Childe Lee born.

January 1847–June 1848—serves on the staff of General Scott during the Mexican War.

September 1852–March 1855—serves as superintendent of the U.S. Military Academy, West Point.

March 1855–November 1857—promoted to lieutenant colonel with 2nd Cavalry, serving in Texas, to stop Comanche and Mexican bandit raids; travels to sit on court-martials.

1858–1860—acts as executor of G. W. Custis's estate.

October 18, 1859—commands marines who capture John Brown at Harpers Ferry, Virginia.

Winter 1860–March 1861—serves as head of the U.S. Army's Department of Texas.

April 20, 1861—resigns from the U.S. Army.

April 22, 1861—accepts command of Virginia forces.

September 12–15, 1861—defeated by General Rosecrans at Battle of Cheat Mountain.

1862

June 1—given command of the Army of Northern Virginia.

June 25–July 1—defeats General McClellan in Seven Days' Battle near Richmond.

August 28–30—defeats General Pope at Second Battle of Manassas.

September 17—fights to a stalemate at Antietam, the bloodiest single day in American history.

October 20—daughter Annie dies.

December 13—routs General Burnside at Fredericksburg.

1863

May 1–6—defeats General Hooker at Chancellorsville.

June—son Rooney wounded and captured.

July 1–3—defeated by General Meade at Gettysburg.

1864

May 5–7—meets Grant in first battle of Overland Campaign at the Wilderness.

May 8–26—armies clash again at Spotsylvania Court House and North Anna River.

May 31–June 12—more slaughter at Cold Harbor.

Mid-June—siege begins outside Petersburg.

1865

April 9—surrenders the Army of Northern Virginia to General Grant at Appomattox Court House.

September—accepts job as president of Washington College.

December 1868—regains his United States citizenship rights.

October 12, 1870—dies at his home in Lexington, Virginia, following a stroke.

1975

August 5—by act of Congress, President Gerald Ford officially restores Lee's citizenship in a ceremony at Arlington House, the Robert E. Lee Memorial.

SOURCE NOTES

The abbreviation "LFDA," used in many of the notes, refers to the Lee Family Digital Archive. Most works are cited by author's name only. Complete publication information can be found in the Bibliography.

CHAPTER ONE: ESCAPING FAMILY HISTORY

"I do solemnly swear . . ." Lee's West Point oath, quoted in Pryor, *Reading the Man*, 58.

"quickness of talent . . ." / "dazzling and always at command" George Washington Custis on Henry Lee, quoted in Nelligan, 152.

"with caution . . ." / "appearance of inhumanity" / "excite resentment" George Washington to Henry Lee, July 9, 1778, LFDA.

"an eloquence . . ." George Washington Custis on Henry Lee, quoted in Nelligan, 152.

"unhappy rage . . ." Same as above, 153.

"The period for payment . . ." George Washington to Henry Lee, January 25, 1798, LFDA.

"First in war . . ." Henry Lee, Washington's eulogy, in Hughes.

"from the claim . . ." Charles Carter, quoted in Pryor, *Reading the Man*, 12.

"The eyes . . ." / "our unfortunate little Smith" / "Do not disappoint me" Ann Lee to Henry Lee, July 6, 1806, LFDA.

"that swindling Henry Lee" Quoted in Pryor, *Reading the Man*, 16.

"by the World forgot" Ann Lee, quoted in Pryor, *Reading the Man*, 13.

"this depot of misery" Henry Lee, quoted in Pryor, *Reading the Man*, 14.

"Those insects" Thomas Jefferson, quoted in Pryor, *Reading the Man*, 16.

"all of my expenses . . ." / "to the great discomfort . . ." Ann Lee to Carter Lee, July 17, 1816, whole letter in Pryor, *Reading the Man*, 20.

"I am determined . . ." Carter Lee to Ann Lee, June 20, 1819, LFDA.

"a well tried disciple . . ." Henry Lee IV to Ann Lee, June 11, 1818, LFDA.

"Major H Lee . . ." Nelly Custis Lewis to Elizabeth Bordley Gibson, quoted in Brady, 107.

"You have no doubt heard . . ." E. H. Randolph, quoted in Pryor, *Reading the Man*, 36.

"escape pollution" Nelly Custis Lewis, quoted in Brady, 110.

"escape the sins . . ." / "I hope the blame . . ." Robert Lee to Mary Custis, quoted in deButts, "Lee in Love," 535.

"honnoured by the President" Robert Lee to John C. Calhoun, April 1, 1824, LFDA.

"You know what I have lost . . ." Ann Lee, quoted in Pryor, *Reading the Man*, 27.

CHAPTER TWO: CORPS OF CADETS

"I hope to see . . ." Ann Lee to Smith Lee, April 10, 1829, LFDA.

"well boiled" / "a pudding with sauce" Quoted in Pappas, 144.

"awful 200" Robert Lee to Martha "Markie" Custis Williams, in Lee, *To Markie*, 25.

"The practice of chewing . . ." Quoted in Pappas, 141.

"Young Men from whom . . ." President John Quincy Adams, quoted in Pryor, *Reading the Man*, 64.

"walking the area" / "Unsoldierlike and disorderly conduct" Quoted in Pappas, 140.

"a wearisome & painful season" Robert Lee to Markie Williams, in Lee, *To Markie*, 40.

"Thirteen men were under . . ." George Ticknor, quoted in Pappas, 163.

"from Olympian Jove" Benjamin Ewell, quoted in Pryor, *Reading the Man*, 65.

"I pray you may have . . ." / "*courageous heart*" Robert Lee to his son Custis Lee, April 18, 1851, quoted in Pryor, *Reading the Man*, 60.

CHAPTER THREE: "WORTHY OF EACH OTHER"

"Do you ever think of me . . ." Robert Lee to Mary Custis, May 13, 1831, quoted in deButts, "Lee in Love," 540.

"sweet modest girl . . ." Nelly Custis Lewis, quoted in Brady, 138.

"There are few worthy . . ." Same as above, 191.

"if she thinks . . ." Robert Lee to Carter Lee, May 8, 1830, LFDA.

"not yet made up his mind . . ." Robert Lee to Carter Lee, September 22, 1830, LFDA.

"If *you* 'felt so grateful' . . ." Robert Lee to Mary Custis, quoted in deButts, "Lee in Love," 535.

"And now My sweet Mary . . ." Same as above, 525.

"Now call us lazy" Same as above, 536.

"I thought & intended . . ." Same as above, 541.

"The truth is . . ." Same as above, 517–18.

"then I should have . . ." Mary Custis to Robert Lee, quoted in deButts, "Lee in Love," 517.

"the wickedness of men . . ." Robert Lee to Mary Fitzhugh Custis, quoted in deButts, "Lee in Love," 531.

"too late to change" Same as above, 548.

"one of them . . ." Robert Lee to Mary Custis, quoted in deButts, "Lee in Love," 546.

"I am sure . . ." Same as above.

"oozing out" / "Do not let it all escape" Same as above, 548.

"the change from Arlington . . ." Same as above, 550.

"nor anything uncommon . . ." Robert Lee to Andrew Talcott, July 13, 1831, LFDA.

"bold as a sheep" Same as above.

"They are worthy of each other" Zaccheus Collins Lee to Carter Lee, July 6, 1831, quoted in Pryor, *Reading the Man*, 84.

"When I left today . . ." Robert Lee to Andrew Talcott, quoted in Pryor, *Reading the Man*, 86.

"order & methodology" Robert Lee, quoted in Pryor, *Reading the Man*, 87.

"your nice mode . . ." Mary Lee to Robert Lee, quoted in Pryor, *Reading the Man*, 86.

"Do not be uneasy . . ." Same as above.

"I do not know . . ." Robert Lee to Mary Lee, quoted in Pryor, *Reading the Man*, 148.

"unwilling hands to work" Robert Lee, quoted in Pryor, *Reading the Man*, 263.

"useless trouble" Robert Lee, quoted in Pryor, *Reading the Man*, 148.

"*recommend* her . . ." Robert Lee, quoted in Fellman, 63.

"In the meantime . . ." Robert Lee to Mary Lee, quoted in Pryor, *Reading the Man*, 148.

"What would I give . . ." Mary Lee to her mother, quoted in Coulling, 7.

"This will never do . . ." Robert Lee to Mary Lee, quoted in Pryor, *Reading the Man*, 87.

"This is a terrible life . . ." Same as above, 88.

"some comfort at home" Mary Lee to her mother, quoted in Pryor, *Reading the Man*, 89.

CHAPTER FOUR: "THE LITTLE LEES"

"I still feel the glow . . ." Robert Lee to his son Rooney Lee, November 1, 1856, LFDA.

"from the performance . . ." Robert Lee to Mary Lee, August 21, 1835, quoted in Coulling, 8.

"much shattered" Robert Lee to Carter Lee, quoted in Pryor, *Reading the Man*, 100.

"your affectionate father" Robert Lee, quoted in R. E. Lee Jr., 56–7.

"in his bright, entertaining way" Rob Lee, quoted in R. E. Lee Jr., 9.

"No tickling, no story" Robert Lee, quoted in R. E. Lee Jr., 10.

"You do not know . . ." Robert Lee to Mary Lee, quoted in R. E. Lee Jr., 16.

"Oh, what pleasure I lose . . ." Same as above.

"Our last romp . . ." Robert Lee to Mary Lee, September 10, 1837, quoted in Coulling, 10.

"Annie is getting . . ." Robert Lee to Mary Lee, June 23, 1849, quoted in Coulling, 27.

"Where is my little boy?" Robert Lee, quoted in R. E. Lee Jr., 4.

"I have been made a horse . . ." Robert Lee to John Mackay, March 18, 1841, quoted in Pryor, *Reading the Man*, 97.

"scarcely get a moment . . ." Mary Lee, quoted in Pryor, *Reading the Man*, 97.

"It seemed to be a great comfort . . ." Robert Lee to Mary Fitzhugh Custis, June 22, 1850, quoted in Pryor, *Reading the Man*, 209.

"You must be No. 1 . . ." Robert Lee to Custis Lee, February 1, 1852, quoted in Pryor, *Reading the Man*, 104.

"never feel assured . . ." Robert Lee to Mary Lee, December 20, 1856, LFDA.

"obedience, regularity . . ." Robert Lee to Mary Lee, November 5, 1855, LFDA.

"If he is *made* . . ." Same as above.

"*regular, orderly & energetic* . . ." Robert Lee, quoted in Pryor, *Reading the Man*, 104.

"They *can* if they *try* . . ." Robert Lee, quoted in Pryor, *Reading the Man*, 104.

"I hope you will always . . ." Robert Lee to Annie Lee, February 25, 1853, quoted in R. E. Lee Jr., 15.

"I noticed that you spelt . . ." Robert Lee to Mildred Lee, April 1, 1861, LFDA.

"most vulnerable" Robert Lee to Mary Fitzhugh Custis, March 17, 1852, quoted in Pryor, *Reading the Man*, 105.

CHAPTER FIVE: "HERE WORKING FOR MY COUNTRY" PART I

"Here Working For My Country" Robert Lee to John Mackay, June 27, 1838, complete letter in Pryor, *Reading the Man*, 10.

"The object is . . ." Same as above, 108–10.

"give direction to . . ." Same as above, 109.

"crowding, squeezing . . ." Robert Lee, quoted in Nelligan, 224.

"a rough country" / "most marvelously" Robert Lee to John Mackay, June 27, 1838, complete letter in Pryor, *Reading the Man*, 108.

"will be repaid . . ." Robert Lee, quoted in Pryor, *Reading the Man*, 117.

"you could cultivate . . ." Robert Lee to John Mackay, October 22, 1837, quoted in Pryor, *Reading the Man*, 119.

"plenty of Indians" Robert Lee to Mary Lee, September 10, 1837, quoted in Fellman, 60.

"somewhat amusing" Robert Lee to Mary Fitzhugh Custis, November 7, 1839, quoted in Fellman, 55.

"a swaggering . . ." Same as above.

"higher order" / "engrossed . . ." / "uninteresting" Robert Lee to Carter Lee, quoted in Fellman, 55–56.

"I felt so elated . . ." Robert Lee to Hill Carter, January 25, 1840, LFDA.

"The manner in which . . ." Robert Lee to John Mackay, June 27, 1838, complete letter in Pryor, *Reading the Man*, 109.

"Oh we have been . . ." Robert Lee to John Mackay, June 22, 1836, quoted in Pryor, *Reading the Man*, 185.

"give our dear children . . ." Robert Lee to Mary Fitzhugh Custis, March 24, 1838, quoted in Nelligan, 223.

"I never felt poorer . . ." Robert Lee to Carter Lee, April 1842, LFDA.

"I shall make . . ." Robert Lee to Carter Lee, March 18, 1848, LFDA.

"I am waiting . . ." Robert Lee to Andrew Talcott, February 2, 1837, quoted in Pryor, *Reading the Man*, 188.

"like a ripe pear" Same as above.

"I do not know . . ." Robert Lee to Mary Lee, quoted in Pryor, *Reading the Man*, 182.

"has become so jealous . . ." Robert Lee to Mary Lee, January 18, 1846, quoted in R. E. Lee Jr., 7.

"My thoughts are engrossed . . ." Robert Lee to Markie Williams, in Lee, *To Markie*, 26.

CHAPTER SIX: WAR WITH MEXICO

"I wish to assure you . . ." Robert Lee to Mary Lee, April 18, 1847, complete letter in Pryor, *Reading the Man*, 155–56.

"gentle Annie" / "more in want of aid . . ." Lee's will, quoted in Coulling, 17.

"fanatical intolerance" Quoted in Time-Life Books, *The Spanish West*, 197–200.

"of extending slavery . . ." Massachusetts legislature, quoted in McPherson, 51.

"better satisfied . . ." Robert Lee to Mary Lee, May 12, 1846, quoted in Pryor, *Reading the Man*, 158.

"distinction & honour" Robert Lee to Mary Lee, December 25, 1846, quoted in Pryor, *Reading the Man*, 170.

"well-weighed words" / "his own services . . ." Lt. Isaac Ingalls Stevens, quoted in Pryor, *Reading the Man*, 161.

"the very best soldier . . ." Winfield Scott, quoted in Pryor, *Reading the Man*, 161.

"so beautiful in their flight . . ." Robert Lee to Mary Lee, quoted in Stern, 78.

"I . . . am at a loss . . ." Same as above.

"my heart bled . . ." Same as above.

"It was a beautiful operation . . ." Robert Lee to Mary Lee, April 18, 1847, entire letter in Pryor, *Reading the Man*, 155–56.

"the greatest feat . . ." Winfield Scott, quoted in Stern, 83.

"tantalizing" Robert Lee to Mary Lee, December 7, 1846, quoted in Pryor, *Reading the Man*, 167.

"good Santa Claus . . ." Robert Lee to sons Custis and Rooney Lee, December 24, 1846, quoted in Coulling, 19.

"Off Lobos" / "The surf . . ." / "The fish . . ." Robert Lee to Dear Major (G. W. Custis), February 28, 1847, LFDA.

"It is a beautiful country . . ." Robert Lee, quoted in Pryor, *Reading the Man*, 168.

"free opinions . . ." Same as above.

"Here I am once again . . ." Robert Lee to Smith Lee, June 30, 1848, quoted in R. E. Lee Jr., 4.

CHAPTER SEVEN: "HERE WORKING FOR MY COUNTRY" PART II

"I can advise . . ." Robert Lee to Markie Williams, September 16, 1853, in Lee, *To Markie*, 37.

"I learn with much regret . . ." Robert Lee, quoted in Stern, 89.

"perfectly enormous" Agnes Lee, July 20, 1853, quoted in deButts, editor, *Journal of Agnes Lee*, 18.

"my precious Arlington" Agnes Lee, August 26, 1853, quoted in Coulling, 21.

"200 demerits . . ." Robert Lee, quoted in Pappas, 289.

"We always have a no. of cadets . . ." Agnes Lee, February 9, 1854, quoted in deButts, editor, *Journal of Agnes Lee*, 32.

"I must sit up . . ." Same as above.

"I do not know what . . ." Robert Lee to Annie Lee, February 25, 1853, quoted in Robert E. Lee, Jr., 15.

"We know almost all . . ." Agnes Lee, February 9, 1854, quoted in deButts, editor, *Journal of Agnes Lee*, 33.

"the greatest lady's man" Same as above.

"a perfect bore" Annie Lee to Helen Bratt, 1855, quoted in Coulling, 44.

"had a good many too . . ." Agnes Lee, March 11, 1855, quoted in deButts, editor, *Journal of Agnes Lee*, 47.

"stretched out . . ." Mary Lee, quoted in Pappas, 292.

"carried to such an extent" Edward Hartz, February 17, 1853, quoted in Pryor, *Reading the Man*, 217.

"what is granted to one . . ." Robert Lee, quoted in Pappas, 290.

"master their Course . . ." Same as above.

"I hope not many" Robert Lee to Markie Williams, in Lee, *To Markie*, 40.

"I fear we shall lose . . ." Robert Lee to Rooney Lee, June 15, 1853, LFDA.

"Two nice lads too . . ." Same as above.

"but to my great satisfaction . . ." Agnes Lee, June 18, 1854, quoted in deButts, editor, *Journal of Agnes Lee*, 37.

"The blow was so sudden . . ." Robert Lee to Markie Williams, in Lee, *To Markie*, 31.

"We are all in the hands . . ." Robert Lee to Mary Lee, September 1, 1856, LFDA.

"I enjoyed the Mountains . . ." / "The views were magnificent . . ." / "How thankless . . ." Robert Lee to Mary Lee, August 4, 1861, LFDA.

"He is now in Texas . . ." Agnes Lee, March 16, 1856, quoted in deButts, editor, *Journal of Agnes Lee*, 77.

"humanize" / "more hideous . . ." Robert Lee to Mary Lee, April 12, 1856, LFDA.

"a world of trouble" / "they are not worth it" Robert Lee to Mary Lee, August 28, 1856, LFDA.

"wandering over the plains" Robert Lee to Custis Lee, May 30, 1859, quoted in Pryor, *Reading the Man*, 248.

"chastised them severely" / "It is a distressing state . . ." Robert Lee to Mary Lee, January 24, 1857, LFDA.

"glad of it, & only wish . . ." Robert Lee to Major Earl Van Dorn, 1860, quoted in Fellman, 61.

"The Sun was fiery hot . . ." Robert Lee to Mary Lee, August 4, 1856, LFDA.

"I know it is useless . . ." Robert Lee to Annie Lee, February 22, 1860, entire letter in Pryor, *Reading the Man*, 242.

"I almost dread . . ." Mary Lee, February 19, 1857, quoted in Nelligan, 337.

"dearest Mary . . ." Robert Lee to Mary Lee, December 20, 1856, LFDA.

"but he should conceal . . ." Robert Lee to Cousin Anna, quoted in Pryor, *Reading the Man*, 252.

"God knows . . ." / "I do not know . . ." Robert Lee to Edward Lee Childe, November 1, 1856, LFDA.

"We are now assured . . ." Robert Lee to Mary Lee, December 27, 1856, LFDA.

"Are we to be chastised . . ." / "our Southern masters" William Cullen Bryant, quoted in McPherson, 150.

"The vulgar Abolitionists . . ." / "they must be . . ." *Richmond Enquirer*, June 9, 1856, quoted in McPherson, 151.

"much pleased with . . ." Robert Lee to Mary Lee, December 27, 1856, LFDA.

"interfere with & change . . ." / "evil" / "unlawful" / "irresponsible" Same as above.

"He has left me . . ." Robert Lee to Custis Lee, July 2, 1859, quoted in Fellman, 67.

CHAPTER EIGHT: TROUBLE WITH "THE PEOPLE"

"Slavery as an institution . . ." Robert Lee to Mary Lee, December 27, 1856, LFDA.

"sad, suffering & sick" / "kindness & affection" Robert Lee, quoted in Nelligan, 344.

"Negro property" G. W. Custis, quoted in Nelligan, 315.

"comfortable homes . . ." / "And truly in many . . ." Markie Williams (quoting G. W. Custis), quoted in Pryor, *Reading the Man*, 267.

"I may own" Quoted in Pryor, *Reading the Man*, 262.

"kind friends" Mary Lee to W. G. Webster, February 17, 1858, quoted in Fellman, 71.

"cares and trouble" Mary Lee, quoted in Pryor, *Reading the Man*, 262.

"ingratitude & bad conduct" Mary's diary, May 1, 1858, quoted in Pryor, *Reading the Man*, 264.

"disposed of . . . to the best advantage" Robert Lee to Mr. Winston, quoted in Nolan, 10.

"all the little Ebony bipeds . . ." Robert Lee to Carter Lee, May 2, 1836, LFDA.

"considerate & kind . . ." / "make them do their duty" Robert Lee to Edward Turner, February 13, 1858, LFDA.

"The painful discipline . . ." Robert Lee to Mary Lee, December 27, 1856, LFDA.

"two thousand years . . ." Same as above.

"trouble with some of the people" / "Reuben, Parks & Edward . . ." / "They resisted . . ." Robert Lee to Rooney Lee, May 30, 1858, quoted in Pryor, *Reading the Man*, 266.

"tampering with the servants . . ." Mary Lee to W. G. Webster, February 17, 1858, quoted in Pryor, *Reading the Man*, 268.

"If he means well . . ." Robert Lee to Mary Lee, December 27, 1856, LFDA.

"Not satisfied . . ." Wesley Norris, *National Anti-Slavery Standard*, April 14, 1866, LFDA.

"The *N.Y. Tribune* . . ." Robert Lee to Custis Lee, July 2, 1859, quoted in Fellman, 67.

"the most villainous attacks . . ." Mary Lee to Elizabeth Stiles, February 9, 1861, LFDA.

"not a word of truth . . ." / "bad treatment" Robert Lee to E. S. Quick, March 1, 1866, quoted in Fellman, 67.

CHAPTER NINE: "I SHALL MOURN FOR MY COUNTRY"

"I Shall Mourn For My Country" Robert Lee to Rooney Lee, January 29, 1861, LFDA.

"I only see . . ." Robert Lee to Markie Williams, January 22, 1861, in Lee, *To Markie*, 58.

"they shall be kept in safety" Robert Lee to John Brown, October 19, 1859, Lee's letter to Brown.

"the attempt of a fanatic . . ." Robert Lee, quoted in Pryor, *Reading the Man*, 282.

"the crimes of this guilty land . . ." John Brown, quoted on National Park Service website.

"'Poor fly . . .'" Robert Lee to nephew Henry Lee, December 6, 1859, LFDA.

"she was as dear . . ." / "affectionate nature" / "atractive manners" Robert Lee to Carter Lee, February 20, 1864, LFDA.

"I succeed badly" Robert Lee, quoted in Pryor, *Reading the Man*, 262.

"I believe that the South . . ." Robert Lee to Markie Williams, January 22, 1861, in Lee, *To Markie*, 59.

"The South . . . has been aggrieved . . ." Robert Lee to Rooney Lee, January 29, 1861, LFDA.

"I feel the aggression" Same as above.

"the equal rights . . ." Robert Lee to Custis Lee, December 14, 1860, quoted in Nolan, 32.

"Ours are the institutions . . ." Speech of William Yancey, 1860, quoted in McPherson, 215.

"Black Republican" *Richmond Semi-Weekly Examiner*, Novmber 9, 1860, quoted in McPherson, 232.

"If Judge Douglas . . ." Robert Lee to Major Earl Van Dorn, quoted in Fellman, 82.

"a party founded . . ." *Richmond Semi-Weekly Examiner*, November 9, 1860, quoted in McPherson, 232.

"ought to be cheerfully . . ." Robert Lee to Custis Lee, December 14, 1860, quoted in Fellman, 84.

"Secession is nothing but . . ." Robert Lee to Rooney Lee, January 29, 1861, LFDA.

"denies the right of property . . ." Mississippi Declaration of Causes.

"our patriot fathers" / "God alone can save us . . ." Robert Lee to Markie Williams, January 22, 1861, in Lee, *To Markie*, 58.

"no rights & privileges . . ." Mary Lee to Elizabeth Stiles, February 9, 1861, LFDA.

"if they will not join them" Robert Lee to Custis Lee, December 14, 1860, quoted in Fellman, 81.

"While I wish to . . ." Same as above.

"maintained by swords . . ." Robert Lee to Rooney Lee, January 29, 1861, LFDA.

"If a disruption takes place . . ." Robert Lee to Markie Williams, in Lee, *To Markie*, 58.

"the recognition of political equality . . ." Texas Declaration of Causes.

"upon the great truth . . ." Alexander Stephens, "Cornerstone Speech."

"between a state of . . ." Robert Lee to Mary Lee, February 23, 1861, quoted in Fellman, 86.

"May God spare us . . ." Same as above, 87.

"I must try & be patient . . ." Same as above.

"hold, occupy and possess . . ." Abraham Lincoln, First Inaugural Address, March 4, 1861.

"You can have . . ." / "You have no oath . . ." / "The mystic chords . . ." Same as above.

"was a determined man . . ." Robert Lee, quoted in Pryor, "Thou Knowest Not," 289.

"perverted . . ." / "not only to the injury . . ." Virginia Secession Ordinance.

"worn and harassed" Daughter Mary Custis Lee, quoted in Pryor, "Thou Knowest Not," 289.

"could not conscientiously perform" Robert Lee to Smith Lee, April 20, 1861, LFDA.

"under orders" Same as above.

"the struggle it has cost me . . ." Robert Lee to Winfield Scott, April 20, 1861, LFDA.

"I suppose you all think . . ." Daughter Mary Custis Lee, quoted in Pryor, "Thou Knowest Not," 290.

"a conservative, or 'Union' family" Same as above.

"D'ont mention Robert Lee's name . . ." Winfield Scott, quoted in Pryor, "Thou Knowest Not," 291.

"With all my devotion . . ." Robert Lee to Anne Lee Marshall, April 20, 1861, LFDA.

"I know you will blame me . . ." Same as above.

"to treat with Traitors" Elizabeth Blair Lee, quoted in Pryor, *Reading the Man*, 292.

"I am willing . . ." Robert Lee to Carter Lee, March 14, 1862, LFDA.

Chapter Ten: The First Year

"The Confederate States . . ." Robert Lee to Andrew Magrath, December 24, 1861, LFDA.

"Where are our ranks . . ." Robert Lee to Mary Lee, April 30, 1861, LFDA.

"could scarcely be endured" Mary Lee quoted in deButts, "Mary Custis Lee's 'Reminiscences,'" 315.

"I grieve at the necessity . . ." / "Be content . . ." Robert Lee to Mary Lee, May 8, 1861, quoted in Nelligan, 392.

"This is a lovely morning . . ." Mary Lee to Robert Lee, May 9, 1861, LFDA.

"You had better Complete . . ." Robert Lee to Mary Lee, May 11, 1861, LFDA.

"I would not stir . . ." Mary Lee to Mildred Lee, May 5, 1861, quoted in Nelligan, 392.

"on your return . . ." General Irvin McDowell to Mary Lee, May 30, 1861, LFDA.

"Captured from Arlington" Quoted in R. E. Lee Jr., 337.

"Dear A----" Robert Lee to Markie Williams, in Lee, *To Markie*, 42–43.

"any other place . . ." Same as above.

"wiped from the earth . . ." Robert Lee to one of his daughters, December 25, 1861, quoted in Nelligan, 409.

"degraded" / "those who revel . . ." Same as above.

"not been grateful . . ." Robert Lee to Mary Lee, May 25, 1861, quoted in R. E. Lee Jr., 32.

"My commission in Virginia . . ." Robert Lee to Jefferson Davis, quoted in Davis, 293.

"constant instruction & discipline" Robert Lee to Commanders of Va. Regiments, quoted in Fellman, 101.

"rigid discipline & obedience to orders" Robert Lee to Col. George H. Terrett, May 10, 1861, quoted in Fellman, 102.

"Petty jealousies . . ." / "criminal and contemptible" Robert Lee to Captain Payton, August 19, 1861, quoted in Fellman, 103.

"I am pained . . ." Robert Lee to Mary Lee, September 17, 1861, LFDA.

"I am very anxious . . ." Robert Lee to Mary Lee, July 12, 1861, LFDA.

"broken down a little" Same as above.

"mortified at my absence" Robert Lee to Mary Lee, July 27, 1861, LFDA.

"supposed him insane" Robert Lee to Mary Lee, August 4, 1861, LFDA.

"calmed down amazingly" Robert Lee to Jefferson Davis, June 3, 1862, LFDA.

"regret & mortification" Robert Lee to Mary Lee, September 17, 1861, LFDA.

"another forlorn hope expedition . . ." Robert Lee to Mildred Lee, November 15, 1861, LFDA.

"I am aware . . ." Robert Lee to General Samuel Cooper, January 8, 1862, quoted in Fellman, 106.

"energy & activity" / "same selfishness . . ." Robert Lee to Custis Lee, May 23, 1862, quoted in Fellman, 108.

"the necessity of endurance . . ." Robert Lee to Mary Lee, May 23, 1862, quoted in Fellman, 108.

"I tremble to think . . ." Robert Lee to Andrew Magrath, December 24, 1861, LFDA.

"I am dreadfully disappointed . . ." Robert Lee to Custis Lee, December 29, 1861, LFDA.

"but are willing . . ." Robert Lee to Mary Lee, December 22, 1861, LFDA.

"the whole country . . ." / "humbled & taught . . ." Robert Lee to Mary Lee, February 8, 1862, LFDA.

"but the lower . . ." Robert Lee to Carter Lee, March 14, 1862, LFDA.

"He never gets any credit . . ." Mary Lee to Eliza Stiles, March 8, 1862, LFDA.

"I hope our Son . . ." Robert Lee to Mary Lee, March 15, 1862, LFDA.

"in the hands of the enemy . . ." Robert Lee to Agnes Lee, May 29, 1862, quoted in Coulling, 103.

CHAPTER ELEVEN: "VALOUR FORTITUDE & BOLDNESS"

"Our people are opposed . . ." Robert Lee to Jefferson Davis, June 5, 1862, complete letter in Pryor, *Reading the Man*, 317–18.

"Our position requires . . ." Robert Lee to Jefferson Davis, June 5, 1862, quoted in Davis, 297.

"I shall feel obliged . . ." Same as above.

"TOO cautious . . ." George McClellan to Abraham Lincoln, quoted in Reardon, 312.

"feverish and excited" Robert Lee to Carter Lee, March 14, 1862, LFDA.

"Now that Pa . . ." Rooney Lee to Charlotte Lee, June 3, 1862, LFDA.

"valour fortitude & boldness" Robert Lee to Jefferson Davis, June 5, 1862, complete letter in Pryor, *Reading the Man*, 317–18.

"I have heard with great delight . . ." Robert Lee to Mary Lee, June 10, 1862, LFDA.

"the Staff of my right hand" Robert Lee, quoted in Reardon, 326.

"I fear all was not done . . ." Robert Lee to Jefferson Davis, quoted in Davis, 298.

"imbued every man . . ." Quoted in Pryor, *Reading the Man*, 323.

"our so-called *timid*? . . ." Walter Taylor, August 30, 1862, *Wartime Letters*, 41.

"Well, my man . . ." / "Why, General, don't . . ." / "much amused at . . ." Rob
    Lee, in R. E. Lee Jr., 77.

"This army achieved . . ." Robert Lee to Jefferson Davis, August 30, 1862, LFDA.

"change the character . . ." Lee to Davis, June 5, 1862, complete letter in Pryor,
    Reading the Man, 317.

CHAPTER TWELVE: "WE CANNOT AFFORD TO BE IDLE"

"Hark! . . ." From "Fredericksburg," a poem by Thomas Bailey Aldrich, in
    Negri, 32.

"cowards of the army" Robert Lee to Jefferson Davis, September 7, 1862,
    LFDA.

"Still, we cannot afford . . ." Robert Lee to Jefferson Davis, September 3, 1862,
    LFDA.

"which is a great comfort" Robert Lee to Mary Lee, October 12, 1862, LFDA.

"gaunt starvation . . ." Mary Bedinger Mitchell, quoted in McPherson, 535.

"the groans & hisses . . ." Walter Taylor, September 28, 1862, *Wartime Letters*,
    46.

"all persons held . . ." / "shall then be in . . ." Abraham Lincoln, January 1,
    1863, Emancipation Proclamation.

"is doing nothing . . ." Rob Lee to Mary Lee, October 30, 1862, LFDA.

"Pa is looking . . ." Rob Lee to Mildred Lee, November 26, 1862, LFDA.

"I do not like your establishing . . ." Robert Lee to Mary Lee, September 29,
    1862, LFDA.

"O Mildred . . ." Agnes Lee to Mildred Lee, October 20, 1862, LFDA.

"My darling Annie . . ." Mary Lee to her daughter Mary, quoted in Pryor,
    Reading the Man, 365.

"overcome with grief . . ." Walter Taylor, *Four Years*, 76.

"I Cannot express . . ." Robert Lee to Mary Lee, October 26, 1862, LFDA.

"In the quiet hours . . ." Robert Lee to Daughter, quoted in R. E. Lee Jr., 80.

"picked up on the last battle field . . ." Robert Lee to Mary Lee, November 22,
    1862, LFDA.

"It was a pitious sight . . ." Same as above.

"as glorious as it is terrible" Walter Taylor, *Four Years*, 80.

"They suffered heavily . . ." Robert Lee to Mary Lee, December 16, 1862, LFDA.

"to liberate all of them" Robert Lee to Mary Lee, December 7, 1862, LFDA.

"fond of his blankets" / "I hope he will . . ." / "& get in the service . . ." Same as above.

"can be furnished . . ." Robert Lee to Mary Lee, December 21, 1862, LFDA.

"Any who wish to leave . . ." / "The men could . . ." Same as above.

"to do what is right . . ." Same as above.

"to close the whole affair . . ." Same as above.

"are already free" Same as above.

"at the death of every one . . ." Robert Lee to Mary Lee, December 25, 1862, LFDA.

"Oh if our people . . ." Same as above.

"that little child . . ." Lee to Mary, December 16, 1862, LFDA.

"What a cruel thing is war . . ." Lee to Mary, December 25, 1862, LFDA.

CHAPTER THIRTEEN: VICTORY AND DEFEAT

"I am more than usually . . ." Robert Lee to James Seddon, January 26, 1863, LFDA.

"After that is exhausted . . ." Robert Lee to James Seddon, January 26, 1863, LFDA.

"and furnish what . . ." Same as above.

"I do not think it is enough . . ." Robert Lee to James Seddon, March 27, 1863, LFDA.

"more bountifully supplied . . ." Same as above.

"I think this army deserves . . ." Same as above.

"a terrible expenditure . . ." Robert Lee to James Seddon, January 10, 1863, LFDA.

"diminished and exhausted troops" Same as above.

"be allowed to evade his duty" Same as above.

"Old age & sorrow . . ." Robert Lee to Mary Lee, March 9, 1863, LFDA.

"I am so cross . . ." Robert Lee to Agnes Lee, February 6, 1863, LFDA.

"is obliged to do something . . ." Same as above.

"some harshness of manner" Walter Taylor, *Four Years*, 77.

"snapping at his ear" Edward Porter Alexander, quoted in Fellman, 116.

"He is so *unappreciative* . . ." Walter Taylor, August 8, 1863, *Wartime Letters*, 69.

"a cheerful fire" Walter Taylor, November 7, 1864, 203.

"was entirely *too* pleasant . . ." Same as above.

"If we can baffle them . . ." Robert Lee to Mary Lee, April 19, 1863, LFDA.

"Our enemy must . . ." Hooker's order to his troops, quoted in McPherson, 639.

"the only man . . ." Stonewall Jackson, quoted in R. E. Lee Jr., 95.

"Ah: don't talk about it . . ." Reported by Captain R. E. Wilbourn, quoted in Krick, 370.

"General: It is necessary . . ." Robert Lee to General J. E. B. Stuart, May 3, 1863, LFDA.

"with deep grief" / "But while we mourn . . ." Lee General Orders No. 61, May 11, 1863, LFDA.

"Any victory would . . ." Robert Lee to Mary Lee, May 11, 1863, LFDA.

"is fearful odds" Robert Lee to Carter Lee, May 24, 1863, LFDA.

"Our ranks are . . ." Same as above.

"the spirit of our enemies . . ." Robert Lee to Mary Lee, June 14, 1863, LFDA.

"atrocious outrage" Robert Lee to Markie Williams, in Lee, *To Markie*, 71.

"young cousin . . ." Mary Lee, quoted in deButts, "Mary Custis Lee's 'Reminiscences,'" 315.

"I do not recall . . ." Quoted in Coulling, 126.

"As some good is . . ." Robert Lee to Charlotte Wickham Lee, June 11, 1863, in R. E. Lee Jr., 98.

"If we can defeat . . ." Robert Lee to Jefferson Davis, July 6, 1864, quoted in Pryor, *Reading the Man*, 347–48.

"fight him when opportunity offers" Abraham Lincoln to Joseph Hooker, quoted in McPherson, 651.

"The commanding general considers . . ." Lee General Orders No. 73, June 27, 1863, LFDA.

"Making use of the eyes of others" Robert Lee to Jefferson Davis, August 8, 1863, LFDA.

"if he found it practicable" Lee's order to Ewell, July 1, 1863, in Nolan, "R. E. Lee and July 1 at Gettysburg," 493.

"If the enemy is . . ." Robert Lee to James Longstreet, quoted in Longstreet, 388–89.

"under a subdued excitement . . ." Same as above.

"Never mind, General . . ." Robert Lee, quoted in Fellman, 143.

"The charm of . . ." George Templeton Strong diary, quoted in McPherson, 664.

"That rebel army fights . . ." Montgomery Meigs, quoted in Pryor, *Reading the Man*, 358.

"I have heard with great grief . . ." Robert Lee to Mary Lee, July 7, 1863, LFDA.

"We must expect reverses . . ." / "The general remedy . . ." / "take measures . . ." / "I do not know . . ." Robert Lee to Jefferson Davis, August 8, 1863, LFDA.

"demand an impossibility" Jefferson Davis to Robert Lee, August 11, 1863, LFDA.

CHAPTER FOURTEEN: "A MERE QUESTION OF TIME"

"I . . . feel the growing . . ." Robert Lee to Jefferson Davis, August 8, 1863, LFDA.

"I want you badly . . ." Robert Lee to James Longstreet, quoted in Trudeau, 524.

"causes me to weep . . ." Robert Lee to Charlotte Wickham Lee, July 26, 1863, quoted in Fellman, 183.

"the anguish her death will cause . . ." Robert Lee to Mary Lee, December 27, 1863, LFDA.

"has caused an aching . . ." Robert Lee to Carter Lee, February 20, 1864, LFDA.

"Our enemies are very strong . . ." Robert Lee to Elizabeth Stiles, November 25, 1863, LFDA.

"grievous punishment" Same as above.

"every exertion . . ." Robert Lee to Jefferson Davis, April 12, 1864, quoted in R. E. Lee Jr., 123.

"*devoted to necessary* wants" Same as above.

"redeem themselves . . ." / "past crimes" Robert Lee, Special Orders No. 96 to HD Army of Northern Va., April 7, 1864, LFDA.

"demands all our thoughts . . ." Robert Lee to Rooney Lee, April 14, 1864, LFDA.

"every man at his place . . ." Same as above.

"Peace can be had . . ." Edwin M. Stanton, quoted in Gallagher, "Another Look," 278.

"What a position . . ." Catherine Ann Devereux Edmondston, June 11, 1864, quoted in Gallagher, "Another Look," 279.

"and many persons . . ." Unknown South Carolinian, quoted in Gallagher, "Another Look," 280.

"now opposed [by] a General . . ." *Charleston Daily Courier*, quoted in Gallagher, "Another Look," 279.

"We can alarm & embarrass . . ." Robert Lee to Jefferson Davis, February 3, 1864, quoted in Trudeau, 524.

"We must strike fast & strong . . ." Robert Lee to Rooney Lee, April 24, 1864, LFDA.

"Wherever Lee goes . . ." Ulysses Grant to George Meade, quoted in McPherson, 722.

"It never occurred to me . . ." / "Would bring us . . ." Rob Lee, in R. E. Lee Jr., 124.

"We have got to whip them . . ." Walter Taylor, April 3, 1864, *Wartime Letters*, 148.

"If the tyrant . . ." Georgia newspaper, quoted in McPherson, 721.

"General Lee, go . . ." Stern, 191.

"hissing fire . . ." Walter Taylor, *Fours Years*, 131.

"terrible record . . ." / "such a brute" / "holds on longer . . ." Walter Taylor, May 23, 1864, *Wartime Letters*, 162.

"A more zealous . . ." Robert Lee to Mary Lee, May 16, 1864, LFDA.

"superior in weight . . ." Robert Lee to Jefferson Davis, May 18, 1864, LFDA.

"The importance of this campaign . . ." Same as above.

"It is the more aggravating . . ." Lee to Mary, May 29, 1864, LFDA.

"the head and front . . ." Jubal Early, quoted in R. E. Lee Jr., 127.

"full of fight . . ." Charles Blackford, quoted in Blackford, 249.

"I think Grant . . ." General Meade to his wife, quoted in McPherson, 735.

"We must destroy this army . . ." / "If he gets there . . ." Robert Lee to Jubal
    Early, quoted in Trudeau, 537.

CHAPTER FIFTEEN: SIEGE AND SURRENDER

"Our numbers are daily . . ." Robert Lee to James Seddon, August 23, 1864,
    LFDA.

"The enemy has a strong . . ." Robert Lee to Jefferson Davis, June 21, 1864, LFDA.

"No doubt the majority . . ." Walter Taylor, August 1, 1864, *Wartime Letters*,
    179.

"unreasonable and provoking" Walter Taylor, August 15, 1864, *Wartime
    Letters*, 182.

"Do you recollect . . ." Robert Lee to Mary Lee, June 30, 1864, LFDA.

"hard to maintain . . ." Charles Blackford, quoted in Blackford, 272.

"The struggle now . . ." Robert Lee, quoted in R. E. Lee Jr., 142.

"the consequences . . ." Robert Lee to James Seddon, August 23, 1864, LFDA.

"There must be more men . . ." Same as above.

"cowardly conduct" Robert Lee, General Orders (no number), October 1864,
    LFDA.

"some brave officers . . ." Same as above.

"is a painful tedious process . . ." Robert Lee to Jefferson Davis, August 13,
    1864, LFDA.

"the same as white soldiers?" Ulysses Grant to Robert Lee, October 2, 1864,
    LFDA.

"all captured soldiers . . ." / "negroes belonging . . ." / "cannot be returned . . ."
    Robert Lee to Ulysses Grant, October 3, 1864, LFDA.

"This being denied . . ." Ulysses Grant to Robert Lee, October 2/3, 1864,
    quoted in Fellman, 206.

"must lead to peace . . ." *Charlotte Mercury*, quoted in McPherson, 772.

"*and prevent military success* . . ." Same as above.

"We must . . . make up our minds . . ." / "to cleanse us . . ." Robert Lee to
    Mary Lee, November 12, 1864, quoted in Fellman, 187.

"enjoying ice water . . ." Robert Lee to Mary Lee, January 29, 1865, LFDA.

"acted so nobly . . ." / "will bring us calamity" Robert Lee to J. C.
    Breckinridge, February 24 and 28, 1865, quoted in Fellman, 176–77.

"make headway against . . ." Robert Lee to Secretary of War, quoted in Fellman, 188.

"at present in this Country" / "the best that can exist . . ." Lee to Andrew Hunter, January 11, 1865, LFDA.

"If slaves will make good soldiers . . ." Howell Cobb (Georgia politician), January 8, 1865, quoted in Fellman, 213.

"access to a large . . ." Robert Lee to Andrew Hunter, January 11, 1865, LFDA.

"convert the able bodied . . ." Same as above.

"I think therefore . . ." Same as above.

"My own opinion . . ." Same as above.

"moral influence" / "our negroes" Same as above.

"It would disappoint . . ." Same as above.

"Every day's delay . . ." Same as above.

"I did not volunteer . . ." W. Albright, quoted in Fellman, 215.

"It makes me sad however . . ." Walter Taylor, February 16, 1865, in Taylor, *Wartime Letters*, 223–24.

"I pray we may not be overwhelmed . . ." / "will you remain . . ." / "who does not always . . ." Robert Lee to Mary Lee, February 21, 1865, LFDA.

"nothing untried . . ." Robert Lee to Ulysses Grant, quoted in Gallagher, *Appomattox Court House*, 30.

"bidding them do their duty . . ." Bettie Saunders, quoted in Taylor, *Wartime Letters*, 242.

"Tired and hungry . . ." / "It is now a race . . ." William M. Owen, quoted in Gallagher, *Appomattox Court House*, 52.

"to shift from myself . . ." Ulysses Grant to Robert Lee, April 7, 1865, quoted in Marshall, 254.

"bushwhacking, the only . . ." Robert Lee to Edward Porter Alexander, quoted in Fellman, 224.

"If there is any hope . . ." Edward Porter Alexander, quoted in Gallagher, *Appomattox Court House*, 62.

"and I would rather . . ." Robert Lee, quoted in Gallagher, *Appomattox Court House*, 68.

"accompany my chief . . ." Walter Taylor, *Four Years*, 153.

"Let them surrender . . ." Abraham Lincoln to Ulysses Grant, quoted in
    Gallagher, *Appomattox Court House*, 41.
"I felt . . . sad . . ." Ulysses Grant, quoted in McPherson, 849–50.
"to yield to overwhelming . . ." Lee General Orders No. 9, quoted in R. E. Lee
    Jr., 153–54.
"avoid the useless sacrifice . . ." Same as above.

CHAPTER SIXTEEN: "THE COWARD LOOKS BACK"

"I shall be very sorry . . ." Robert Lee to Captain Matthew F. Maury,
    September 8, 1865, LFDA.
"How can I write it? . . ." Catherine Edmondston, quoted in Gallagher,
    "Another Look," 281.
"wish we were all dead . . ." A Florida woman, quoted in Gallagher, "Another
    Look," 281.
"We have all been very quiet . . ." Mary Lee to Lucy Ann Taylor, April 26,
    1865, LFDA.
"the courtesy of . . ." Same as above.
"the greatful hearts . . ." William H. Platt to Robert Lee, May 5, 1865, LFDA.
"tempted to think . . ." Mary Lee to "My dear Caroline," July 18, 1865, LFDA.
"for the misery . . ." Mary Lee, in deButts, "Mary Custis Lee's
    'Reminiscences,'" 313.
"savage cruelty" Mary Lee to Louisa Snowden, April 16, 1865, complete letter
    in Pryor, *Reading the Man*, 426–27.
"Future generations may . . ." / "We are all unsettled . . ." Same as above.
"sense of justice . . ." Thomas Cook to Robert Lee, April 23, 1865, LFDA.
"It is unfortunate . . ." *New York Herald*, April 29, 1865. (All quotes in this
    section are from Lee's interview with Thomas Cook.)
"up to the very door" Mary Lee, quoted in deButts, "Mary Custis Lee's
    'Reminiscences,'" 318.
"My heart will never . . ." Same as above, 321.
"some humble but quiet . . ." Robert Lee to Rooney Lee, July 29, 1865, LFDA.
"permitted by the victor" Robert Lee to Armistead L. Long, May 1865, quoted
    in Fellman, 228.

"conciliatory manner" Robert Lee to John Letcher, August 28, 1865, LFDA.

"I shall avoid no prosecution . . ." Robert Lee to Markie Williams, June 20, 1865, in Lee, *To Markie*, 62–63.

"I can do but little . . ." Same as above.

"The thought of abandoning . . ." Robert Lee to Matthew F. Maury, September 8, 1865, LFDA.

"all their support . . ." Robert Lee to Walter Taylor, quoted in Coulling, 149.

"The duty of its citizens . . ." Robert Lee to John Letcher, August 28, 1865, LFDA.

"give full scope . . ." Robert Lee to A. M. Keiley, September 4, 1865, quoted in Fellman, 276.

"I think it wiser . . ." Robert Lee to David McConaughy, August 6, 1869, LFDA.

"in this trying hour" Quoted in Pryor, *Reading the Man*, 435.

"little desire to recall . . ." Robert Lee to Edward A. Pollard, January 24, 1867, quoted in Fellman, 298.

"one of the most important . . ." Robert Lee to Rev. G. W. Leyburn, March 20, 1866, LFDA.

"an object of censure" / "injury" Robert Lee to Trustees of Washington College, August 24, 1865, LFDA.

"advantageous to the College . . ." Same as above.

"the arch traitor Lee" / "in more treason" Quoted in Crenshaw, 154.

"the bloodiest and guiltiest . . ." Theodore Tilton, quoted in Preston, 54–55.

"life is indeed gliding away . . ." Robert Lee to Mary Lee, October 9, 1865, quoted in R. E. Lee Jr., 189.

"You know the comfort he is to me," Robert Lee to Markie Williams, December 22, 1866, in Lee, *To Markie*, 74.

"the quiet and rest . . ." R. E. Lee Jr., 279.

"might be of service . . ." Robert Lee to Rooney Lee, October 30, 1865, quoted in Fellman, 229.

"The coward looks back . . ." Robert Lee to Rooney Lee, November 1, 1856, LFDA.

CHAPTER SEVENTEEN: "GENERAL LEE'S COLLEGE"

"We have but one rule here . . ." Robert Lee to an unnamed student, quoted in Fellman, 250.

"of prime importance . . ." Washington College Catalogues, 1869, quoted in
    Preston, 63.

"looking forward to . . ." Same as above, 64.

"practical chemistry" / "experimental philosophy" / "applied mathematics"
    Quoted in Preston, 62.

"the most important interest . . ." Robert Lee to the Finance Committee of the
    Board of Trustees, January 8, 1869, quoted in Preston, 96.

"I think it afforded me . . ." Robert Lee to Mary Lee, March 27, 1863, LFDA.

"General Lee's College" E.L. Godkin, quotd in Preston, 67.

"hatred to the Union" *Chicago Daily Tribune*, April 7, 1868, quoted in
    Preston, 75.

"the blood of tens of thousands . . ." Theodore Tilton, March 12, 1868, quoted
    in Preston, 75.

"You should not force . . ." Robert Lee, quoted in Fellman, 250.

"I wished he had . . ." / "blubbering like a baby" A student at Washington
    College, quoted in Pryor, *Reading the Man*, 439.

"I think every boy . . ." Robert Lee to Mrs. Carter, April 2, 1869, quoted in
    Fellman, 255.

"I hope this severe lesson . . ." Robert Lee to Lewis Parsons, March 8, 1867,
    quoted in Fellman, 256.

"very busy, and full of work" Robert Lee to Rooney Lee, October 19, 1868,
    quoted in R. E. Lee Jr., 329.

"We are all as usual . . ." Robert Lee to Rooney Lee, December 2, 1869,
    quoted in R. E. Lee Jr., 374.

"A farmer's motto . . ." Robert Lee to Rob Lee, March 12, 1868, quoted in R.
    E. Lee Jr., 305.

"I can help you . . ." Robert Lee to Rob Lee, October 26, 1867, quoted in R. E.
    Lee Jr., 282.

"becoming in a Virginia girl . . ." / " rational amusements" Robert Lee to
    Mildred Lee, January 27, 1867, quoted in R. E. Lee Jr., 253.

"persuade some . . ." Robert Lee to Agnes Lee, March 28, 1868, quoted in R.
    E. Lee Jr., 309.

"To me he seems a Hero . . ." Mildred Lee diary, August 21, 1888, quoted in
    Fellman, 235.

"shone in his happiness" Robert Lee to Mary Lee, November 29, 1867, quoted in R. E. Lee Jr., 287.

"There was a great crowd . . ." William Wickham to Elizabeth Fry and Anna Leigh, December 4, 1867, LFDA.

"as his custom is" / "an air of sadness . . ." Same as above.

"gloomy night . . ." Robert Lee to Rooney Lee, December 21, 1867, quoted in R. E. Lee Jr., 293.

"a load of sorrow" Same as above.

"You know how agreeable . . ." Robert Lee to Mildred Lee, January 8, 1870, quoted in R. E. Lee Jr., 380–81.

"All the world may know . . ." *New York Times*, October 17, 1865, LFDA.

CHAPTER EIGHTEEN: "PEACE IS NOT RESTORED"

"Do you think . . ." Lee testifying before the Joint Committee on Reconstruction, February 17, 1866, LFDA.

"They hate us and despise us . . ." John Richard Dennett, April 1866, quoted in Kohlmetz, 551.

"although the freedman . . ." Carl Schurz, summer 1865, quoted in Kohlmetz, 551.

"for the action of President Johnson . . ." Robert Lee to Smith Lee, January 4, 1866, LFDA.

"excite the Radicals . . ." Same as above.

"I am considered now . . ." Robert Lee to Markie Williams, April 7, 1866, in Lee, *To Markie*, 68.

"How do the people . . ." Robert E. Lee's Testimony Before the Joint Committee on Reconstruction, February 17, 1866, LFDA. (All following questions and answers are from the same source.)

"all persons in their rights . . ." The Reconstruction Act of March 1867.

"of whatever race . . ." Same as above.

"declared by Congress . . ." Same as above.

"all persons entitled . . ." Robert Lee to Judge Robert Ould, March 29, 1867, quoted in Fellman, 283–84.

"the South is to be placed . . ." Robert Lee to Edward Childe, January 16, 1868, LFDA.

"The purpose for which . . ." / "present policy" / "would have been tolerated . . ."
Same as above.

"The Conservatives . . ." Robert Lee to Edward Childe, January 5, 1867, LFDA.

"counterbalance the Conservative votes . . ." / "the party in power . . ." Robert
Lee to Edward Childe, January 16, 1868, LFDA.

"with all the dignity . . ." / "The certain fact . . ." Robert Lee to Edward Childe,
January 22, 1867, LFDA.

"every good in my power" Robert Lee to Rob Lee, March 12, 1868, quoted in
R. E. Lee Jr., 306.

"I have always observed . . ." Robert Lee, quoted in R. E. Lee Jr., 168.

"our material, social . . ." Robert Lee to Rob Lee, March 12, 1868, quoted in
R. E. Lee Jr., 306.

"stolen by a set . . ." Mary Lee to Benson Lossing, June 12, 1867, LFDA.

"no greater evil . . ." Same as above.

"their Northern friends . . ." Same as above.

"malignant enemies" / "The country that allows . . ." Mary Lee to Mrs. R. H.
Chilton, March 19, 1867, quoted in Fellman, 293.

"a candid statement . . ." September 8, 1868, White Sulphur Manifesto. (All
quotes in this section are from the same source.).

"The whole people of the South . . ." *Staunton Spectator*, September 8, 1868,
quoted in Rosecransheadquarters.org.

"honor and self-respect" Address of Lee, November 26, 1866, quoted in
Fellman, 259.

"commit outrages . . ." Same as above.

"every Northern man . . ." *Independent*, April 2, 1868, quoted in Preston, 86.

"Damn Yankee bitch . . ." Quoted in Pryor, *Reading the Man*, 454.

"none would countenance . . ." Robert Lee to J. B. Strickler, May 10, 1868,
quoted in Fellman, 261.

"disturb the public peace . . ." Robert Lee (Notice on Washington College
bulletin board), quoted in Preston, 82.

"universal amnesty and pardon . . ." President Johnson's universal amnesty.

"imposed disfranchisement . . ." Robert Lee to Edward Childe, February 16,
1869, LFDA.

"though I shall never see it" Same as above.

CHAPTER NINETEEN: "ONLY THE HERO OF A LOST CAUSE"

"The toils of his crowded . . ." Mary Lee to Letitia Burwell, November 15, 1870, LFDA.

"great weariness and depression" R. E. Lee Jr., 379.

"I take no pleasure . . ." Robert Lee to Edward Childe, July 10, 1868, LFDA.

"to visit my dear . . ." Robert Lee to Mildred Lee, March 21, 1870, quoted in R. E. Lee Jr., 385.

"mournful, yet soothing . . ." Robert Lee to Mary Lee, April 2, 1870, quoted in R. E. Lee Jr., 390.

"Lee! Lee!" Agnes Lee to her mother, April 3, 1870, quoted in R. E. Lee Jr., 392.

"He is mightily . . ." Same as above.

"I do not think travelling . . ." Robert Lee to Mary Lee, April 17, 1870, quoted in R. E. Lee Jr., 395.

"die of eating" Agnes Lee to her mother, April 3, 1870, quoted in R. E. Lee Jr., 392.

"the affection and feeling . . ." Same as above, 392.

"Papa has borne . . ." Same as above, 394.

"Agnes threatens . . ." Robert Lee to Mildred Lee, May 7, 1870, quoted in R. E. Lee Jr., 403.

"the most pleasant part . . ." Robert Lee to Edward Childe, June 3, 1870, LFDA.

"the depression . . ." Robert Lee to Edward Childe, June 3, 1870, LFDA.

"He kept his suffering . . ." Mildred Lee, quoted in Pryor, *Reading the Man*, 459.

"to remove a weakness . . ." Lee in conversation with William Allan, professor at Washington College, 1868, in Allan, 12.

"the imperfect, halting way" / "gave victory . . ." Same as above, 14.

"the opinion which posterity . . ." Lee to his cousin Cassius Lee, June 6, 1870, LFDA.

"for the maintenance . . ." Same as above.

"I had no other guide . . ." Robert Lee to George Jones, March 22, 1869, quoted in Fellman, 282.

"a true history . . ." Robert Lee to his cousin Cassius Lee, June 6, 1870, LFDA.

"expecting too much . . ." Robert Lee to Edward Childe, August 22, 1870, LFDA.

"You look very tired . . ." Mary Lee to Carter Lee, October 7, 1870, complete letter in Pryor, *Reading the Man*, 460–61.

"looked so beseechingly . . ." Mildred Lee, quoted in Pryor, *Reading the Man*, 464.

"he was so much worse . . ." / "& the struggles . . ." Mary Lee to Carter Lee, October 13, 1870, LFDA.

"In the midst . . ." Agnes Lee to "My Dear Lizzie," December 27, 1870, complete letter in Pryor, *Reading the Man*, 461.

"no one speaking . . ." William Nalle to his mother, October 16, 1870, LFDA.

"looked to be reduced . . ." Same as above.

"The mournful tidings . . ." *Charleston Daily News*.

"so rarely gifted . . ." *New York Times* Obituary, LFDA.

"*A gallant foeman in the fight . . .*" "Robert E. Lee," a poem by Julia Ward Howe, in Negri, 2–3.

Epilogue: Myth Building

"Tell Hill he must . . ." / "Strike the tent" Quoted in R. E. Lee Jr., 439.

"bathed in the white light . . ." Fanny Downing, quoted in Nolan, 4–5.

"the sun as it rises and sets . . ." / "beyond description" Charles Francis Adams Jr., quoted in Pryor, *Reading the Man*, 467.

"sacred duty" / "pious work" Jubal Early Speech, in Gallagher, *Lee the Soldier*, 73.

"at the Confederate Capital . . ." Same as above, 73.

"renegade to their comrades . . ." Same as above, 72.

"a crime against the white . . ." UDC historian Mildred Rutherford, quoted in Cox, 107.

"truths of Confederate history" *A Measuring Rod*.

"all scholastic and library . . ." Same as above.

"Reject a book . . ." Same as above.

"instructed . . ." Kentucky chapter of UDC, quoted in Cox, 130.

"What was the cause . . ." *The Confederate Catechism*.

"be lifted to . . ." Woodrow Wilson, quoted in Connelly, p. 99.

"Perhaps no man . . ." Mary Williamson, *The Life of General Robert E. Lee*, quoted in Connelly, 113.

BIBLIOGRAPHY

Allan, William. "Allan; Memoranda of Conversation with Lee," in *Lee The Soldier*, edited by Gary W. Gallagher. Lincoln: University of Nebraska Press, 1996.

Armes, Ethel. *Stratford Hall: The Great House of the Lees*. Richmond, VA: Garrett and Massie, 1936.

Ayers, Edward L. "The Road to Disunion and War, Slavery, Economics, and Constitutional Ideals," in *Appomattox Court House*. Washington D.C.: Division of Publications, National Park Service Handbook, No. 160.

Blackford, Susan Leigh, and Charles Minor. *Letters from Lee's Army*. Lincoln: University of Nebraska Press, 1998.

Blight, David W. "Legacies and Memory: An America Transformed," in *Appomattox Court House*. Washington D.C.: Division of Publications, National Park Service Handbook, No. 160.

Brady, Patricia, editor. *George Washington's Beautiful Nelly: The Letters of Eleanor Parke Custis Lewis to Elizabeth Bordley Gibson, 1794–1851*. Columbia: University of South Carolina, 1991.

Connelly, Thomas L. *The Marble Man: Robert E. Lee and His Image in American Society*. New York: Alfred A. Knopf, 1977.

Coulling, Mary P. *The Lee Girls*. Winston-Salem, NC: John F. Blair, 1987.

Cox, Karen L. *Dixie's Daughters: The United Daughters of the Confederacy and the Preservation of Confederate Culture*. Gainesville: University Press of Florida, 2003.

Crenshaw, Ollinger. *General Lee's College*. New York: Random House, 1969.

Davis, William C. "Lee and Jefferson Davis," in *Lee the Soldier*, edited by Gary W. Gallagher. Lincoln: University of Nebraska Press, 1996.

deButts, Mary Custis Lee, editor. *Growing Up in the 1850s: The Journal of Agnes Lee*. Chapel Hill: University of North Carolina Press, 1984.

deButts, Robert E. Lee, Jr. "Lee in Love: Courtship and Correspondence in Antebellum Virginia." *Virginia Magazine of History and Biography*, Vol. 115, No. 4 (2007).

———. "Mary Custis Lee's 'Reminiscences of the War.'" *Virginia Magazine of History and Biography*, Vol. 109, No. 3 (2001).

Early, Jubal. "The Campaigns of Gen. Robert E. Lee: An Address by Lieut. General Jubal A. Early, before Washington and Lee University, January 19th, 1872," in *Lee the Soldier*, edited by Gary W. Gallagher. Lincoln: University of Nebraska Press, 1996.

Fellman, Michael. *The Making of Robert E. Lee*. New York: Random House, 2000.

"Funeral of Mrs. G. W. P. Custis and Death of General R. E. Lee, Described in Contemporary Letters." *Virginia Magazine of History and Biography*, Vol. 35, No. 1 (1927).

Gallagher, Gary W., editor. *Lee the Soldier*. Lincoln: University of Nebraska Press, 1996.

———. "From Petersburg to Appomattox: An End and a New Beginning," in *Appomattox Court House*. Washington D.C.: Division of Publications, National Park Service Handbook, No. 160.

———. "Another Look at the Generalship of R. E. Lee," in *Lee the Soldier*, edited by Gary W. Gallagher. Lincoln: University of Nebraska Press, 1996.

Kohlmetz, Ernest, editor. *The Study of American History, Volume 1*. Guilford, CT: Dushkin Publishing Group, 1974.

Krick, Robert K. "Lee at Chancellorsville," in *Lee the Soldier*, edited by Gary W. Gallagher. Lincoln: University of Nebraska Press, 1996.

Lee, Captain Robert Edward [Jr.]. *Recollections and Letters of Robert E. Lee*. New York: Dover, 2007. Originally published by Doubleday, Page & Co., New York, 1904.

Lee, Robert E. *"To Markie": The Letters of Robert E. Lee to Martha Custis Williams*, edited by Avery Craven. Cambridge, MA: Harvard University Press, 1934.

Longstreet, General James. "Lee in Pennsylvania," in *Lee the Soldier*, edited by Gary W. Gallagher. Lincoln: University of Nebraska Press, 1996.

Marshall, Charles. *An Aide-De-Camp of Lee*. Boston: Little, Brown, 1927.

May, Robert E. *The Southern Dream of a Caribbean Empire, 1854–1861*. Athens: University of Georgia Press, 1989.

McPherson, James. *Battle Cry of Freedom*. New York: Oxford University Press, 1988.

Negri, Paul, editor. *Civil War Poetry: An Anthology*. Mineola, NY: Dover Publications, 1997.

Nelligan, Murray H. *Arlington House: The Story of the Robert E. Lee Memorial*. Burke, VA: Chatelaine Press, 2005.

Nolan, Alan T. *Lee Considered*. Chapel Hill: University of North Carolina Press, 1991.

———. "Robert E. Lee and July 1 at Gettysburg," in *Lee the Soldier*, edited by Gary W. Gallagher. Lincoln: University of Nebraska Press, 1996.

Pappas, George S. *To The Point: The United States Military Academy, 1802–1902*. Westport, CT: Praeger, 1993.

Preston, Walter Creigh. *Lee: West Point and Lexington*. Yellow Springs, OH: Antioch Press, 1934.

Pryor, Elizabeth Brown. *Reading the Man: A Portrait of Robert E. Lee Through His Private Letters*. New York: Penguin Books, 2008.

———. "Thou Knowest Not the Time of Thy Visitation: A Newly Discovered Letter Reveals Robert E. Lee's Lonely Struggle with Disunion." *Virginia Magazine of History and Biography*, Vol. 119, No. 3 (2011).

Reardon, Carol. "From 'King of Spades' to 'First Captain of the Confederacy': R. E. Lee's First Six Weeks with the Army of Northern Virginia," in *Lee the Soldier*, edited by Gary W. Gallagher. Lincoln: University of Nebraska Press, 1996.

Rozear, Martin E., Wayne Massey, et al. "Robert E. Lee's Stroke." *Virginia Magazine of History and Biography*, Vol. 98, No. 2 (1990).

Schroeder, Patrick. *Thirty Myths About Lee's Surrender*. Lynchburg, VA: Schroeder Publications, 2016.

Schwarz, Philip J. *Twice Condemned: Slaves and the Criminal Laws of Virginia, 1705–1865*. Baton Rouge: Louisiana State University Press, 1988.

Seale, William. *A Guide to Historic Alexandria*. Alexandria, VA: Office of Historic Alexandria, 2000.

Stern, Philip Van Doren. *Robert E. Lee, the Man and the Soldier, A Pictorial Biography*. New York: Bonanza Books, 1963.

Taylor, Walter. *Four Years with General Lee*. Bloomington: Indiana University Press, 1996. Originally published 1877.

———. *Lee's Adjutant: The Wartime Letters of Colonel Walter Herron Taylor, 1862–1865*, edited by R. Lockwood Tower with John S. Belmont. Columbia: University of South Carolina Press, 1995.

Thomas, Emory. "The Lee Marriage," in *Intimate Strategies of the Civil War, Military Commanders and Their Wives*, edited by Carol K. Bleser and Lesley J. Gordon. New York: Oxford University Press, 2001.

Time-Life Books, *The Spanish West*. New York: Time Inc., 1976.

Trudeau, Noah Andre. "'A Mere Question of Time': Robert E. Lee from the Wilderness to Appomattox Court House," in *Lee the Soldier*, edited by Gary W. Gallagher. Lincoln: University of Nebraska Press, 1996.

Zimmer, Anne Carter. *The Robert E. Lee Family Cooking and Housekeeping Book*. Chapel Hill: University of North Carolina Press, 1997.

ONLINE RESOURCES

Lee Family Digital Archive, a vast collection of Lee family papers, letters, and information, from the 1700s to the present:

   leefamilyarchive.org/family-papers

Arlington House, The Robert E. Lee Memorial, National Park Service:

   nps.gov/arho/index.htm

For quick Civil War battle information, I used National Park Service sites and the American Battlefield Trust sites:

   civilwar.org/learn/civil-war/battles/antietam
   nps.gov/frsp/learn/historyculture/chist.htm
   civilwar.org/learn/civil-war/battles/wilderness
   nps.gov/pete/index.htm
   nps.gov/rich/learn/historyculture/cold-harbor.htm
   civilwar.org/learn/civil-war/battles/second-manassas
   nps.gov/apco/index.htm
   civilwar.org/learn/civil-war/battles/gettysburg
   nps.gov/hafe/index.htm

Harpers Ferry National Historical Park, John Brown's Raid
    nps.gov/articles/john-brown-raid.htm
    battlefields.org/learn/biographies/john-brown

Editorial on Lee's death, *Charleston Daily News*:
    rarenewspapers.com/view/596995>

Johnson's "universal amnesty and pardon":
    presidency.ucsb.edu/ws/?pid=72360>

The White Sulphur Springs Manifesto:
    rosecransheadquarters.org/Rosecrans/WhiteSulphurManifesto/Lee.htm

Lincoln's First Inaugural Address:
    avalon.law.yale.edu/19th_century/lincoln1.asp

Emancipation Proclamation:
    civilwar.org/learn/primary-sources/abraham-lincolns-emancipation-
        proclamation

A Measuring Rod:
    archive.org/stream/measuringrodtot00ruth#page/n1/mode/2up

Declaration of Causes by the Seceding States:
    civilwar.org/learn/primary-sources/declaration-causes-seceding-states>

Lee's interview with Thomas Cook, April 1865:
    civilwartalk.com/threads/post-war-interview-with-robert-e-lee-
        part-1-2.23379/

Proclamation to the People of Maryland:
    leefamilyarchive.org/9-family-papers/725-robert-e-lee-to-the-people-of-
        maryland-1862-september-8

Document of January 2, 1863, in which Lee promises freedom to the Custis slaves:
    encyclopediavirginia.org/media_player?mets_
        filename=evm00001861mets.xml

The Virginia Secession Ordinance:
    civilwar.org/education/history/primarysources/declarationofcauses.html>

Alexander Stephens "Corner Stone" Speech:
    teachingamericanhistory.org/library/document/cornerstone-speech/

The Reconstruction Act of March 1867:
    teachingamericanhistory.org/library/document/first-reconstruction-act/>

The Confederate Catechism:
    scv.org/pdf/ConfederateCatechism.pdf

Hughes, Hillary. "First in War, First in Peace, and First in the Hearts of His Countrymen." The Digital Encyclopedia of George Washington, accessed 9/12/2017.
    mountvernon.org/digital-encyclopedia/article/first-in-war-first-in-peace-
        and-first-in-the-hearts-of-his-countrymen/

Special Orders No. 191:
    leefamilyarchive.org/9-family-papers/454-special-orders-no-191-1862-
        september-9

INTERVIEWS
Matthew Penrod, National Park Ranger and historian at Arlington House, The Robert E. Lee Memorial. March 2017.
Lucy Wilkins, Director of University Collections and Lee Chapel and Museum, Washington and Lee University. March 2017.
Tom Clemens, historian, Antietam Battlefield and Harpers Ferry, West Virginia. March 2017.

PICTURE CREDITS

Courtesy of **Arlington House, The Robert E. Lee Memorial**: 42, 48, 64 (bottom), 92, 93, 96, 118, 122, 123, 148, 164 (left and right), 206, 219

Courtesy of **Independence National Historical Park**: 18

Gift of **Dr. Lee, Courtesy of Lee Chapel Collections, Washington and Lee University**, Lexington, Virginia: 215

Gift of **Dr. George Bolling Lee, Washington and Lee University**, Lexington, Virginia: 155, 188 (left and right)

Bequest of **Mrs. Robert E. Lee III, Washington and Lee University**, Lexington, Virginia: 52

Library of Congress, Prints and Photographs Division, LC-DIG-cwpb-04402: 10; LC-DIG-ppmsca-12376: 14; LC-USZ62-110010: 46 (left); LC-DIG-pga-03106: 64 (top); LC-DIG-pga-09394: 68; LC-USZ62-14216: 70; LC-DIG-pga-02604: 72; LC-USZC4-9950: 73; LC-DIG-cwpb-01470: 98; LC-DIG-ppmsca-23763: 102; LC-USZ62-126970: 104; LC-DIG-ppmsca-19610: 109; LC-DIG-cwpbh-04224: 112; LC-DIG-ppmsca-23852: 125; LC-DIG-cwpb-00127: 132; LC-DIG-ds-03251: 136; LC-DIG-ppmsca-21470: 137; LC-DIG-ppmsca-21027: 144; LC-DIG-ds-05168: 145; LC-DIG-pga-01927: 151; LC-DIG-pga-02907: 160; LC-USZ62-118168: 162; LC-DIG-ppmsca-40717: 166; LC-DIG-ppmsca-38007: 168; LC-DIG-ppmsca-35446: 173 (left); LC-DIG-cwpb-04402: 173 (right); LC-DIG-ppmsca-35236: 176; LC-DIG-ppmsca-21457: 179; LC-DIG-Stereo-1s02646: 184; LC-DIG-ppmsca-21320: 196; LC-DIG-cwpb-02764: 199 (top); LC-DIG-ppmsca-08230: 199 (bottom); LC-DIG-cwpbh-03114: 200 (bottom); LC-DIG-ppmsca-07322: 204; LC-DIG-cwpbh-03111: 205; LC-USZ62-39952: 208; LC-DIG-ds07129: 229; LC-DIG-ppmsca-05704: 230; LC-DIG-pga-08560: 245; LC-DIG-pga-03338: 251

Bequest of **Mr. Francis A. MacNutt, Washington and Lee University,** Lexington, VA: 25

Mads Madsen of Colorized History: 256

Brandon Marie Miller (author): 26

National Archives and Records Administration: 59, 103, 116, 130, 135, 195, 212

National Park Service/Fort Pulaski National Monument: 39

Smithsonian American Art Museum, Washington, D.C./Art Resource, NY: 86

Special Collections Department, Washington and Lee University: 211, 214, 221 (top and bottom), 232, 240, 246, 247, 248

Virginia Historical Society: 45, 46 (right), 53, 55

Virginia Military Institute Archives, MS 0277: 74

Courtesy of the **West Point Museum Collection,** United States Military Academy: 30, 36

Wikimedia Commons: 79, 200 (top)

BRANDON MARIE MILLER

visited Gettysburg, her first Civil War battlefield, at age ten. A history fan and expert, she earned a degree in American history from Purdue University and has written award-winning nonfiction titles for young readers on the American West and the Colonial and Revolutionary eras. Miller lives in Cincinnati, Ohio. Learn more at brandonmariemiller.com.